Arabian Hero

Oral Poetry and Narrative Lore from Northern Arabia

Letter from the General Editor

The Library of Arabic Literature makes available Arabic editions and English translations of significant works of Arabic literature, with an emphasis on the seventh to nineteenth centuries. The Library of Arabic Literature thus includes texts from the pre-Islamic era to the cusp of the modern period, and encompasses a wide range of genres, including poetry, poetics, fiction, religion, philosophy, law, science, travel writing, history, and historiography.

Books in the series are edited and translated by internationally recognized scholars. They are published as hardcovers in parallel-text format with Arabic and English on facing pages, as English-only paperbacks, and as downloadable Arabic editions. For some texts, the series also publishes separate scholarly editions with full critical apparatus.

The Library encourages scholars to produce authoritative Arabic editions, accompanied by modern, lucid English translations, with the ultimate goal of introducing Arabic's rich literary heritage to a general audience of readers as well as to scholars and students.

The publications of the Library of Arabic Literature are generously supported by Tamkeen under the NYU Abu Dhabi Research Institute Award G1003 and are published by NYU Press.

Philip F. Kennedy
General Editor, Library of Arabic Literature

الديوان والأخبار

شايع الأمسح

LIBRARY OF
المكتبة
ARABIC
العربية
LITERATURE

Arabian Hero

Oral Poetry and Narrative Lore from Northern Arabia

Shāyiʿ al-Amsaḥ

Edited and translated by
Marcel Kurpershoek

Volume editor
Philip F. Kennedy

NEW YORK UNIVERSITY PRESS
New York

NEW YORK UNIVERSITY PRESS
New York

Library of Congress Cataloging-in-Publication Data

Names: Ibn Mirdās, Shāyiʻ, author. | Kurpershoek, P. M., translator.
Title: Arabian hero : oral poetry and narrative lore from northern Arabia / Shāyi' al-Amsaḥ ; edited and translated by Marcel Kurpershoek.
Description: New York : New York University Press, 2024. | Series: Library of Arabic literature | Includes bibliographical references and index. | Summary: "The heroic deeds and words of a warrior poet of northern Arabia An epic hero and a poet, the semi-legendary Shayi' al-Amsah was a prominent ancestor of the Shammar tribal confederation that stretches across the Great Nafud desert in the northern Arabian Peninsula. Shayi's corpus of extant poems are preserved in narratives about his chivalrous exploits transmitted orally for centuries. In this volume, Marcel Kurpershoek vividly translates the deeds and verses of this compelling poet, based on recordings of late-twentieth century reciters, a testament to Shayi''s prominence as an embodiment of Bedouin virtue, courage, wiliness, and generosity. Born with one eye, Shayi' presents himself as unattractive and unassuming, only to reveal a hero's strength, sagacity, and wiliness. In a number of stories, he is shown hiding his identity, whether in disguise as an impoverished Bedouin or on a camel deliberately made to look mangy and weak. In the oral culture of the Bedouin, the epic cycle of Shayi' al-Amsah delights and instructs listeners through its unmasking of false appearances and its revelation of the hero's true character. Translated into English for the first time, these engaging tales and poems tell of dangerous desert travel, warlike exploits, chivalrous conduct and its opposite, fears of hospitality that defy belief, and convey nuggets of wisdom from the Bedouin manual of survival, making this collection a colorful compendium of the manners and customs of the tribes of northern Arabia"-- Provided by publisher.
Identifiers: LCCN 2024002124 | ISBN 9781479834167 (hardback ; acid-free paper) | ISBN 9781479834174 (ebook) | ISBN 9781479834181 (ebook)
Subjects: LCSH: Ibn Mirdās, Shāyiʻ--Translations into English. | LCGFT: Poetry.
Classification: LCC PJ7765.I297 A88 2024 | DDC 892.7/14--dc23/eng/20240805

LC record available at https://lccn.loc.gov/2024002124

New York University Press books are printed on acid-free paper, and their binding materials are chosen for strength and durability.

Series design by Titus Nemeth and Stuart Brown.

Typeset in Sakkal Kitab Medium.

Typesetting and digitization by Stuart Brown.

Manufactured in the United States of America
c10 9 8 7 6 5 4 3 2 1

Table of Contents

Introduction

Shāyiʿ al-Amsaḥ

Shāyiʿ al-Amsaḥ is an epic hero and one of the early ancestors of the Shammar tribal confederation in northern Arabia. Among Shammar, his lore is especially treasured and preserved by members of the tribe of al-Rmāl (meaning "the Sands"): intimately associated with the Nafūd Desert, they venerate Shāyiʿ as their first ancestor. His influence can be traced as far afield as the coasts of today's United Arab Emirates: some of his verse migrated into the work of the late-eighteenth-century poet al-Māyidī ibn Ẓāhir. He shares with al-Māyidī characteristics of oral poetry associated with the Banū Hilāl, first discussed by the historian Ibn Khaldūn (732–808/1332–1406). Shāyiʿ's verse and lore also have parallels with pre-Islamic and other early classical poets, such as Imruʾ al-Qays and Ḥātim al-Ṭāʾī. Narratives about him, and some of his verse, contain a sprinkling of historical names and events, much of it clearly anachronistic or lacking in precision. Nevertheless, by taking these elements into consideration, as well as his style and phrasing, one might surmise that his floruit and the origin of his saga occurred in the seventeenth century, perhaps a little earlier than dates associated with al-Māyidī ibn Ẓāhir.[1]

Tribal Background and Historical Context

Shāyiʿ's nickname, al-Amsaḥ, refers to his description as a one-eyed person. One side of his face looked as if a hand had wiped it away (classical Arabic *masḥ*, "wiping off"), causing the eye and eyebrow to disappear. His eye socket was empty. The narrative of his legend starts with Shāyiʿ bringing a raiding expedition to successful conclusion thanks to his one eye: it is so supernaturally powerful that it registers the movements and attire of an enemy tribe a full day's ride away.[2] This thread runs through the entire corpus of narratives-cum-poetry. At first glance, Shāyiʿ is merely remarkable for his unattractive looks and unassuming demeanor. As the story unfolds, this impression is belied by the hero's amazing strength, sagacity, and wiliness. In the oral culture of the Bedouin, the epic cycle of Shāyiʿ al-Amsaḥ delights and instructs the audience by its unmasking of false appearances and reaffirmation of truth.[3] By extension, this also applies to his mounts. Always in the saddle, he is at one with his camel or horse.[4] Invariably, these animate vehicles of the hero's ambition share his inauspicious, scruffy appearance. Initially held in contempt or ignored on account of their looks, they soon baffle those who took them for granted: the shabby camel is an unrivaled sturdy desert cruiser that knows the way to hidden water holes as well as its master does, and the rundown horse with the looks of a mule is a battle-hardened veteran that whisks to safety three men whose racing mounts stumbled (see Chapters 8, 9, and 10). This is the reassuring return to normalcy as the tale winds up. Balance is righted and things once again fall into their proper places. The time-honored codes that are the pride of the Arabian desert achieve a resounding victory over devious and sneaky behavior, pettiness, and outright treachery, all thanks to the resolute interventions of the hero. As the discrepancy between the veil of appearances and the solid truth behind it opens up, the space in between leaves ample room for amusing twists in the plot and enchanting descriptions of Bedouin manners and customs. The outcome is never in doubt.

Yet, despite Shāyiʿ's role as upholder of widely held Bedouin codes, other tribes are not inclined to embrace him as their champion because of rivalries and jealousies inherent in the system. To some extent, this even applies to the Shammar confederation as a whole. Each division and section of Shammar takes pride in its own heroes. Ultimately, Shāyiʿ only fully belongs to the Rmāl, particularly those who directly trace their descent to him.[5] This does not prevent other members of Shammar from taking a lively interest in the legend. The tales, exciting and full of surprises, keep audiences spellbound when told by artful and creative transmitters. Still, his lore's origin in the oral traditions of the Rmāl tribe must be kept in mind when considering the recordings of which this edition is a faithful reflection.[6] What the tradition loses in the way of quality and detail on its migration from the tribe's fountainhead in the Nafūd Desert to distant destinations becomes clear if one compares this text to the tales about Shāyiʿ al-Amsaḥ recorded by R. Montagne from Shammar tribesmen in the Syrian Euphrates region in the 1930s.[7]

In the opening lines of his poetry, Shāyiʿ presents himself as the son of Mirdās. According to the storytellers and genealogists of the Rmāl, Shāyiʿ ibn Mirdās, nicknamed al-Amsaḥ, was born to a lineage that, through a common ancestor,

Khanshar, traces its ancestry to ʿAmīrah, the first father of the Rmāl. ʿAmīrah belonged to the Ghfēlah, a branch of the Sinjārah, one of the four divisions of the Shammar tribal confederation. The main settlement of the Ghfēlah is the town of Mōgag, a commercial center of the area before the rise of the regional capital of Ḥāʾil. As legend has it, ʿAmīrah grew up among his maternal relatives of the Nuʿaym tribe, "somewhere north," and on arrival in Mōgag found employment as a cattle rustler for his kinsmen there.[8] A skillful raider, he often replenished their supply of camels and, when asked from where he had captured his booty, always gave the same reply: "From the sands (*al-rmāl*)"; that is, the Nafūd Desert. Thus, in the end, he was referred to as Ibn Rmāl, "Son of the Sands," the tribal name passed on to his descendants. One day, ʿAmīrah strayed into the shallow depression of Jubbah and hit upon water. He informed his kinsmen of the Ghfēlah that henceforth he would settle there, and he declared his independence from the Ghfēlah lineages in Mōgag. The well in Jubbah was called al-Ḥammāl, or al-Ḥammālī (from CA *ḥamal*, "to carry a burden"), because it provided for all of his descendants. Around its wide rim, he erected nine pairs of beams with rollers and pulley wheels for drawing water, one for each of his nine sons.[9] His eldest, Muḥammad, whose descendants regard themselves as the principal lineage of the Rmāl, was brought up by his maternal uncles of the Kithīr branch of the Banū Khālid tribe, from whose ranks rose the Āl Ḥumayd dynasty of eastern Arabia, commonly known as Ibn ʿUrayʿir.[10] Like ʿAmīrah when he grew up among the Nuʿaym, Muḥammad found that his prowess was not enough to make the other boys accept him as an equal. Unhappy, he urged his mother to tell him about his father. He returned to his tribal home in time to quell an uprising against his father's leadership and soon after inherited his position. Ever since, it is said, the sons of Muḥammad ibn ʿAmīrah have been the shaykhs of the Rmāl settled in Jubbah. The sons of Khanshar ibn ʿAmīrah became shaykhs of the tribe's nomadic branches.

Khanshar had two sons, Gidrān and Mṣabbiḥ. One of the four sons of Mṣabbiḥ was Mirdās, the father of Shāyiʿ. Gidrān had two sons, Midhwad and Rāshid. This volume opens with a sequence of stories and verses that climaxes in a dramatic struggle for power between Rāshid ibn Gidrān, a resolute and capable leader, and Shāyiʿ, who ultimately displaces his kinsman as tribal leader.[11]

Some stories and pieces of verse may be related to kinship ties outside Shammar, as described by the transmitters of this lore. One example is the amalgam of antagonism and respect in two narratives featuring a tug-of-war between

Shāyiʿ and Ibn ʿUrayʿir (ʿRēʿir), the Bedouin rulers in eastern Arabia. This lore may reflect a garbled version of ʿAmīrah's relationship with his in-laws, who came from the Banū Khālid tribe.[12] Claims in narrative and verse that Shāyiʿ was related to the Great Sharifs of Mecca are highly speculative. In Arabian oral tradition, names of well-known families of tribal chiefs, such as al-Jarbā, Ibn Shaʿlān, Sharif of Mecca, and Ibn ʿUrayʿir, are used as a catchall in reference to persons of those kin groups, without information about the person's identity or a particular moment in time (see n. 165). These big names are bandied about to lend luster to a tribal ancestor whose origins and feats have been lost in the haze of legend. At the time of recording, precise genealogies counted for little among the transmitters and partakers of the oral culture. They considered these narratives part of their tribal identity and for that reason took them as a mostly faithful reflection of historical fact (see p. xiii below).

The traditions paint a broad canvas of warfare waged by the Shammar confederation against invading troops of the Sharif of Mecca. Among Shammar leaders, Shāyiʿ is the one most opposed to the sharif's pretensions to lordly preeminence. Oddly, his unbending refusal is based on his own snobbish claims of kinship with the sharif. For the same reason, in victory he magnanimously shows the badly mauled sharif a measure of forbearance. No explanation is given, but the key is found in traditions that trace a more distant descent of the Rmāl to Ruṭayyān al-Sharīf, whereas the other branches of the Ghfēlah, through their forefather ʿAlī, are said to count the sharif Muḥammad al-Ḥārithī among their ancestors.[13] Somewhat confusingly, the long poem about protracted warfare waged by the sharif against Shammar at Ajā has been put into the mouth of the sharif. The fulsome praise the Meccan prince heaps on his Shammar nemesis may sound incongruous, but such conceits are not uncommon in boastful Bedouin poetry (*mufākharah*).

Adorned with conventional rhetorical flourishes, the fantastical tales spun around distant forefathers leave open the question of what, if anything, from this lore reflects the historical life and times of Shāyiʿ al-Amsaḥ. Perhaps the most illuminating fact is what remains unmentioned: the rise of the Ibn Saud dynasty and the Wahhabi movement. In 1754, the alliance between the religious reformer Muḥammad ibn ʿAbd al-Wahhāb and the tribal leader Muḥammad ibn Saʿūd was cemented in the town of al-Darʿiyyah. In 1782, there was an uprising against the first Saudi state in Qaṣīm Province, abetted by Ibn ʿUrayʿir and his Banū Khālid troops, and reinforced with Shammar warriors.[14] In 1791, the Saudi state routed Shammar at al-ʿUdwah, a pivotal battle that caused the large-scale migration of Shammar tribes to Mesopotamia, led by the preeminent shaykhs of the nomadic divisions of Shammar at that time, al-Jarbā. The absence in the text of any reference to these events provides a terminus ad quem for the era in which the legend is situated.[15]

The rule of Āl Ḥumayd of Banū Khālid, known as Ibn ʿUrayʿir, in eastern Arabia lasted from the second half of the seventeenth century until the dynasty was crushed by the onslaught of the House of Saud in 1793. The only name from the narratives that might offer a clue to dating Shayīʿ historically is Muḥammad al-Sharīf. The sharif Zayd ibn Muḥsin (r. 1631–66) had appointed the sharif Aḥmad ibn Muḥammad al-Ḥārith as his representative in the town of al-Shaʿarāʾ in central Najd (1646–70). It is thought that his son, Muḥammad ibn Aḥmad ibn Muḥammad al-Ḥārith ibn Abī Numayy the Second, might have been the sharif who conducted this military campaign against Shammar Mountain.[16] If so, this would point to a date a few decades earlier than the approximate dates given for the floruit of al-Māyidī ibn Ẓāhir (see introd., n. 1). Stylistic and linguistic parallels point in the same direction, as set out below. This is important since in oral tradition legend is often taken as historical fact, as noted above and by Ibn Khaldūn in his comments on the lore of the Banū Hilāl.[17] Sowayan argues:

> Transmitters of oral traditions are often unfamiliar with historical and geographical dimensions. For that reason, unaware of any contradictions, they may present events separated by long intervals of time as if they occurred simultaneously; or places far apart as if they are situated side by side in close proximity. Thus, they may recite a poem attributed to one of the Banū Hilāl that features coffee, tea, tobacco, and firearms, ignorant of the fact that these articles were nonexistent at the time. [. . . .] It is not surprising, therefore, to see some transmitters of popular culture attribute their stories and poems in vernacular to well-known personalities from the pre-Islamic era, who are supposed to speak in classical Arabic, such as ʿAntarah, al-Muhalhil, Kulayb, and Jassās, without the slightest doubt that such was the case. Or they may recite poetry of al-Zanātī Khalīfah, who is presented as a leader of the Berber population of North Africa, in the vernacular of Najd. When it comes to stories told about the westward migration of the Banū Hilāl or the migration of the Ḍayāghim, they take them as historical fact. [. . . .] They make no distinction between legendary tales such as those of Shāyiʿ

> al-Amsaḥ, the ancestor of the Rmāl of the Sinjārah division of Shammar, and chronicled history. This is what Ibn Khaldūn means when he speaks about people of his time attaching belief to the story of al-Jāziyah and the sharif Shukr, saying that "they are in full agreement about the tale of al-Jāziyah and the sharif from one generation to the next. Whoever dares to show any sarcasm or doubt about their veracity is put away as a madman and stands accused of doing wanton harm to its popularity among them."[18]

One way of looking at this corpus of oral traditions is to regard it as an aggregate of influences accrued and grafted over time onto a core legend of a putative early ancestor of the Rmāl tribe. The text amply demonstrates that this process occurred in an environment particularly rich in narrative and poetic traditions, many reaching back to the pre-Islamic period and the early centuries of Islam. To identify the inherited archetypes and motifs woven into the text is an enriching experience by itself. Yet they are no more than elements in a text that demands to be understood on its own terms.

The Poetry of Shāyiʿ al-Amsaḥ

The legend of Shāyiʿ al-Amsaḥ, probably centuries old, and its associated poetry have been transmitted orally. In the absence of early written sources and information about a historical composer, the poetry can only be judged by its intrinsic features as it stands on basis of recordings made in the twentieth century. By comparison to other poetry of its assumed era from the Arabian Peninsula, it can be categorized as early Nabaṭī poetry—that is, a compound of classical poetic idiom and vernacular language, and in a style that first appeared in association with Banū Hilāl. The "westward migration" (*taghrībah*) of this Arabian tribe from its origins to North Africa has spawned a saga (*Sīrat Banī Hilāl*) that has been transmitted over the centuries and in various forms in lands on the tribe's trajectory. Rough-hewn and phrased with deliberate simplicity, the Hilālī cycle of epic storytelling and poetry has been perpetuated in oral circulation in Arabia as a subject of majlis entertainment until recently.[19] First described by the historian Ibn Khaldūn, its most recognizable feature is the signature verse in which the poet proclaims his name and credentials as a poet.[20]

Often, poems in Shāyiʿ's relatively modest collection of 377 verses cap a narrative or episode. Of these, 107 verses have been put in the mouths of other persons: Ibn Gidrān, the shaykh killed by Shāyiʿ (67 verses); a daughter of Shāyiʿ (3 verses); and the sharif (37 verses). Except for the verses recited by the daughter, these poems open with a signature verse, as do poems by the name of Shāyiʿ: "Ibn Gidrān said," "the sharif said," and so on. Seven poems open with the formula "Thus spoke Ibn Mirdās, generous Shāyiʿ" (*yigūl Ibn Mirdās fitā al-jūd Shāyiʿ*), a phrase that in one poem also occurs as the closing verse, and that in another poem has been wedged into the middle of the piece. Almost the same formula opens one of the poems recorded by Ibn Khaldūn in his *al-Muqaddimah* (*Prolegomena*): "These are the words of sagacious and generous Khālid" (*yigūl bi-lā jahlin fitā al-jūd Khālid*).[21] This introduction of the composer as a person primarily motivated by a desire for chivalrous action is followed by various boastful claims. In approximate terms, the signature verse in this style is found in the area's poetry until about the end of the seventeenth century.[22] Ibn Khaldūn explains that people in the eastern part of the Arab world (*al-mashriq*) call this genre "Bedouin poetry" (*shiʿr bi-l-badawiyy*).[23] It is principally associated with the tribe of Banū Hilāl and their western migration from the Arabian Peninsula to North Africa.

In the Najdī tradition of the Banū Hilāl cycle of poetry and narratives, the signature verse is common, for instance in: "Thus spoke the generous Zuʿbī, Dhiyāb ibn Ghānim, his resolve harder than steel of metal rasps."[24] Such verses are also ascribed to the sharif: "Thus spoke Shukr the sharif, son of Hāshim: the sight of deserted camps frightens."[25] Remarkably, the phrase also occurs in a signature verse recorded by Ibn Khaldūn: "Thus spoke the sharif, son of Hāshim, ʿAlī, burning inside from hot moans."[26] And in his war with Shāyiʿ and other Shammar tribesmen: "The sharif composed these exquisite verses" (§5.5, v. 1).[27] The poem recited by Ibn Gidrān upon his return from a dramatic campaign against the Sirḥān tribe north of the Nafūd Desert, and his onward migration to the Banū Ṣagr in today's northern Jordan, is reminiscent of the Hilālī style; so are verses put in the mouth of the sharif in the aftermath of his ill-starred campaign against the Shammar tribe. As in the Banū Hilāl epos, these verses give an enumerative account of the action's episodes, more or less sequenced in the order of the narrative that culminates in the poem. In the verses, as in the narratives, tribal groups are in perpetual movement, punctuated by colorful incidents and chivalrous displays of the main characters. Certain details lend a distinctive Hilālī touch, such as the ubiquity of abundant game and scenes of hunting with cheetahs.

The degree to which poetic content correlates with events in the narratives varies. Some poems celebrate a happy ending following the hero's shrewd maneuvering to beat the odds, such as the verses on Shāyiʿ's deliverance from being held in chains by Ibn ʿUrayʿir. In other verses, the connection is tenuous or less apparent. An example is the poem about girls of the ʿAnazah tribe who vied for the honor of tending to the riding camel of Shāyiʿ and, unable to agree, submitted their dispute to a tribal judge: only one of the twenty-four verses mentions the girls ("Large-eyed beauties, I entrust my mount to you"); otherwise, the poem is about training a mount and riding it on tough raiding expeditions, with many phrasings and images dating back to the pre-Islamic period (§12.2). One poem stands out for its relative artistic finesse and psychological subtlety against a background well known from Arab antiquity (see n. 177 for a similar story and poem from pre-Islamic Arabia). In this case, the narrative serves as an explanatory adjunct to the poem. A lone individual facing an array of natural forces makes for lyrical drama. It pictures the poet alone with his camel in a vulnerable situation, convinced that his last hour has struck. His normally docile camel has run away, startled by the whir of a bird flying up, and he lies down in a self-dug grave, passing the night in dialogue with an owl hooting in a rare nearby tree. He dozes off and is roused from sleep by the persistent calls of an inner voice, a trope reminiscent of Ḥātim's stories.[28] The caller points him to an acacia tree he knows from previous desert crossings. Indeed, he finds his camel, ropes, and halter entangled in the thorny branches, and he continues on his way to home and family he thought he'd never see again. The story is well told, with a whiff of agreeable melancholia. The poem of twenty-four verses has a smooth flow, unmarred by the abrupt transitions that often result from verses gone missing or from originally noncontiguous blocks of verse or single verses having been bolted together (§11.1). It is impossible to tell whether it was composed by a historical figure called Shāyiʿ al-Amsaḥ, or whether it stems from other sources and dates from a more recent period. This particular poem is a far cry from the Hilālī-style poems that sometimes feel as if they are drawn forward on square wooden wheels. This volume's four final poems are stand-alone pieces, all with signature verses that come across as raw, boastful battle cries.

Orally circulating poetry, recorded at dates long after their supposed composition in an early period, "cannot be relied upon in determining the origin of Nabaṭī poetry or in tracing the various stages of its linguistic and thematic development."[29] Nevertheless, a broader stylistic, thematic, linguistic, and prosodic comparison, even across regions as far apart as northern Arabia and the southern Gulf coast, may corroborate certain assumptions concerning the approximate era of the poetry's original versions. And in such cases, it seems likely that at least some of the oral material has preserved parts of its original shape, as also shown by Ibn Khaldūn, albeit as haphazardly scattered remains of ancient structures laid bare in excavations. There are almost identical verses in the diwans of Shāyiʿ and the late-seventeenth-century poet Ibn Ẓāhir, and they have the prevalence of the signature verse in common, as mentioned above.[30] Rhyme shows remarkable correspondences with other Hilālī-style verse of the early centuries of Nabaṭī poetry,[31] and the degree of overlap with rhymes used by Ibn Ẓāhir and poetry of the Banū Hilāl is particularly high.[32] Therefore, the recurrence of vocabulary, imagery, motifs, and themes; sayings and proverbs; and prosodic characteristics argues in favor of such a tentative dating for at least parts of this corpus.

Poems and Narratives

The impression left by the text is overwhelmingly one of action rather than reflection. If Shāyiʿ and his corpus are placed in the classical category of "knight and poet" (*fāris wa-shāʿir*), the balance tilts toward the knight. With few exceptions, the poetry is integrated within the context of a narrative about feats performed by the hero. Storytelling is dominant. Verses are mostly tacked onto the end of a narrative: the crown on the tale, celebrating the successful outcome. The poem may refer to events and incidents in the story, but generally it is a statement in its own right. Many lines offer advice and wisdom taken from the store of sayings in vogue at the time; the prevalent tone is one of unabashed self-congratulation by way of raw tribal boasting and gloating over opponents who come to grief.

The narratives, on the other hand, abound with subtle psychology, humorous situations, sly pleasure, fast movement, and surprising twists in plot and denouement. The character of Shāyiʿ appears in different guises. In the longest story, he deliberately plays the part of underdog, one reason being that among strangers he fears becoming a target for blood revenge given the many men he killed while raiding and in armed clashes. He has covered his empty socket with an eye patch, for fear that otherwise his face would give him away. Therefore, he is called Labbād, "the man with the patch."[33] As guest of the Fuḍūl tribe, he is expected to put up his ragged tent near the dwelling of the shaykh. In the camp, he spends his days collecting camel dung for use as fuel by the camp's women, which he exchanges for a loaf of bread. Therefore, he is looked upon as an itinerant pauper, albeit one strangely married to a beautiful wife. As he studies the camels of the chief's herds, his attention is caught by a wretched-looking white one: he notices that on returning to the camp she is never in a hurry to drink and that she has a predilection for picking up bones from the desert floor as crunchy snacks.[34] His wife, having struck up a friendship with the lady of the shaykh's household, asks for the beast in exchange for some of her jewelry. When the call goes out for men to join a raid, Shāyiʿ makes the animal look as if afflicted by mange, a much-feared infectious disease that requires a horrendously difficult and tiresome treatment. In consequence, none of the raiders accepts his company except two brothers of a peculiar character who are the lowest ranked in the tribal pecking order. This is the first of many tests he carries out. The brothers prove an invaluable support, and gradually the odd threesome takes command of the expedition, in spite of the contempt with which they are initially met. Thanks to his unrivaled experience as a raider and desert guide, Shāyiʿ finds a hidden source of water in a fearsome wilderness and tracks down the camel herds. Acting as a lone scout, he sneaks into an enemy camp and, concealed under a tent flap, listens in on a newlywed couple frolicking in bed. She playfully menaces her husband with his sword, saying that she is Shāyiʿ on the prowl, and orders him to tell her where she can find the camp's herd. Playing along, the husband tells her, including the details of his own animals.

Armed with this knowledge, Shāyiʿ makes his way back and leads the Fuḍūl to their prize, but makes sure to send one herdsman away with the animals of the newlywed couple. Later, it dawns on him that they will inevitably be singled out as the ones who betrayed the camels' whereabouts in collusion with the raiders. Alone, he returns to the camp, where indeed the tribe is in an uproar and the couple is in danger. He makes himself known and explains what happened: he took it as an omen when he heard himself mentioned as a romantic robber knight. His courageous confession achieves its aim. Unmolested, he rejoins his comrades and, on the raiders' triumphant return, his true identity is revealed. Suddenly the despised and ridiculed camel-dung collector is lionized as the star of the camp. Girls flock to the majlis to get a peek at him. Repulsed by his weather-beaten, unappealing looks, they give voice to their disappointment with comments audible to everyone. Stung, Shāyiʿ improvises a song with a proud description of how a life of hardship and endurance in pursuit of noble feats has marked his face. The rude maidens duly humble themselves and beg his forgiveness.

The story draws on Bedouin culture's store of time-honored motifs and images, such as the hero overhearing others mention his name and fame in admiration, and girls who come to take a look at the famous man and give vent to their dismay and letdown at his coarse features. Both motifs are key scenes in the lore of the desert knight and poet Shlēwīḥ al-ʿAṭāwī.[35] Similarly, the glorified pre-Islamic robber poet, *ṣuʿlūk*, ʿUrwah ibn Ward overhears a couple in a tent mention his name, from which he understands that the boy who tends to their herds is in fact his own son.[36]

Certain characteristics recur in most of the tales. At first, matters are not what they seem, and in their dealings with the poet-hero those who meet him are misled by appearances. Sometimes Shāyiʿ secretly delights in wrongfooting them or has reasons to put them to the test, generally in order to prove them wrong in their judgment of him, tilt the balance against them, and gain the upper hand. It also happens that he rubs people the wrong way or others take him for granted until he proves his true mettle and springs a surprise on them.[37] Though Shāyiʿ initially may show humility, his is not a typical revenge of the underdog: the hero's superiority is never in doubt, even if other participants may not at first be aware of it. In several episodes, Shāyiʿ overcomes daunting odds to wrest the leadership of the tribe from a rival branch, led by Ibn Gidrān, who is shown as a determined, capable, shrewd, and creative leader. Forced by drought to migrate north, Ibn Gidrān comes to the aid of friends in al-Jawf.[38] He deals a defeat to the marauding tribesmen of al-Sirḥān, and from there works his way up the Valley of al-Sirḥān with the aim of negotiating grazing rights on the land of the Banū Ṣakhr in what is now northern Jordan. Trapped by his hosts' treachery, he eventually leads his tribe out of captivity by clever employment of a riddle-like message couched in double entendre that the hostage takers take at face value but whose hidden meaning is decoded correctly by his experienced elders to whom it is sent.

Ibn Gidrān appears in a less favorable light when he makes use of Shāyiʿ's prolonged absence in Baghdad. While Shāyiʿ struggles in foreign lands to make enough money to pay the bride-price demanded for his nuptials, Ibn Gidrān and his henchmen put tremendous pressure on his bride-to-be to marry him instead of Shāyiʿ. They finally overcome her resistance by producing proof of Shāyiʿ's death: a *ṣlubī*, a member of a pariah tribe, is instructed to come with the news that while in Baghdad he was told about Shāyiʿ's death in that city. On his way to Iraq and in Baghdad, Shāyiʿ goes through a series of adventures that fall within the category of fantastic tales and are not typical of Bedouin stories.[39] He is given a ride by a well-armed, remarkably handsome traveler who proceeds to slay a giant black slave in a castle after having fought him in an all-night duel. The outcome is decided when Shāyiʿ pulls out his dagger and joins the fray in response to his friend's desperate cries for help.

On his return to their mount, the man is gone: he has transformed back into being a princess.[40] She tells him about the gruesome usurpation of her father's palace and family by the black ifrit. He receives her marriage proposal and is offered all her riches, but he declines and asks for no more than her knightly outfit. Thus armed, he starts raiding wayfarers plying the desert road between Syria and Iraq. An adolescent who insists on joining him is accepted on the conditions put by his anxious mother, who appeals to Shāyiʿ's honor and makes him swear that he will take full responsibility for the boy: another well-known motif. In Baghdad, his ward, a good-looking lad, attracts the attention of a sorceress and disappears. After a search of many years, Shāyiʿ tracks him down with the help of the city's experts in magic and forces her at knifepoint to break the spell that turned his friend into a mindless sex slave. This section represents a rare instance of a Bedouin story with motifs of transformation, monsters, and magic spells that would not be out of place in collections like *The Tales of the Marvelous and News of the Strange* or *The Thousand and One Nights*. When the Bedouin hero is forced to make a trek to the city for economic reasons, this tale from the Nafūd Desert blends in effortlessly with the setting of an urban metropolis and its taste for the fantastic.

Having found employment as a guide for the Iraqi caravan of pilgrims, he approaches his native village on the way to Mecca. From an old woman living alone in a tent, he learns that the nearby loud merriment and ululations, punctuated by the terrifying wails of one woman, stem from the marriage procession of his betrothed. He hides under the marriage tent, a raised camel litter covered with cloth. Her resistance leaves him in no doubt that she is an unwilling victim. When Ibn Gidrān violently throws her down and is about to rape her, she cries out for Shāyiʿ: "My man!" Like a furious lion, he attacks and with his knife rips open Ibn Gidrān's belly from the breastbone to the crotch. The entrails come gushing out and the cadaver is thrown out of the tent, "where the dogs are pulling and tearing at his flesh." With this gripping scene, Shāyiʿ becomes the new shaykh. Feeble attempts to avenge Ibn Gidrān by elderly uncles are easily snuffed out. But a grave setback lies in store. Ibn Gidrān's young son is brought up together with his own, and they are inseparable friends until a disgruntled fellow tribesman informs the adoptive son who killed his father. As in the story of the pre-Islamic poet and knight Qays ibn al-Khaṭīm, nicknamed Qays Abā Yazīd, who is informed by a playmate and makes his mother confess by threatening to impale himself on his own sword, Ibn Gidrān's son feels honor bound to take revenge. He kills the boy, who is like his twin brother, and escapes to Iraq, effectively bringing the Ibn Gidrān lineage to an end.

Intrigue aimed at driving a wedge between husband and wife or separating them from each other has always been a favorite motif in folktales.[41]

Revenge, Settling of Accounts, and Prestige

Revenge is a pervasive motif, as it is in so many tales of al-Iṣfahānī's *Book of Songs* (*Kitāb al-Aghānī*). It comes in various shapes, not always as outright as the killing of Ibn Gidrān or his son's exacting revenge for his father. Restoration of respect due but not given, or violated by a perceived slight, is also a form of getting even. Women provide many of the pieces on the chessboard of revenge. Daughters of renowned knights of the desert are in as high demand as reputed camel studs and their daughters: belief in the importance of the male ancestry on the female side for breeding purposes is deeply ingrained from the early days of the Arabs until today. The equivalence of breeding both superior humans and camels is a thread running through the story and poetry of al-Bijādī's elopement with the daughter of Shāyiʿ. Al-Bijādī, a strapping young man of the Subayʿ tribe in southeastern Najd, is teasingly dared by his father to ask for the daughter of Shāyiʿ in marriage, though they only know him by his storied name. Taking up the challenge, he comes to Shāyiʿ as a single man looking for work (§7.1).[42] He rides a stud camel that sets him apart from other men in similarly humble positions. When Shāyiʿ is asked for his daughter's hand, he finds excuses, but nevertheless Shāyiʿ demands that his she-camel be covered by his guest's stud. This request is dismissed out of hand by al-Bijādī unless he is given the daughter. One day the daughter, who herds her father's camels, contrives to have the she-camel covered by the male. Though al-Bijādī, being a camel expert, realizes what has happened, he keeps silent. On leaving his job, he snatches up the daughter and elopes with her. Shāyiʿ chases them, but his camel is no match for the stud: when spurred, the beast takes a leap that subsequently was measured and marked with cairns by the astounded Rmāl, a place near Jubbah still known as Umm al-Rjām, "Mother of Cairns." Back among the Subayʿ, al-Bijādī meticulously follows the protocol for marriage with a highborn lady: the marriage act is concluded, impressive processions and festivities are held, and a large bride-price is paid. All camels given to the daughter are marked with her father's tribal brand.

Years go by, during which Shāyiʿ nurtures and pampers the daughter of the stud, step by step, until her performance is the spitting image of her father's, only better. Once her training has peaked, he saddles her and lets her make a leap at Umm al-Rjām, with the predictable result that she outjumps her father by an appreciable margin. He tracks down his daughter, who has been expecting him. She tells him that she is pregnant with a second child and that she will be of no use to him for the purpose of getting even.[43] Her substitute is al-Bijādī's favorite daughter by another wife. She entices the girl to meet up with Shāyiʿ in the dark of night, and he seizes her in the way his own daughter was seized, fastening her long tresses to the crosspieces of the wooden saddle. Al-Bijādī and his men go in hot pursuit, following the traces by the light of a fire kept burning in a large cooking pot suspended between two horses. At dawn, only al-Bijādī and his stud are left. Shāyiʿ, though riding a faster mount, the daughter of al-Bijādī's stud, allows him to draw within hearing distance, and they strike up a conversation. Al-Bijādī assures him in the name of all that is holy that the marriage was concluded properly and invites Shāyiʿ to return with him and take al-Bijādī's daughter as his wife. Thus, the balance of honor is restored.

In yet another story, Shāyiʿ is kept in shackles as a prisoner, in the humiliating manner described by nineteenth-century travelers (see n. 194 for Burckhardt's description). He has fallen afoul of the Bedouin rulers in eastern Arabia, Ibn ʿUrayʿir, after failing to return their robbed herds. Many years later, his son, called ʿAmīrah after the first ancestor of the Rmāl, comes to free him. Shāyiʿ has been expecting him, counting the years until the son had grown up. In the same way as his daughter advised him in the al-Bijadī story, Shāyiʿ tells ʿAmīrah that making off with him will not set the record straight. To properly right the balance sheet, he should lift the young son of Ibn ʿUrayʿir from the tent where he sleeps alone with his mother: that night is not her turn, and her husband is sleeping with one of his other wives. Also, Shāyiʿ is itching to savor the spectacle of Ibn ʿUrayʿir's despair. On his return to Shammar Mountain with the kidnapped boy, ʿAmīrah demands the release of his father. In addition, he exacts huge damages. One condition leaves Ibn ʿUrayʿir nonplussed: the horses should cover the distance treading on carpets. Once the riddle is solved—that is, shoeing the horses with pieces of carpet—accounts are duly settled. In yet another story, the same apparently impossible clause is part of the conditions laid down by a son of Ibn ʿUrayʿir, who ordered his uncle to repair a broken promise his father made to Shāyiʿ.[44]

The hero unfailingly emerges as the winner from his trials, but the cycle of narratives-cum-poetry offers sufficient suspense and colorful detail to sustain the audience's attention, though everyone knows that the outcome is not in doubt. In Bedouin culture, blood revenge or obtaining the stipulated amount of blood money for killing a person in ways not allowed by the desert code is regarded as a hallowed duty for the victim's relatives in the male bloodline to a certain degree of kinship. Blood revenge makes for an engrossing subject in oral lore, but the cycle of Shāyiʿ steers mostly clear of it in favor of more lighthearted entertainment and instruction: a mixture of the genre of marvelous tales and the quasi-realistic Bedouin narratives told until recent times. These aspects are evident in another story in which the balance has gone awry and is not righted. That is, the hero gets away with an infringement he has committed against others. Again, the tale is loaded with motifs redolent of earlier usage, harking back to pre-Islamic times. ʿAmīrah, the son of Shāyiʿ, works his way into a camel train of the Banū Khālid of Ibn ʿUrayʿir on the march. He accosts the huge male camel carrying the howdah of the shaykh's daughter. On seeing the dashing, handsome lad who wears his hair Bedouin-style in long greased tresses, she has no hesitation in extending her protection to him. Having spent the night in her tent, he rejoins his fellows. To their alarm, a strong scent of her costly ambergris perfume wafts about him and his clothes. They order him to pull his cloak over his head in the majlis and pretend that he is not feeling well. The shaykh's daughter tells her father that the visitor must be ashamed of his poor dress, and she brings him one of her own cloaks. At this, the tribe's young men start exchanging malicious glances and whispers. Sensing imminent danger, the visitors make their escape at night, aided by one of the Rmāl who is staying as a protected neighbor with al-ʿUrayʿir. The audacious love affair in the howdah is reminiscent of verses by the pre-Islamic bard Imruʾ al-Qays on his reckless cavorting with ʿUnayzah in her howdah. Similarly, a ribald knight of the Ẓafīr tribe is betrayed by a special perfume reserved for the aristocratic lady who seduced him to clamber into her howdah.[45] Without exception, they got away with it, perhaps as part of the script for the motif.

Hospitality and Women's Heroism

Storytellers like to take the displays of hospitality by Shāyiʿ al-Amsaḥ to almost impossible extremes, casting him in the mold of Ḥātim al-Ṭāʾī. They do not ascribe to him Ḥātim's supernatural ability to send dinner to guests who appeal to him for food at his grave, a scene that was included in *The Thousand and One Nights*. Yet Shāyiʿ does not fall far short of such feats. One tale in particular seems to have been lifted straight out of Ḥātim's playbook. As happened to Ḥātim, Shāyiʿ is left to his own devices by his fellow tribesmen, who are fed up with him capturing booty only to waste everything on lavish roasts for all and sundry. Unruffled at being dumped by their kin, Ḥātim and Shāyiʿ accept their fate as a matter of pride and persist in practicing their reckless virtue with brio. Their wives and children calmly put up with the outrageous quirks of the family head.

On a bitterly cold and rainy winter night, ten kinsmen arrived at the tent of Shāyiʿ, claiming that they had been despoiled of their mounts by an enemy tribe. In fact, they had decided to test if Shāyiʿ could uphold his unbounded liberality when he was hard up. They had hidden their riding camels at a little distance in a dip of the terrain behind some sandy knolls and arrived on foot. Naturally, they were warmly welcomed. In the absence of his son, and knowing that he had no animal to slaughter, Shāyiʿ consulted his two wives. He told the younger one that he had no choice but to slaughter her and serve her flesh to the guests. As she threatened to scream, he went to his first wife, saying that it must be her fate, though she was less meaty than the younger co-wife. She told him not to act the fool and how to find out whether their story was true or not. The trick worked: the ten camels were discovered, slaughtered, and cooked, and fed to the unsuspecting guests, beginning with the camels' hearts and kidneys. They quickly understood and left in a panic. The meat was distributed among the area's population and his kinsmen hastened to readmit him to their embrace so as to prevent worse.[46]

Often, Shāyiʿ's wife, Kʿēb al-Ẓabiy, features as his enabler. Self-assured, clever, and socially adept, her bearing has a whiff of higher-class airs. While her husband potters about, wearing an eye patch and collecting dung, she strikes up a friendship with the shaykh's wife, whom she overawes with her good looks, jewelry, savoir vivre, and shrewd advice on how to bend her powerful man to her wishes. She is prompted to work her magic by an urge to comfort Shāyiʿ and his soaring ambition, and she is the one who makes his true identity known. Patient and faithful like Penelope, Kʿēb al-Ẓabiy is steadfast in warding off suitors during her wait of many years. In desperate straits, she cries out the words that seal Ibn Gidrān's fate and elevate Shāyiʿ to a position of command (§2.8). Likewise, the daughter of Shāyiʿ, as desirous as her mother to satisfy her father's appetite for superior camels, secretly has her she-camel impregnated by the stud of the suitor whom her father refused (§7.2). She thereby precipitates her own abduction but procures a mount for her father that outstrips all others, and she sees to it that her father in his turn abducts the abductor's child, thereby restoring the balance.

A daughter is falsely accused of a tryst in the dunes by her stepmother, when in fact she is searching the night skies for flashes of lightning (§1.3). In doing so, she acts out the well-known motif of a daughter assisting her father in determining where rains fall and grazing is found. A daughter may also assist a stranger against a relative who wronged her father. The daughter of a friendly shaykh of the Banū Ṣakhr, for example, warns Ibn Gidrān about the evil designs of his wicked successor by surreptitiously sending a rill of water his way (§1.10). Similarly, the wife of the former chief of al-ʿUrayʿir alerts her son that his ruling uncle has failed to honor his father's promises to Shāyiʿ regarding compensation for the exceptional mare he was forced to cede (§10.5).

Spouses (except stepmothers), daughters, and unrelated daughters of men who would have kept their word are faithful to given pledges and feel honor bound to do whatever is within their power to assist the hero in his unrelenting battle against evil, improper conduct, treachery, and miserliness. Tellingly, in this corpus the only action that does not redound to the hero's credit as a gallant knight, but counts as a daredevil act of ribaldry, is ʿAmīrah's lovemaking in a swaying howdah. This rakish episode in the style of Imruʾ al-Qays happened, according to the narrative, at the instigation of the noble-born, self-willed daughter of Ibn ʿUrayʿir, as mentioned above. She is punished twice: she loves the hero and loses him; and she takes her relatives' blame for debasing her tribe's currency and giving other tribes reason to gloat. But unlike men unhappy in love, she does not go down with flying colors in the annals of passion as a martyr of love. Her relation to the hero is one of romantic doom. One view is to see them as partners in crime; the other to chalk it up as an act of sexual raiding. This impression is reinforced by lines of poetry recited by ʿAmīrah as he is about to enter the woman's tent in foul weather and sees a wolf prowling around the camp's sheep: "Wolflike I prowl under cover of night, each of us claiming his God-allotted prey." There are many such examples of a correlation between attractive young women and the howling or appearance of a wolf. As Sowayan explains:

> There is a remarkable metaphorical relation between the bite of a wolf's jaws and the piercing of the hymen: both involve the spilling of blood and a dent in value and reputation. [. . . .] The wolf's bite causes loss of value to the untouched young female that becomes faulty and is therefore best avoided in the view of possible takers, exactly as suitors do not come forward if a girl has lost her virginity [. . . .] As in the verse: "Lord Almighty, I moved toward the sheep, snatching the wolf's ewe from between the tents' ropes."[47]

Shāyiʿ al-Amsaḥ: Avatar of Ḥātim al-Ṭāʾī

From the stories and poetry of his legend, perpetuated in the oral tradition of the Bedouin until recently, Shāyiʿ emerges as an avatar of Ḥātim al-Ṭāʾī: the Arabian archetype of generosity and hospitality, qualities that hold pride of place among the cardinal virtues of Arab tradition.[48] The heroic feats and rough-hewn verse of both champions are set against the background of the granite rocks of the Ajā mountain range that looms from the desert just north of the regional capital of Ḥāʾil. In pre-Islamic days, Ajā was called the Mountain of Ṭayy after the tribe of Ḥātim. In more recent centuries, the area has become known as the Mountain of Shammar, Jabal Shammar.[49] As late as the nineteenth century, tribal areas and names across the Arabian interior remained in a state of flux. Even Shammar, a tribe with a strong sense of identity and a contiguous, well-defined tribal homeland, firmly anchored to their remarkable mountain ranges, is not regularly mentioned in the chronicles before the eighteenth century. Yet the legend's durability is not only rooted in geographical continuity. Branches of Ṭayy were absorbed within the broad and diverse Shammar tribal system. In modern times, the tribe of Ṭayy is mostly found in the northern confines of Syria. In Arabia, their memory has been preserved in stories and verse that, suitably romanticized, tell how Ṭayy was evicted by Shammar from their mountain stronghold. Therefore, it can hardly be coincidence that the ideas, themes, motifs, and even phrasing and vocabulary of the lore associated with these men of action and poetry have much in common.

Ḥātim's legend took wing from the mountain to spread from the Arabian Peninsula to far-flung domains of the Islamic world, appearing in Saadi's *Gulistan* and other Persian works, *The Thousand and One Nights*, and *The Adventures of Ḥātim Ṭayy* from the Indian subcontinent, and beyond to Boccaccio's *Decameron* and Goethe's *West-Östlicher Divan*.[50] Proverbial for his boundless hospitality, Ḥātim's name became a byword for an extravagantly generous disposition. His tribal background hardly plays a role anymore. By contrast, the renown of Shāyiʿ al-Amsaḥ remained mostly limited to tribal areas of the Arabian interior, primarily the domains of Shammar along the sands of the Nafūd Desert and further north.

Unlike Shāyiʿ, Ḥātim al-Ṭāʾī has a well-marked tomb in Ajā Mountain. It is a matter of local pride that through him the area of Shammar Mountain lays claim to being at the core of the hallowed concept of hospitality. In consequence, not only Shammar, but all inhabitants of the province, no matter their background, sing his praises and consider him one of their own. The voluminous sculptures at the entrance to many cities, representing the traditional set of coffeepots and utensils around the fireplace, are a tribute to Ḥātim's legacy in its place of origin. Shāyiʿ al-Amsaḥ's case is different. Among the tribes of inner Arabia, the reputation of Shāyiʿ is that of a latter-day manifestation of a Ḥātim al-Ṭāʾī syndrome: compulsive and extreme generosity that may inflict severe losses and hardship on the hero, and in almost equal measure on his beloved ones, dependents, and fellows.

Misers as Fair Game for the Generous: Honor and Cleansing the Dross

The essence of much of Ḥātim's and Shāyiʿ's poetry is captured pithily by a verse of Ḥassān ibn Thābit: "I preserve my honor with my wealth, not soiling it; wealth without honor is not blessed by God."[51] While Ḥassān connects the concepts of honor and faith, for Ḥātim and Shāyiʿ honor (*ʿirḍ*) is mostly a stand-alone value that needs to be pursued for its own sake. Ḥassān's verse is phrased by Ḥātim as: "With my wealth I shield my honor, earning credit: that is the gain I need."[52] And the seventeenth-century Nabaṭī poet Ibn Ẓāhir says: "The noble-hearted use money for honor's sake, not the reverse: selling honor for material gain."[53] Shāyiʿ echoes this ethical principle ("My honor is sparkling clean, free of blemish; munificent, my hands are liberal with gifts" §7.13, v. 19), but pairs it with readiness to wage war and embark on raiding expeditions (§15.2, vv. 2–4):

I love din of battle, faithful to my struggle
to keep honor unstained by ignoble deeds.
I feed my neighbors and pamper guests,
though beset by hunger and starvation.
I love raiding, loot of lean-bellied camels,
a tight-knit band speeding along in my wake.

As Bishr Farès states, the pre-Islamic concept of honor, *ʿirḍ*, "was in its origin associated with fighting." Hence, power was its foundation and weakness the opposite. Though many of its elements found a place within the Islamic system, *ʿirḍ* and its associated values "lost their original character: they are no longer capable of being the cause of boastfulness" and became "connected with religion or with a moral principle emanating from religion." Yet "among the modern Bedouins we still find *ʿirḍ* with almost all its pre-Islamic force."[54] Warlike generosity is subsumed in the ambition to attain glory, *majd*, as in the verse of the pre-Islamic poet Imruʾ al-Qays: "I am one to aim for glory pure and simple: true glory is attained by the likes of me."[55] Similarly, glory pure and simple is the overarching ambition of Shāyiʿ, who boasts (§6.6, vv. 2–3):

I soar away from the contemptible below:
my abode is lofty heights, now as of old.
If all who aspire to those heights there alight,
they'd be crowded with poultry, fast asleep.

If Shāyiʿ is an avatar of Ḥātim among the latter-day Arabs, he is also heir to the defiant and bellicose rhetoric of Imruʾ al-Qays and other pre-Islamic poets of the famous *Muʿallaqāt* collection.[56] For Shāyiʿ and his earlier counterparts, the aim of warfare is to capture booty, mostly camels, and to redistribute the spoils among visitors and the indigent. In Bedouin lore, the word for "wealth," *māl* (nowadays "capital, money"), is practically synonymous with "camels."[57] In this respect, these heroes' legends might be compared to that of Robin Hood, "the good outlaw who did poor men much good,"[58] or to the pre-Islamic brigand hero, *ṣuʿlūk*. The crucial difference is that while these are antiestablishment figures who spend much time outside, preying on society from a base in the wilds, Ḥātim and Shāyiʿ are firmly rooted in the mainstream tribal world. Their exceptionalism may seem irrational, sometimes bordering on madness, but it is not. In fact, they seek to embody their society's highest ideals and show their zeal by taking them to such extremes that the well-being of their tribal group comes under threat. The pursuit of these ideals beyond reasonable limits upholds their claim to be champions of society's ethical norms. Society may lose patience and signal unwillingness to put up with certain excesses by shunning these extremists or leaving them alone for a while, but they are never formally expelled, and in difficult situations they are a considerable asset to the group.

Thus, Ḥātim and Shāyiʿ are not colorful outlaws like Robin Hood or the *ṣaʿālīk* poets. In their parlance, a *ṣuʿlūk* is a poor vagabond or a good-for-nothing who scrounges on others.[59] Shāyiʿ recites, in reference to himself: "Be kind to vagabonds (*ʿashīr ṣuʿlūkin*), poor in camels; implacable foe of misers rich in herds" (§4.2, v. 6). With an unswerving eye on legacy, their ultimate goal is to be remembered as having had a character of stainless mettle. To be seen by posterity as the epitome of what it means to be a good man is the guiding principle of their actions. Ḥātim's poetry was said to be like his generosity: "His deeds were true to his words."[60] They were not motivated by an afterlife as envisaged by Islam; rather, their aspiration was to bow out from the world stage with a shining reputation earned through courage and exertion. Death is on Ḥātim's mind as the ultimate and humbling human test and experience:

Listen, Māwiyah, riches are of no avail to a fellow
    when death rattles strangle his breast;
When the ones I love lower me
    into the smooth sides of a dusty grave;
Hastily they leave, shaking sand from their hands,
    and grumble, "Digging made my fingers bleed."

Likewise, Shāyiʿ advertises a final advice in anticipation of breathing his last (§6.6, vv. 19–21):

Keep tent flaps open; don't shut neighbors out!
    Food not shared by neighbors is forbidden fare,
Until my shroud's measurements are taken and I,
    dressed in loincloth, jaws tightly closed,
Lie abandoned in haste, like a loaf baked in hot ashes
    by impatient travelers, keeping still forever.

The road to that lofty last station is both austere and lavish. The means for lavish banquets of roast meat, a requisite for fame, should come from raiding expeditions targeting herds owned by misers.[61] Heartless and tightfisted hoarders have turned their back on humankind: their fire is extinguished and they are doomed to disappear from earth without leaving a trace. Their opposite, an openhanded and munificent person (*al-jawwād*), always adds fuel to a fire that stands for a life lived well.[62] After braving hardships and dangers, the hero distributes the spoils among his kin and anyone in need—"even if they are jinn and shaitans," says Ḥātim—or as gifts to the worthy. The booty hauled in also serves to cement his position as shaykh at the head of a tribe.[63] Wealth not spent during one's lifetime lies fallow and serves no useful purpose; nor does leaving an inheritance.[64] The items a hero may proudly bequeath are a warrior's tools: in the case of Ḥātim, a coat of mail, his warhorse, a strong-shafted spear, and an Indian sword.[65] For Shāyiʿ, his spear and sword bear witness to his heroism: "They testify for me about battles we fought, saying, 'The deeds of Ibn Mirdās speak loudly indeed!'" By living this virtuous routine, the champion builds stone by stone the castle of glory, even at the cost of being shunned and forsaken by his kin.[66] Fame in the tribal world is the pre-Islamic equivalent of the scales that weigh one's sum total at the Last Judgment. From this perspective, fame is measured by the balance of human opinion. As expressed by Ḥātim:

A miser at his funeral is trailed by low regard and heirs claiming his camels.
  Do as you say, for one is followed on his bier by what he built.[67]

And Shāyiʿ, with supreme hyperbole (§15.3, v. 16):

To die in obscurity, short of eternity's rock,
  is to cut a poor figure among God's folk.

Poets do not shy from boasting about how true they are in deeds to their words. Ḥātim proclaims:

Peerless is my way of doing things, except if people are like me:
  never my glorious feats, unrivaled munificence, were achieved before.[68]

Imruʾ al-Qays claims no less for his name:

On the mount, a knight earth never carried before,
  utterly devoted to covenants, truest of friends.[69]

And, to take one sample from Shāyiʿ's ample array of chest-thumping dithyrambs (§15.4, v. 3):

I'm the last of a long line of honorable men;
the rest of my kinsmen are odious rogues.

In the resolutely extroverted style of Imru' al-Qays, Shāyiʿ boasts (§13.5, v. 20):

Extreme in exuberance, extravagant in loot,
he outdid his ancestors, doughty warriors all.

In their traditional summing up of three primordial virtues, he and Ḥātim agree on the first: the imperative of protecting and respecting women of the tribe and neighbors. Next for Ḥātim is faithfulness to trust placed in him, and being well thought of by visitors who enjoyed his hospitality. Shāyiʿ lists three cardinal sins: abusing women, cowardice, and reminding people of favors rendered (§6.7, v. 10, §15.4, v. 4). Generosity's glow stems from its innate power, regardless of the response it elicits.[70]

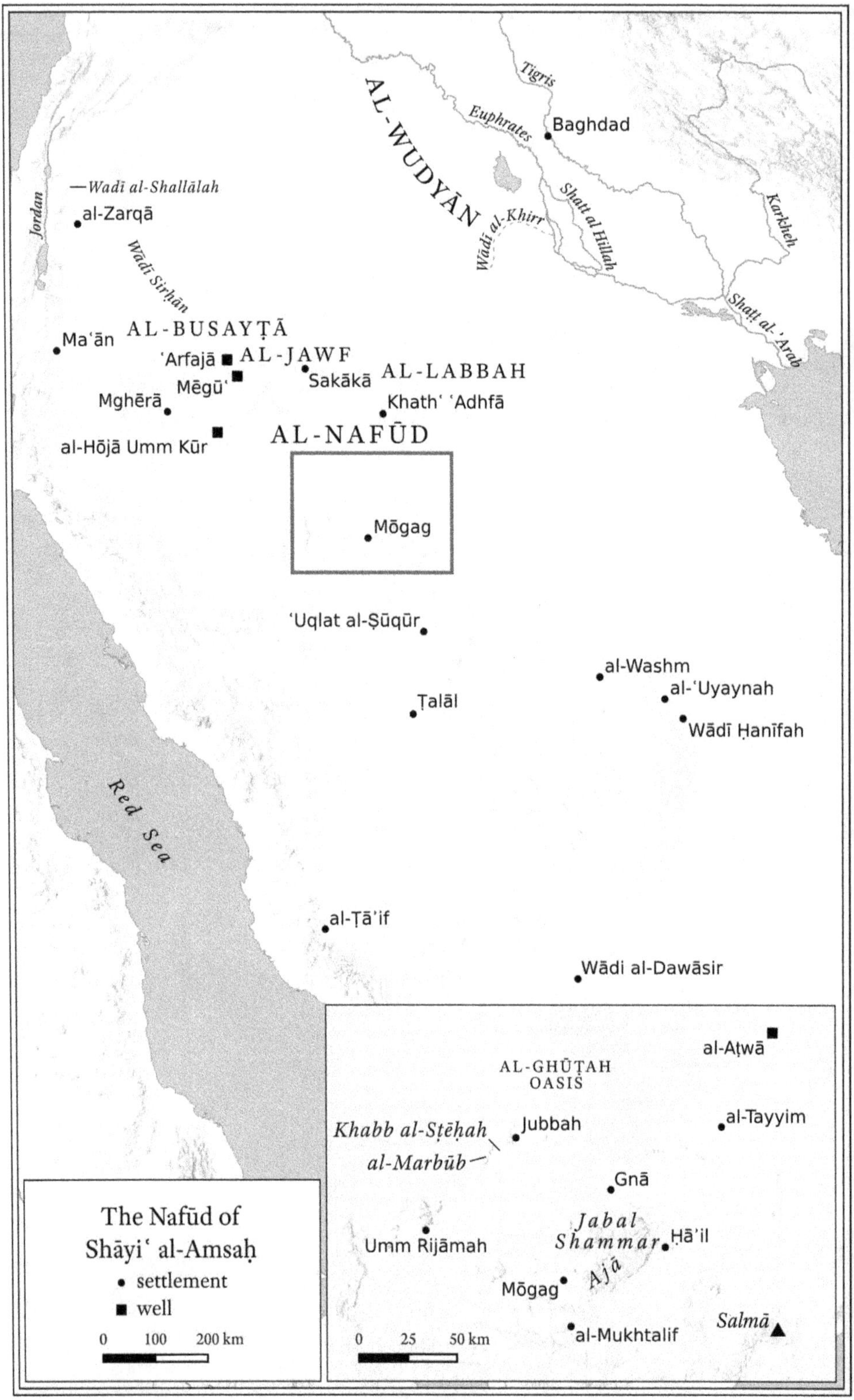

Tigris
Euphrates
Baghdad
AL-WUDYĀN
Wadī al-Shallālah
Jordan
al-Zarqā
Wādī Sirḥān
Wādī al-Khirr
Shatt al Hillah
Karkheh
Shaṭṭ al-'Arab
AL-BUSAYṬĀ
Ma'ān
'Arfajā
AL-JAWF
Mēgū'
Sakākā
AL-LABBAH
Mghērā
Khath' 'Adhfā
al-Hōjā Umm Kūr
AL-NAFŪD
Mōgag
'Uqlat al-Ṣūqūr
al-Washm
al-'Uyaynah
Ṭalāl
Wādī Ḥanīfah
Red Sea
al-Ṭā'if
Wādi al-Dawāsir
al-Aṭwā
AL-GHŪṬAH OASIS
Khabb al-Sṭēḥah
Jubbah
al-Tayyim
al-Marbūb
Gnā
Jabal Shammar
Umm Rijāmah
Ḥā'il
Ajā
Mōgag
Salmā
al-Mukhtalif
0 25 50 km
The Nafūd of Shāyi' al-Amsaḥ
settlement
well
0 100 200 km

Note on the Text

The Arabic Text

The cycle of narratives and poetry featuring the adventures and poetry of Shāyiʿ al-Amsaḥ, the ancestor of the tribe of Rmāl, has been in oral circulation among transmitters of the Nafūd Desert and Shammar Mountain in northern Arabia until recently.[71]

This volume's edition follows the Arabic text and edition, based on audio recordings, in Saad Sowayan's monumental *Ayyām al-ʿarab al-awākhir: Asāṭīr wa-marwiyyāt shafahiyyah fī l-taʾrīkh wa-l-adab min shamāl al-jazīrah al-ʿarabiyyah maʿa shadharāt mukhtārah min qabīlat Āl Murrah wa-Subayʿ* (*The Days of the Latter Arabs: Legends and Oral Traditions Relating to the History and Culture of the Northern Part of the Arabian Peninsula with Some Sections from the Āl Murrah and Subayʿ Tribes*). Running to 1143 densely printed pages, it is the edited repository of the largest collection of oral tradition and literature from northern Arabia in existence. In his Introduction, Sowayan explains his method and the nature of the recorded materials.

> Recording started in 1982 and continued over a number of years. A vast amount of material, hundreds of hours of recordings on cassette tapes, was digitized for computer use in preparation for the production of thousands of pages: the written version of the text as spoken in the original vernacular of the transmitters.[72]

By the time of the work's publication in 2010, almost all the transmitters from whom the material was recorded had passed away. In *The Days of the Latter Arabs*, the chapter devoted to Shāyiʿ al-Amsaḥ runs to forty-five pages and is based on recordings from twelve transmitters. As Sowayan explains, he constructed a text as complete, detailed, and well told as possible, drawing on the various versions to fill gaps and clear up obscurities.

> As a general rule, I have not introduced any element of my own making, but only used the words spoken by the transmitters. One

> might say that I have made myself the "super-transmitter," which is a legitimate procedure because each and every transmitter goes about it in this manner. After all, the only way to learn the stories and poetry, and commit them to memory, is by hearing them a number of times from several transmitters and different sources before embarking on the construction of one's own particular version based on these elements.

An edition of poetry collected and edited by ʿAbd al-Raḥmān al-Suwaydāʾ, *Min Shuʿarāʾ al-jabal al-ʿāmmiyyīn* (*Popular Poetry from the Mountain*, 1988), includes poetry and a line-by-line explanation of vocabulary and meaning of the verses. As in other early collections, the poems are sometimes accompanied by a bowdlerized version of a background story, invariably rendered in Modern Standard Arabic stripped of its most expressive and colorful elements.

Transmitters from whom I recorded are also among those listed in *The Days of the Latter Arabs*. Thirty years later, when I was in the Nafūd area for research and a documentary on oral poetry for the Al Arabiya TV channel, including that of Shāyiʿ al-Amsaḥ, some of my informants were the sons of my hosts during the earlier visit. Foremost among them was Ibrāhīm al-Hamazānī, the son of the poet Sʿayyid al-Hamazānī.[73] His generous assistance was crucial in clarifying countless obscure or not fully understood parts of the text. No edition of the narratives-cum-poetry in the exact words of the most proficient transmitters at the time of recording comparable to that of Sowayan is in existence.

During fieldwork in the area of the Nafūd in 1988, poetry of Shāyiʿ al-Amsaḥ was recited to me and recorded, and I was given handwritten papers with narratives and verses from his legend. The handwriting is coarse and not easily legible, and the text exhibits the usual orthographic deviations from accepted standard Arabic spelling.[74] These may reflect vernacular pronunciation. The *ḍād* and *ẓāʾ*, which have merged in the Najdī and Gulf dialects, are substituted for one another at random. As is common in these dialects, *sīn* is frequently pronounced as a more emphatic *ṣād*. The *tāʾ marbūṭah* is often substituted for *tāʾ*, even in the suffixed pronouns of verb endings. For example, *w-in ʿisht* is written وان عشة (§11.4, v. 15).

The poetry in this handwritten version corresponds to a varying extent with this volume's text. Three of the five poems are identical with regard to the number of verses. Also, the order of verses and phrasing is similar, and these three poems are relatively coherent and structured in a way that reflects the thrust of the narrative (Chapters 11, 13, and 16). The accompanying narratives are rendered in a mixture of vernacular and language that approximates standard Arabic usage. They summarily explain the occasions that gave rise to the compositions. Surprisingly, the narrative attached to the other two poems distributes key elements of the lore's stories in ways that significantly differ from this volume's text. In one story (Chapter 8), Shāyiʿ and his wife lodge with another tribe, where he is called al-Labbād, "man with the eye patch." In this volume, the tribe is identified as al-Fuḍūl, and his adventures as the tribe's protected guest are spun out in colorful detail in a long sequence of narrative threads and verse. In the handwritten version, the tribe is Subayʿ (Sbēʿ) and their chief Abū Thnēn. In both versions, the story ends with the capture of camels through the miraculous talents of Shāyiʿ, but for the verses the handwritten version substitutes lines that in this volume stem from another story (§1.2, v. 1). The poem celebrating the triumph of Shāyiʿ over fellow tribesmen who tried to deceive him with the aim of putting his hospitality to the test has expanded from twenty-one to seventy-two verses, mostly dithyrambs on Shammar, including more verses asserting an affiliation of the Rmāl with the Meccan Hashimites (Chapter 6).

The handwritten version from the Nafūd area may represent a selection of poetry that has gained wider circulation because of its popular appeal. In the 1930s, the French orientalist Robert Montagne published poetry and narratives of Shāyiʿ al-Amsaḥ, together with other materials, while working in the French government's service during the period of the mandate over Syria and Lebanon accorded by the League of Nations to France. Montagne recorded these versions in the Syrian Upper Euphrates region from Bedouin transmitters of the ʿAbdah and Khriṣah divisions of Shammar that had migrated from northern Arabia to the Mesopotamian lands between Euphrates and Tigris. In contrast to the handwritten version received in the Nafūd area, Montagne's versions are almost exclusively devoted to two of these better-known narratives, with one tale rounded off by a few mangled verses (Chapters 7 and 8). Though instantly recognizable as reflective of Arabian Bedouin idiom, the text is shot through with features of Syrian dialect. The stories are reasonably coherent, but many episodes and much detail found in this volume are missing. As Sowayan observes:

> It is apparent from the titles of the stories that they belong to the literary expression circulating in Najd. But the Najdī oral narratives I heard, some of which I recorded, are very different from the ones presented by Montagne. It would seem that the specimens collected

> by Montagne are not up to the mark as far as literary value is concerned, but still they are of much better quality than the poems collected by the American researcher H. H. Spoer [. . . .] in southern Palestine and Transjordan and attributed by him to Nimr ibn ʿAdwān.[75]

The Translation

The Days of the Latter Arabs remains the standard for this lore, and this edition and translation are based solely on it. The original edition is mostly pure text, without explanatory notes, except for the glosses put by the transmitters themselves during recording, and without a critical apparatus. For the purpose of translation of this edition, and the one preceding it, *Bedouin Poets of the Nafūd Desert*, informants in the area of Shammar Mountain have been consulted on issues of vocabulary, language, and interpretation of the area's lore. The volume of detail gained from these sources is vast and, though it has informed the translation, only a small part of it has found its way into the Introduction and the endnotes. Occasionally, the translation has been cross-referenced with early Nabaṭī poetry of Shāyiʿ al-Amsaḥ's era, and the early classical period from about AD 500 to 800.[76] The English translation closely follows the Arabic original, but it is far from a literal translation.

Sowayan refers readers to his earlier publications, which may assist in better understanding the text of *The Days of the Latter Arabs*. For Arabists and general readership alike, *The Arabian Oral Historical Narrative: An Ethnographic and Linguistic Analysis* (1992) is key. Its Arabic text, fully vocalized and included in *The Days of the Latter Arabs*, has been translated and annotated; an extensive Introduction and Glossary assist in interpreting the Arabic and English text. This work and Sowayan's *Nabaṭi Poetry: The Oral Poetry of Arabia* (1985) offer everything an Arabist and a nonspecialist might wish to know about the subject, and make for delightful reading. A more demanding study, the Arabic *Nabaṭī Poetry: Popular Taste and the Authority of the Text* (*Al-Shiʿr al-Nabaṭī, dhāʾiqat al-shaʿb wa-sulṭat al-naṣṣ*, 2000), covers and analyzes Nabaṭī poetry's history, linguistics and prosody, manuscripts, and other aspects in great detail. A comprehensive catalog of poets and poems is Sowayan's *Catalog of Nabaṭī Poetry* (*Fihrist al-shiʿr al-nabaṭī*, 2001). Finally, a cultural, social, and anthropological overview of the material in this book, and the Najdī tradition in general, is found in *The Arabian Desert: Its Culture and Poetry over the Centuries;*

An Anthropological Reading (*Al-Ṣaḥrāʾ al-ʿarabiyyah: Thaqāfatuhā wa-shiʿruhā ʿabra al-ʿuṣūr; qirāʾah anthrūbūlūjiyyah*, 2010).

In the Introduction to *The Days of the Latter Arabs*, Sowayan refers the reader specifically to the latter study as a compendium with the requisite background to *Ayyām al-ʿarab*. I had the opportunity to meet with Dr. Sowayan a number of times and we remained in touch, often almost daily, by WhatsApp to discuss this edition's text. However, the final responsibility for the text, including its shortcomings, rests solely with me.

Language

At the level of language, features discussed in *The Arabian Oral Historical Narrative*'s chapters "The Oral Narrative Style and Technique" and "Syntax of the Oral Narrative" are illustrated in the Introduction to *The Days of the Latter Arabs*, with examples drawn from its Arabic text. Both works stem from the same cultural and linguistic environment, and these chapters of the earlier work fully apply to this edition's text as well. The examples illustrate well-known characteristics of the oral narrative style and linguistics, such as repetition and other redundancies; the enlivening of the storytelling by use of narrative imperative; gestures and other body language accompanied by matching words; direct address to the audience meant to better involve it in the imagined action of the story, and direct address to the narrative's subject as if the person were present; devices for disambiguation, making sure the audience does not lose the plot and understands whom the narrator is talking about; the use of what Sowayan has termed the *-k* of courtesy, the second-person pronoun suffix, used as if the narrator addresses one listener in particular, but in fact a narrative routine even in large gatherings; and the use of the pseudo-dative when the preposition *l-* is followed by a pronominal suffix that might be doubled (for example, *luh luh* or *buh luh*).

One of the pitfalls in approaching these texts is to proceed on the assumption that the Arabic can be read in the same way as classical Arabic (CA). Knowledge of classical Arabic, especially early poetry from the Arabian desert, is a great advantage in trying to understand it. In addition to lending depth to the reading, it offers a bridge to the later poetic idiom. Arabists wishing to take a closer look at the Arabic text might familiarize themselves with features of most frequent occurrence. For instance, *ilā*, also *lā*, *lyā*, and *yā*, is used as a particle with a subordinate function equivalent to CA *idhā*, "when, if"; and *yōm* not only as CA *yawm*, "day," but frequently as a conjunction introducing a subordinate clause, "when." Noteworthy is the ubiquitous occurrence of the internal passive, resembling CA usage, in the verbal forms.

In the Introduction to *The Days of the Latter Arabs*, Sowayan briefly lists linguistic aspects peculiar to the northern dialect of the Shammar tribe and explains how these and other more general vernacular characteristics of the text are reflected in his Arabic notation. For instance, the equivalent of the classical diphthong *-aw* is pronounced as *-ō*, and the presence of this diphthong is highlighted in the notation by a vowel *fatḥah* over the preceding consonant. The letter *yā'* is written as *alif maqṣūrah* if it is pronounced that way. For example, *wālī al-aqdār* ("the Lord of Destiny") is pronounced *wāl al-agdār*, written والى الاقدار, but the *qāf*, though not pronounced as in CA, is still written with the classical *qāf*. In the Arabic text, the word for "son of," *ibn*, is pronounced and written as such, where in standard Arabic it is written as بن. Except for text taken from Sowayan's earlier work, the Arabic text has been voweled sparingly and selectively. In the present edition, a modest number of short vowel signs, *sukūn*, *tashdīd*, and *tanwīn*, have been added, mostly in the poetry, to assist reading. Some of the vocabulary has been explained with the help of an unpublished dictionary of Bedouin language by the Swiss scholar J. J. Hess in the Archive of the Orient Institute of the University of Zurich. For further information on the linguistic and prosodic aspects of the text, readers are referred to the works of Sowayan.

Notes to the Introduction

1 In al-Māyidī ibn Ẓāhir's verses, there is a reference to the Omani ruler of the Ya'āribah dynasty, Sayf ibn Sulṭān al-Ya'rubī (r. 1692–1711) (Kurpershoek, *Love, Death, Fame*, xii). For more detail on the dating of the Shāyi' al-Amsaḥ lore, see below under the heading "The Poetry of Shāyi' al-Amsaḥ."

2 This is a supernatural trait Shāyi' shares with the pre-Islamic brigand-poet Ta'abbaṭa Sharran, whose hearing and eyesight are equally miraculous (*min asma' al-'arab*, "possessed of the sharpest hearing among the Arabs," and *min abṣar al-nās*, "no one has such eyesight") (al-Iṣfahānī, *Kitāb al-Aghānī*, 21:131, 135, 166).

3 Aspects of the legend of Shāyi' show a remarkable likeness to the oral narratives transmitted about the amazing feats of al-Māyidī ibn Ẓāhir (cf. Kurpershoek, *Love, Death, Fame*, xxxiii–iv). The poetry of al-Māyidī, however, is completely different in character.

4 Verses such as "In the saddle, scalded by midsummer's glare, I'm happier than in dense gardens' deepest shade" (§12.2, v. 20) are also characteristic of a nineteenth-century desert knight, Shlēwīḥ al-'Aṭāwī, one of whose famous pieces opens with "I have given my heart to the speedy riding camels, as though it was bound by cinches to the saddle" (Kurpershoek, *The Story of a Desert Knight*, 165).

5 Even among this relatively narrow group, individual transmitters often differ in their presentation of genealogical details with alternative readings that reflect favorably on the quality of their more immediate ancestral lineage.

6 See the Note on the Text for further detail on how these poems and oral traditions have been preserved.

7 See the Bibliography for the titles.

8 For this section on the tales of origin, orally transmitted and recorded from tribal elders, see the chapters "Al-Ghfēlah, ansābhum, wa-wsūmhum, wa-shyūkhhum" ("Al-Ghfēlah, Their Lineages, Camel Brands, and Shaykhs"); "Qarāyā al-Ghfēlah" ("The Villages of al-Ghfēlah") with the subheadings "Mōgag," "Jubbah," "Gnā wa-Umm al-Gilbān," and "'Igdah," in Sowayan, *Ayyām al-'arab al-awākhir*, 224–47.

9 In central Arabia, these constructions are called *zarānīg*; among Shammar, their name is *migām*, pl. *migim*.

10 See p. xiii and Kurpershoek, *Love, Death, Fame*, xviii.

11 As expressed by the transmitter, the descendants of Shāyiʿ "grew into full-fledged tribes," whereas the other branch "came to extinction, but for a very few of them" (§2.16).

12 The first names of the Ibn ʿUrayʿir chiefs in the narratives do not make their identity unambiguously clear. See n. 165 to §10.1.

13 Sowayan, *Ayyām al-ʿarab*, 228, 233. The name Ruṭayyān is not found in the list of names of the Great Sharifs of Mecca.

14 Philby, *Saʿudi Arabia*, 72.

15 This confirms the anachronism of certain figures or facts in the tales that are known to belong to a later date, e.g., the nineteenth century.

16 See the chapter "The Campaigns of the Sharifs against Shammar Mountain" in al-Suwaydāʾ, *Manṭiqat Ḥāʾil ʿabra al-taʾrīkh*, 296–307. This chapter's principal sources are authors from the Hejaz who chronicled the history of the sharifs.

17 Ibn Khaldūn writes that popular taste for this lore "would dismiss as an utter lunatic and a complete fool anyone casting any doubt or expressing any disbelief in the story, because of its overwhelming popularity among them" (Sowayan, "The Hilali Poetry in the *Muqaddimah*: Its Links to Nabaṭi Poetry," 282).

18 The chapter "Entwinement of History and Legend" in *al-Ṣaḥrāʾ al-ʿarabiyyah*, 286–87.

19 As Sowayan observes, "nomadic life itself is in a sense a living epic and the nomads live a heroic age, which is no different from the Hilalis" ("The Hilali Poetry in the *Muqaddimah*: Its Links to Nabaṭi Poetry," 288). For a relatively recent account on the state of Najdī oral tradition with regard to Banū Hilāl, see Lerrick, *Taghribat Banī Hilāl Al-Diyāghim: Variation in the Oral Epic Poetry of Najd.*

20 For more on the signature verse, see Kurpershoek, *Love, Death, Fame*, xix–xxii.

21 Ibn Khaldūn, *al-Muqaddimah*, 590. The pronunciation at the time is not precisely known, but the phrase could also be read as in classical Arabic: *yaqūlu bi-lā jahlin fatā al-jūdi Khālidu*. The honorific *fatā*, which in another opening verse in *al-Muqaddimah* is the female *fatāh*, means "young man, a strong youth; generous, honorable, bountiful man."

22 See Kurpershoek, *Love, Death, Fame*, xx.

23 Ibn Khaldūn, *al-Muqaddimah*, 586. Ibn Khaldūn adds that this "Bedouin" poetry comes in two sorts, al-Ḥawrānī and al-Qaysī, and that the urban Arabs of North Africa call it by another name, al-Aṣmaʿiyyāt, after the famous philologist and transmitter al-Aṣmaʿī. It is clear that Ibn Khaldūn regarded Nabaṭī Bedouin poetry as the natural continuation of the pre-Islamic mode of poetic composition (Sowayan, "The Hilali Poetry in the *Muqaddimah*: Its Links to Nabaṭi Poetry," 286).

24 Sowayan, *Ayyām al-ʿarab*, 1039. The practice is also associated with versions of the saga that feature versified dialogue of the characters: "Because verse sections of *Sīrat Banī*

Hilāl are almost always direct discourse of one or more characters, the first hemistich of a verse section usually begins with the formula 'so-and-so said'" (Ayoub, in *Sirat Beni Hilal: Actes de la permière Table Ronde Internationale sur la Geste des Béni Hilal*, 92).

25 Sowayan, *Ayyām al-ʿarab*, 1034.

26 *Qāla l-Sharīf ibn Hāshim ʿAlī, tarā kabdī ḥarrā shakat min zafīrihā* (Ibn Khaldūn, *al-Muqaddimah*, 587).

27 *Qāla l-Sharīf min ḥaliyyāt al-amthāl, barraqt bi-l-dunyā wa-ana qabli fākir.*

28 The story seems copied from the tale of the pre-Islamic poet ʿAbīd ibn al-Abraṣ, whose riding camel ran away at night and who was about to perish from thirst when he was told by a secret voice (*hātif*, belonging to a snake he had earlier rescued by sharing his water) in a dream about a mount that brought him back to safety (al-Iṣfahānī, *al-Aghānī*, 22:85).

29 Sowayan, "The Hilali Poetry in the *Muqaddimah*: Its Links to Nabaṭi Poetry," 289, with specific reference to "poems connected with the [Hilāli] *sīrah*, as well as those oral poems connected with other epics, like the Ḍayāghim epic or Shāyiʿ al-Amsaḥ."

30 Kurpershoek, *Love, Death, Fame*, xii, 242n175, 255n248, 267n344, 273n381.

31 The poems have a single rhyme at the end of each verse, as in classical poetry. In the nineteenth century, poets generally followed the requirement of composition with a separate rhyme for each column of hemistichs. They are composed "in the classical *ṭawīl* meter, which is called the *hilālī* meter by the people of Najd, *hilālī* being a designation they apply to anything ancient, or considered to be of great antiquity, exactly in the same sense that the adjective *ʿād* is used in classical times" (Sowayan, "The Hilali Poetry in the *Muqaddimah*: Its Links to Nabaṭi Poetry," 287).

32 See "Ibn Ẓahir, Jabrīd, and Other Early Nabaṭī Poetry: Frequency of Rhymes" in the online "Glossary of Style, Themes, and Motifs" at https://www.libraryofarabicliterature.org/assets/Glossary-of-Style-Themes-and-Motifs.pdf.

33 This is one of the two stories recorded by Montagne in Syria, though shorn of much narrative development and detail. In Montagne's version, he is not called Labbād but Jallāl, "collector of camel dung" (*jallah*).

34 In other words, the camel's appearance is as deceptive as that of Shāyiʿ.

35 See "A Face Marked by the Sun" and "The Beginning of a Raid Commander's Career" in Kurpershoek, *The Story of a Desert Knight*, 152–55, 168–75. For girls' disappointment at the features of a fabled desert knight, see "Encore: The Ugly Knight and the Happy Bedouin" in Kurpershoek, *A Saudi Tribal History*, 714–17.

36 Al-Iṣfahānī, *al-Aghānī*, 3:86–88.

37 In this and other respects, Shāyiʿ shows parallels with his near contemporary Ibn Ẓāhir, whose "habitual dissemblance (*tanakkur*) is a thread that runs through all tales" (Kurpershoek, *Love, Death, Fame*, xxxiv).

38 This probably refers to tribesmen of the Rmāl who settled in the oasis of al-Jawf. See n. 14 to §1.7.

39 As to the question of how Hilālī poems and episodes circulating in Najd came to show names and thematic elements from distant urban centers in Syria, Egypt, and North Africa, Sowayan speculates that the Najdī guild of cattle merchants, *ʿgēl* (ʿUqayl), would listen to them while waiting for weeks, and even months, in cafés in urban centers where epics were recited. "Back home in Arabia, they would recast and reversify whatever episodes they could recollect of such epics in a diction and a form that would suit the local taste and blend in with the already existing epic version" (Sowayan, "The Hilali Poetry in the *Muqaddima*: Its Links to Nabaṭi Poetry," 288–89). Such influences might have engendered the *Thousand and One Nights* style elements in this episode.

40 "The very broad category of transformation is one of the most fundamental in storytelling. [. . . .] In tales the world over, people shape-shift into the opposite sex. [. . . .] No real difference seems to exist between transformation and enchantment." (Gary and El-Shamy, *Archetypes and Motifs in Folklore and Literature: A Handbook*, 125–26.)

41 Al-Iṣfahānī, *al-Aghānī*, 6:129–39. As for al-Muraqqash and Asmāʾ, and ʿUrwah ibn Ḥizām and ʿAfrāʾ (*al-Aghānī*, 24:145–66), lack of money to pay the bride-price caused the initial obstacle in the way of marriage. But unlike these classical fools of love and al-Mutalammis (*al-mutayyamūn*), Shāyiʿ and his beloved, Kʿēb al-Ẓabiy, refuse to become martyrs of love: they overcome the odds stacked against them to become united in a happy marriage.

42 The ruse is a familiar one; see n. 124 for the story of Khalaf al-Dʿējā.

43 "I am of no use for the purpose of settling accounts with him" (§7.8).

44 As the daughter of the former chief of al-Sirhān warns off Ibn Gidrān against the treacherous new chief (§1.10), the son of the former chief of the Ibn ʿUrayʿir clan forces the new chief to honor his father's pledges and to pay a high additional price for reneging on the promise given to Shāyiʿ (§10.7).

45 Sowayan, *al-Ṣaḥrāʾ al-ʿarabiyyah*, 281.

46 Ḥātim al-Ṭāʾī, his mother, ʿUtbah, and sister, Saffānah, similarly revel in displays of self-destructive generosity, obstinately ignoring their fellow tribespeople's pleadings to temper their zeal. Like Shāyiʿ, they are eventually looked upon with exasperated endearment and their eccentricities are tolerated, and even viewed with pride when "the marvels of Ḥātim" (*ʿajāʾib Ḥātim*) bring their tribe wide renown. Ḥātim is voted the man who outperforms all others "in generosity and poetry" (*akramukum wa-ashʿarukum*), a variation of the more common "as a poet and knight" (*shāʿir wa-fāris*), a mantle here claimed by Shāyiʿ (al-Iṣfahānī, *al-Aghānī*, 17:380–95).

47 Sowayan, *al-Ṣaḥrāʾ al-ʿarabiyyah*, 644–45. Similarly, the daughter of Ibn Ẓāhir bemoans her lost youth in a roughly contemporary verse: "If you don't look after a fat sheep and slaughter it, a wolf bites its throat and does the work for you" (Kurpershoek, *Love, Death, Fame*, 141).

48 In poetry, generosity and courage hold pride of place as desirable qualities, often presented in such a way as to make it clear that they are inseparable. See, for example, the final counsels of the early pre-Islamic poet and knight (*shāʿirun fārisun min qudamāʾ al-shuʿarāʾ fī l-jāhiliyyah*) Dhū l-Iṣbaʿ al-ʿAdwānī to his son Asīd as described in the *Kitāb al-Aghānī* (al-Iṣfahānī, *al-Aghānī*, 3:98–99); or, as put succinctly by ʿAmr ibn Kulthūm, "We are known for feeding guests whatever we have, wiping out enemies who bother us" (al-Zawzanī, *Sharḥ al-muʿallaqāt al-sabʿ*, 134).

49 As put by Shāyiʿ in his verses: "I hail from the Mountain, visible from afar; tall and proud, it dominates the surrounding land: / Granite rock dwelling of Ḥātim al-Ṭāʾī, of generous disposition, hospitality's paragon. / May rains of the Pleiades shower his land" (§15.3, vv. 9–11).

50 A well-known Arabic saying, meaning that something is almost impossible, is "more generous than Ḥātim" (*askhā min Ḥātim*) (al-ʿUbūdī, *al-Amthāl al-ʿāmmiyyah fī Najd*, 1:104). See Dorothee Metlitzki, "On the Meaning of 'Hatem' in Goethe's West-Östlicher Divan."

51 *Aṣūnu ʿirḍī bi-mālī lā udannisuhu, lā bāraka llāhu baʿda l-ʿirḍi fī l-mālī* (*Sharḥ dīwān Ḥassān ibn Thābit al-Anṣārī*, 327).

52 *Wa-ajʿalu mālī dūna ʿirḍiya junnatan, li-nafsī fa-astaghnī bi-mā kāna min faḍlī* (Ḥātim al-Ṭāʾī, *Dīwān*, 75).

53 *Krāmin yihūn al-māl dūn aʿrāḍiha, wa-lā tittugī bi-l-ʿirḍ dūn amwālihā* (Kurpershoek, *Love, Death, Fame*, 89).

54 The article "ʿIrḍ," *The Encyclopaedia of Islam*, vol. 4. Leiden: E. J. Brill, 1978.

55 *Wa-lākinnamā asʿā li-majdin muʾaththalī, wa-qad yudriku l-majda l-muʾaththala amthālī* (Imruʾ al-Qays, *Dīwān*, 145).

56 See §2.8 for a gory passage that rivals the bloody exploits of Aias in *The Iliad*.

57 The concepts of glorious prestige, wealth, and camels are metaphorically connected by al-Ḥuṭayʾah: "Unfailingly, camels of their solid glory return at night, and their wise generosity takes no leave from home" (*lan yaʿdamū rāʾiḥan min irthi majdihim, wa-lan yabīta siwāhum ḥilmuhum ʿazabā*), where glory is compared to a camel that always heads home to its owners from the pasture in the evening (*raʾiḥ*), and their intelligent generous disposition is compared to a camel that does not stay away from home with others on a distant pasture (*ʿazaba*) (al-Ḥuṭayʾah, *Dīwān*, 12).

58 The last stanza of *The Gest of Robyn Hode*.

59 Ḥātim al-Ṭāʾī, *Dīwān*, 30, 51, 82; al-Iṣfahānī, *al-Aghānī*, 386. Ḥātim uses *taṣaʿluk* simply with the meaning of "poverty," as contrasted with *ghinā*, "wealth" (*Dīwān*, 51).

60 Al-Iṣfahānī, *al-Aghānī*, 366. Perhaps for this reason Ḥātim al-Ṭāʾī was said to be a man of few words and long silences, in accordance with his adage: "Unless something is necessary, leave it!" (*Dīwān*, 26).

61 The pre-Islamic outlaw hero ʿUrwah ibn Ward aided the weak and poor who had been left behind in a drought-stricken area by raiding for booty with his bands of tribal flotsam, *al-ṣaʿālīk*, targeting those who "obstinately tightfisted, clung to their possessions" (al-Iṣfahānī, *al-Aghānī*, 3:79).

62 Al-Iṣfahānī, *al-Aghānī*, 17:390.

63 As expressed in Ḥātim al-Ṭāʾī's verse: "They said, 'You're wasting your wealth, be thrifty!' If I were as they wish, I wouldn't be chief" (*Dīwān*, 41).

64 Ḥātim al-Ṭāʾī, *Dīwān*, 38.

65 Ḥātim al-Ṭāʾī, *Dīwān*, 41. In nineteenth-century northern Arabia, this ethos was still adhered to by ʿUbayd ibn Rashīd, the strongman of the Ibn Rashīd dynasty, albeit in Wahhabi guise. Anne Blunt reported from her visit in 1879 that "he left no property behind him, having given away everything during his lifetime—no property but his sword, his mare, and his young wife" (*Pilgrimage to Nejd*, 194).

66 Ḥātim al-Ṭāʾī, *Dīwān*, 76. The metaphor of building glory is embroidered upon by the Umayyad Bedouin poet Shabīb ibn al-Barṣāʾ, who takes his stand on the lofty battlements constructed by his ancestors and continues: "Battlements of glory where, on death, we soar to a bastion of blessed heights, / impervious to rock throwers, out of reach of archers' arrows" (*buyūta l-majdi thumma namūtu minhā, ilā ʿalyāʾa mushrifati l-qadhālī / tazillu hijāratu l-rāmīna ʿanhā, wa-taqṣuru dūnahā nablu l-niḍālī*) (al-Iṣfahānī, *al-Aghānī*, 12:273). And al-Ḥuṭayʾah: "He builds their glory, a good place to be, and to pasture one's animals" (*fa-yabnī majdahum wa-yuqīmu fī-hā, wa-yumshī in urīda bihi l-mashāʾū*) (al-Ḥuṭayʾah, *Dīwān*, 1987, 86); and Kurpershoek on the metaphor of "building" glory (https://www.libraryofarabicliterature.org/assets/Glossary-of-Style-Themes-and-Motifs.pdf).

67 Ḥātim al-Ṭāʾī, *Dīwān*, 73.

68 Ḥātim al-Ṭāʾī, *Dīwān*, 76.

69 Imruʾ al-Qays, *Dīwān*, 95.

70 Reminding people of having done them a good turn is considered a serious infringement on the code of good conduct. Al-Ḥuṭayʾah: "They are liberal with what they have, and their gifts come without ado or strings attached" (*w-in kānat al-naʿmāʾu fī-him jazaw bi-hā, wa-in anʿamū lā kaddarūhā wa-lā kaddū*) (*Dīwān*, 66).

71 In the documentary series *al-Raḥḥālah al-akhīr* (*The Last Traveler*, 2017) by Al Arabiya television, two transmitters, one at the northern edge of the Nafūd near the oasis of al-Jawf and the other at the southern edge near Jubbah, are seen reciting poetry by Shāyiʿ al-Amsaḥ. One of them, who was also one of the transmitters of this volume's text, Ṭalāl Rumayḥ al-ʿArūj from Jubbah, has since passed away. The tradition of this lore's oral transmission may have become extinct by now.

72 Sowayan, *Ayyām al-ʿarab*, 19; similarly, *The Arabian Oral Historical Narrative*, xi.

73 On the occasion of my first visit to Ḥā'il, Sʿayyid and his friends had composed a poem on a difficult rhyme, his specialty, in this case the rhyme *-aklī*, to test my understanding of Nabaṭī poetry: an example of the local penchant for indulging in playful half-mocking, half-serious challenges testing friends and visitors.

74 See the Notes on the Text in the volumes *Arabian Satire*, *Arabian Romantic*, and *Love, Death, Fame* for more detail and examples.

75 Sowayan, *al-Ṣaḥrā' al-ʿarabiyyah*, 295. Yet the tales collected by Montagne are remarkable for their correspondence with this volume's text with regard to certain details that lend a particular color. Such phrases and vocabulary stand out sufficiently to survive the journey from the hero's native tribe to other faraway divisions of Shammar. These two narratives correspond to this edition's Chapters 7 and 8.

76 These volumes have not been as extensively cross-referenced as *Love, Death, Fame* by al-Māyidī ibn Ẓāhir (see its Note on the Translation, xlix), but as it stems from the same era and largely draws on the same literary sources, much of it also applies to the lore and poetry of Shāyiʿ al-Amsaḥ.

الديوان والأخبار

Arabian Hero

شيخة ابن قدران بالرمـالـــ

١،١ عـلى دور راشد ابن قدران، يوم ابن قدران هو امير العرب، غزوا الرمال على الاساعده من عتيبه وغزى معهم شايع الامسح. يوم غزوا ويجون لهم تلٍّ بديار عتيبه ويرقبونه شايع الامسح ومعه رقيبة ثاني، اثنين او هم ثلاثه. قال: تشوفون شي؟ قالوا: لا، ما نشوف شي. قال: انا اشوف عرب. قالوا: أجل يالله نخبّر خويانا. وهم يخبرون خوياهم وهم يمشون. ويإخذون يوم كامل وهم ما وصلوا العرب. يوم جا العصر قال: هذا اثر قنيص شفتهم مدّوا من العرب يوم ينزلون. وهم يقضبون جرّتهم. يوم جوهم وهم يتذابحون هم واياهم، هم تسعةٍ القنيص، ويذبحون من القنيص ثمانيه ويبقى واحد مِتّقٍي له بصخره، مْتَغَبّي، ويضرب حدى القدران يا ذابحه. ويوم ذْبِحُه وهي تجي العرب فزعة على الرمي. وصار بينهم وبين عتيبة كون ما هو زين. تذابحوا بمحلٍّ يقال له خب العطاف، هاللي عند النقا. يقولون المسولفة انهم اربعين جوز اخو اللي ذِبْحوا به من ساعده من عتيبه. والعطف اللي مع الغازيه قصّمن به، هاللي سمي خب العطاف. وارجعوا يالاساعده مفاليس. هذولاك باللوى ببقعا، الاساعده، وابن قدران وربعه بعزهم وبديرتهم. يقصد عاد شايع يقول:

٢،١ يا خـال شفت الشوف قبل يشوفني ... مـمشـــــاة يومٍ للذلول اهـذالــــ
يقول بالعــيـنـين مــا زال زايــل ... واقول بالعــين الوحيـــــده زالـــ
والله يالولا خوف شمّـاتـة العـدا ... لاقول هجين وعلى ورك الهجين نعالـــ
ولاقول بالبــطحـا بـيوت تبـنى ... ولاقول عنــــــد البيوت جمـالـــ
ولاقول بالبــطحـا شبّوا نارهــم ... ولاقول دلال وعـند الدلال رجالـــ

Ibn Gidrān: Shaykh of the Rmāl

At the time of Rāshid ibn Gidrān's leadership, the tribesmen of the Rmāl carried out a raid against the Asāʿidah, a clan that is part of the ʿUtaybah confederation.[1] One of the raiders was Shāyiʿ al-Amsaḥ. Close to the territory of ʿUtaybah, Shāyiʿ al-Amsaḥ and one or two others climbed a hill to spy out the country. "Do you see anything?" "No, we don't." "I see some people in the distance." "In that case," the other two said, "we must inform our comrades." They did so and continued on their way, but after a full day's march they still had not reached the people observed by Shāyiʿ. Late in the afternoon, they hit on the tracks of hunters. He said, "These must be the men I saw from afar as they set out from their camp."[2] They followed the tracks until they encountered the hunters and made their attack, killing eight of the nine. One of them took cover behind a rock and shot one of Ibn Gidrān's men. At the sound of shots, the alarm went out and the hunters' allies came rushing in.[3] A fierce battle ensued at a place called the Vale of the Howdahs, Khabb al-ʿIṭāf, near al-Nigā. It is told that forty pairs of brothers were slain at that spot, all of them tribesmen of the Asāʿidah of ʿUtaybah. Their howdahs were wrecked, hence the name given to the battleground. Defeated, the Asāʿidah withdrew to their base at al-Liwā, near Bagʿā, while Ibn Gidrān and his men returned victorious. On that occasion, Shāyiʿ composed these verses: 1.1

Hear! I saw them before they saw me:[4] 1.2
fast camels take a day trotting so far.
"No sign of life to be seen," he said;
"With only one eye, I espy human shapes," I replied.
By God, but for fear of peevish gloaters,
I'd say: I see cameleers, feet on haunches;
In a valley's sandy bottom lofty tents,
ringed by the camp's camel herds;
Flicker of fires lit across yonder vale,
dapper lads handling shining coffeepots;

ولاقول حطّابـاتهـم يوم مـدّن   بنـاتٍ بيلبّـاتهـن حـبالـ
ولاقول روّايـاتهـم يوم مـدّن   عبـداتٍ عـلى ظهورهـن ابـلالـ

يعني قِرَّب لهم.

ولاقول قنـيصهـم يوم مـدّوا   لاقول تسعـه يشْتِوون غـزالـ
عـدينا عليهم عـدوة حنيش مع الغَبا   يا حنـا واياهـم شـباط رجـالـ

شباط يعني مشاجر، تشابكوا بالايدين.

وذبحنـاهـم كلهـم غير واحـد   مـاكر حـرار وضـاري لافعـالـ
وردّه عليـنا وذبح ابن قـدران خـيّر   عليـه العـذارا دفّقن ابـلالـ

دفقن دموع.

والجـبو ما يملاوه طشٍّ من المطـر   ولا يستوي رجـلٍ بغـير افعـالـ
والسيف ما ينِّقـل بليـا جَـنايـد   ولا ينِّطِـح جـمعٍ بغـير رجـالـ
ولا ينقـل اليـنقوش رجـل طـيب   ولا ياكل الزبـد المـذاب رجـالـ

الينقوش النميمه. الزبد المذاب كناية عن المرة اللي ما تحفظ شرفها.

رحـنا بالدنيـا حـبالٍ نحوشـه   وراحت بنـا الدنيـا بغـير حـبالـ
يا قـاعـد بالظِـل زاح ظـلك   ويا قـاعـد بالشمس جاك ظـلالـ

٣،١ وينزلون حروة النقا، النقا هو هذا طعسٍ شرقٍ من جبه، شرق شمال، وسط النفود. صارت عليهم هذيك السنة محل ما وقع مطر عندهم. وبنت ابن قدران

Swarms of maidens out gathering wood,
bodies wound about with lengths of rope;
I'd say: I see skins heavy with hauled water,
slung over servant girls' shoulders.

—He means, their skins filled with water from the well.

I'd say: Hunters pulling out of camp,
nine of them: one roast gazelle sates them all.
We leapt at them, as an uncoiling viper
strikes lightning fast from its lair;[5]

—"We leapt at them": they are coming to blows, hand-to-hand combat.

We slew them all, except for one:
a noble falcon, ferocious killer of prey:
He turned, struck, slew one of Ibn Gidrān:
wailing girls sprinkled him with tears.

—They are shedding copious tears.

Rock holes aren't filled by a drizzle;[6]
without feats, one can't stand tall.
To carry a sword one needs a scabbard;
it takes stout fighters to storm an enemy.[7]
The virtuous abstain from slander;
honest men decline to gorge on melted fat.[8]

—"Slander" means slanderous gossip. Here, melted fat stands for a woman of questionable virtue.

We rush to catch the world in nets of rope;
the world needs no rope to catch us.[9]
Don't forget: your spot in the shade may yet fade
and be taken by one who bakes in scorching heat.[10]

They set up camp in the area of al-Nigā, a high dune to the northeast of Jubbah in the middle of the Nafūd Desert. They suffered from severe drought: a year without a drop of rain. In the morning, the daughter of Ibn Gidrān would take the camels to browse on whatever they could find. Springtime had come 1.3

تسرح بالزمل. يوم جا آخر الوقت، الربيع، انتهى وقت الربيع ما طاح المطر. وليا مار بنته تصير مع البل. يوم روّحت ليلة من الليالي وهي تنط النقا، طعس بشمالي جبه، وكَفّت له نياقٍ من راس النبا. يوم نطّت النقا يا والله هذاك البرق يلوح بالشمال. وهي تدلّي تِخِيلُه. وسبعة أيام كل ما تغيب الشمس تروح زمله تسري وتنط الطعس وتخيل البرق.

٤،١ ثاري امه من الكْتاب، يعني مرة لابوه ما هي ام له، شكّت به وقالت هذي وكاد تروح يم عشقِه. وهي تجي وهي تخبر ابوه، قالت: بنتك تسري من له سبعة ايام يم الطعس ولا ادري وشي تسري عليه، وكاد انه خاونيْه. قال: لا، ما تخاون. قالت: اقضب علمي، بنتك خاونيْه، افطن له، الى هْجَعت الناس اطرق البال عليَه، تسري له يم لعيب. قال: يا راحت علّمين. يوم جا وسط الليل الى مير يوم انه انسلت مثل السحله، يوم راحت وهي تعلّمُه. وهو يتجنّد سيفُه وهو يجي ويدلّي يَتِلْيَه على الشوف، يشوفه. وهي تناحر الطعس وتنط الطعس، طعس طويل. قال: هذا وْعَدَه، أكيد، هذا الوعد اللي بينه هي وايا رفيقه. يوم اقبل عليَه يا مار براس هالطعس لحاله ولا عنده احد. ويوم تصنّت لكلامه يا مير تقول عزك، حيّ هالنور. يوم بحّر يا هذاك البرق. يا والله يوم دلت تمثل.

٥،١ سـرى البـرق يابوي يا موَدِّتي   برقٍ بعيد ومن شفا البعد اخايلـه
أخيله من النبك الشمالي لعرفجا   لشيبا وميقوعٍ وهـذي مخايلـه
ان انحدر يِندي فلقين من الغضا   ويسقي سعـاف العـراق اوايلـه

الفلق مهازع النفود والمطامن. وسعاف العراق حدود العراق.

٦،١ التفت ليا هذا البرق بس مثل شلع الخام، يلوح. قال: آه، متى شفتي هذا؟ قالت: والله يايبه لي سابع ليله. قال: والله كان انا ابوك كود ارعى من مرعاوه

and was almost gone with no sign of rain. One night, as she drove the herd home, she ascended al-Nigā, the highest dune north of Jubbah, to collect some camels that had wandered off. On the top, she was surprised by a flicker of lightning far to the north. She sat down, gazing at the view in amazement. For seven days, this became her routine: as soon as she had delivered the camels back home, she went out in the dark to marvel at the spectacle of the faraway flashes of lightning from that dune.

Her stepmother, a woman of the Ktāb tribe married to her father, grew distrustful of her movements. She suspected the girl of stealing away at night for a tryst with a lover and shared her doubts with the father. "Are you aware that on each of the past seven nights your daughter has headed to that high dune for some unknown business of hers? She must have been up to no good."[11] "No," he said, "she is not that sort of girl." "Mark my words," she said. "Keep an eye on her! Once people have bedded down for the night, keep a close watch on her. She wanders off to do some mischief." "When you see her go out, tell me," he said. Around midnight she slunk off. She slipped away into the dark, stealthily like a snail. As soon as she had gone, his wife alerted him. Girded with a sword, he followed her without losing her form from view. She headed straight for the tall sand hill. Ah, he thought, this must be her rendezvous: no mistake, she is going to see her lover. On drawing closer, he discovered that it was nothing of the kind. She was sitting alone by herself, murmuring. He listened intently: "Great God, a hearty welcome to this wondrous light!" He turned his gaze toward where she was looking and could not believe his eyes: flashes of lightning, indeed! Thereupon, she recited these verses: 1.4

Dear father, lightning cleaves dark of night. 1.5
See, it flickers over the horizon from afar!
Flashes beckon north of al-Nabk to ʿArfajā,
Shaybā, and Mēgūʿ—a spellbinding spectacle.
Come, drench the sandy dells with their *ghaḍā* shrubs
once you've soaked Iraqi plains!

—The "dells" are the dips in the terrain between the chains of sand hills. The "plains" of Iraq are the Iraqi borders.

He turned his gaze to the distant flashes and watched, spellbound. It was as if streaks of lightning were shredding white cloth in the sky.[12] "Well," he said, "how long ago did you first notice this?" "Really, Father, the first time was seven 1.6

واشرب من ماه. يوم رجع قال لمرته: روّحي لهلك، روحي لهلك، يالله، ما لك مقعادٍ عندنا. وهو يجي وهو يصيّف على التيّم، جَوٍّ هالحين لعبدة بلغف حايل من شمال، هكالحين يقال له الزبيدي، الزبيدي نويزياتٍ دون التيم. ويصيّرون على الزبيدي، هالقليب اللي بالتيم. التيم هو هذا هالحين ورا الخطه، شرقٍ منه. يوم نزلوا التيم وهي تِجَرّد الاساعدة عليهم يوم قربوا لهم. وهي تجرد يبون يكينون عليهم. قال ابن قدران: حنا نزلنا هالمنزل هذا عندهم وتجرّدوا علينا، إما نذبحهم مثل الذبحة الاوله والا يذبحوننا يتقاضون ياخذون ثارهم مرتين، لكن حنا نبي نوسّع روحنا واللي يبي يِطلِبنا يبي يعيننا الله عليه.

٧،١ ويجيه من اهل الجوبة هكالخطّ، انت يابن قدران: إن كان انك رفيقٍ لنا مثل اول – لهم رفقةٍ اول بينهم وبين اهل سكاكا – فانت لا تخلينا ترى الرجال وِطونا. الرجال السِرْحان. كتّوا الوادي عليهم السرحان وهذولاك، أهل الجوبه، ما هم كثير وبغوهم، السرجان بغَوا ياخذون اهل الجوبه. قال ابن قدران للعرب: بلّوا الصميل. هم بالقيض. وعلّق عليّه من الزبيدي وانزع من حدريّ التيّم وحِل مع الخَلّ وسنّد، استشملوا مع النفود ويحولون على الاطوا، قليب يقال له الاطوا، وعلى شَيقِر، قِلْبان يقال لهن شيقر، وعلى الجوبه، سكاكا. ويرِد عليهم على الخِصِم، الخصم مغَيرا وخوعا وصوَير والجوبه، مْناشاعات الجوبه. هذولي يصيرون منازل بدو. يوم جوا الجوبه، جفرة قِبْلِيّه نفود وشماليّه حْجَره وهي بله هوبه. يا مار السرحان قاضبين لهم الما ويتناوخون وسبع ليال وهم معقّلين البل. وياخذون ما ادري وش كثرهن ليال، وهم قاهرينهم عن الما. واحقلوا عليهم. قالوا: هالحين وشلون؟ ذبحنا العطش وهم والينِ الما. قال ابن قدران: وش الراي؟ قالوا: والله بكيفك.

nights ago." "By God," he said, "as true as I am your father, nothing will keep me from pasturing our animals on those rainfed meadows and letting them quaff its pure water." On his return, he told his wife, "Pack up and leave at once! Off and away with you to your own family! Go back to your kin! I don't want you around here with us any longer." He moved camp with the intention of spending early summer at al-Tayyim, a flat expanse of land owned by the ʿAbdah tribe of Shammar at the northern end of Ḥā'il's line of foothills.[13] In those days, it was known by the name of al-Zubaydī, an area of small sandy outcrops on the way to al-Tayyim. They spent early summer at the well of al-Tayyim, beyond what is now called al-Khuṭṭah to its east. No sooner had they settled down at al-Tayyim than the Asāʿidah marched on them. They massed nearby, ready for the attack. Ibn Gidrān said, "Now that we have pitched our tents in their land, they're coming for us. Either we cut them up as we did the first time or they will avenge their earlier losses twofold. We'd better make ourselves scarce, and whoever wants to lay his hands on us, God help him."

It so happened that at that time he was sent a note by the people of al-Jawf, 1.7
saying: "Ibn Gidrān, if we can count on your friendship as before"—they used to maintain bonds of friendship with the people of Sakākā in al-Jawf—"don't leave us under the yoke of our tribal oppressors."[14] They meant the tribesmen of the Sirḥān, who had come roaring down the valley toward them. The population of al-Jawf was small and the clans of the Sirhān had designs on their possessions. Ibn Gidrān told his men, "Fill your waterskins"—it was midsummer—"and load up your riding camels!" They pulled out of al-Zubaydī, away from al-Tayyim, journeying over a track running through the sands and upcountry. They made their way north through the sand desert toward the well of al-Aṭwā and the water holes of Shēgir until they reached al-Jōbah, Sakākā. They steeled themselves to square up to their adversaries: clans settled in Mghērā, Khōʿā, Ṣwēr, and other outlying districts where Bedouin had struck roots in al-Jawf—the large depression that at its southern end touches the great sands and in the north shades into stony plains. The tribesmen of the Sirḥān stood their ground at the well. Having hobbled their camels during seven nights of fighting, they fought pitched battles.[15] For a long time the Sirḥān held firm and would not be budged from the water hole where they had massed their forces. What should we do next? Ibn Gidrān wondered. Here we are, dying of thirst and barred from reaching the water. "Tell me, what is your opinion?" Ibn Gidrān asked. "Whatever you think best," they said. "Fine. In that case, we'll drive our camels in front

قال: الراي اننا ندفع لنا اباعر ونهوش وراه. يا مير غفيلٍي يقال له ابن محمود من الشمروخ من الزميل، شيخ زوبع بالجزيرة هالحين، قال: انا ادفع اباعري. وهم ينوّخون الدبش ويعقّلونه وهم يمشون بالبل. يوم ضاقت محايلهم العرب وهم يسوقون عليهم مغاتير ابن محمود، سوقوا البل عليهم، ساقوَه على المتاريس وهم يدلّون يهوشون وراه يما خْلِطوهم وينصرهم الله على السرحان، ويكسرونهم ويقزّون السرحان عن الجوف. ويقيمون بالديره وهذولاك هَجّوا.

٨،١ والي مير القيض حانٍّ عليهم، القيض راكبهم والنفود قَفْوُهم. قالوا: اغدينا يوم ولينا السرحان نِجْلِد بالجوبه. هم يحبون الشمال. قالوا الآخرين: حنا شويين يا شمر، ما حناب كثير، ذالينٍ تعالم بنا هل الشمال. قالوا: حنا ما حناب ناكسين. قالوا الشيبان: الا نبي نرجع لديارنا، يم ديار شمر، وش لنا بهالقومان هذي نناحيَه! قال ابن قدران: نبي نِرْكِب على السرحان ونبي نِهدي عليهم أغديهم يقبلون الهدو ويصحبوننا ناخذ منهم صحب انهم ما زالنا بديارهم ما يتعرضوننا، ونبي سلوم العرب والقوانين. الناس هكالحين له سلوم، يا أركب الرِكْب على الرجل، عنّز على له حاكم أو شيخ يصحبه لو هم أمس متذابحين. قالوا الشيبان: ما يقبلون منك صحب، رجل زرتهم بمحلاتهم وسقتهم عن ديرتهم الجوبه وتبي تصحب، وهالحين مجتمعة كل هكالديرة، ولا يقبلون منك، وان قبلوا منك الكثير منهم يبوقك. قالوا: أجل حنا وش نسوّي؟ ما نقدر نجلد على الجوبة بين قومان شمر ولا حنا محبّينٍ ننكس للنفود نوبه. وش الراي؟ وش الراي؟ وسبع ليال وهم يتشاورون، سبع حكم. قال ابن قدران: أجل ما لنا الا نفوتهم، نبي نتبع السرحان ونفوتهم، ونحول مع اثرهم يم حدود الاردن ونِرْكِب على بني صخر. قالوا

of us, a wall of animals to shield us until we leap forward from behind the camels and engage them in battle." One of the men was Ibn Maḥmūd, a man of the Ghfēlah who belonged to the Shamrūkh tribe of the Zmēl division of Shammar, those who are now the chiefs of Zōbaʿ between the Tigris and Euphrates rivers in Iraq. He volunteered: "I am going to drive my camels in front." They made all their animals kneel, hobbled them, and made them march thus fettered at an excruciatingly slow pace. Fighters would resort to this ruse if they felt cornered to the point of desperation. With jerky movements, Ibn Maḥmūd's white camels limped along while being driven toward the enemies' barriers.[16] As long as they kept moving forward, the camels served as the warriors' shield until the men came surging from behind the protective wall of animals. A chaotic melee ensued. Warriors fought tooth and nail in close combat. With God's help, the tide of battle turned in their favor and they gained the upper hand. Their resistance broken, the Sirḥān were chased out of al-Jawf. Ibn Gidrān and his men stayed in the district while their opponents made a run for it.

By then they were under the pall of midsummer's oppressive heat, and the scorching sands of the Nafūd Desert lay behind them. They said, "Now that we have sent the Sirḥān packing, we might as well stay here in al-Jawf." They loved the north. Others disagreed: "We, Shammar, are a small group of outsiders here. We should be wary of these northerners conniving against us." The other group objected: "We are certainly not turning back!" But their elders insisted: "Certainly we are! We want to return home to our ancestral Shammar lands. We have no business confronting enemy tribes here." Ibn Gidrān said, "We might send some camels as a present to the Sirḥān. If it is agreeable to them, we will conclude a pact of friendship and receive a promise allowing us to stay in their tribal area without disturbance, in keeping with tribal customs and laws." In those days, the lives of people were ruled by tribal codes and practices. By sending a camel and presents, one appealed to the goodwill of a ruler or shaykh. Such a gesture implied an offer of friendship, no matter how ferociously they might have been fighting only a short time before. The old men said, "They will not accept your offer of friendship. How could they after what you did: marching on their country and evicting them from their abode in al-Jawf? And after that you ask them to be friends? They won't welcome your courtship, and if they do, it will be no more than a pretense meant to betray you at the first opportunity." "So, what to do? We cannot stay indefinitely in al-Jawf surrounded by enemies of Shammar. Nor do we have a mind to cross the Nafūd 1.8

الشيبان: لعن ابوكم كيف تبون تَخَطْرَون ديرة السرحان وانتم مذبّحينهم، الخريمة يسفِرنّه ضباع مغيرا، هذي ما توافق. قال ابن قدران: لازم حلالنا ننجّمه باللي هي به واليوم المرعى والريف يم الاردن.

٩،١ هم من مدة كم من سنه غرّب ابن قدران هو وعربه، غربوا يم الغربيه وقيّضوا لهم عند شيخ عرب على الشلاله حدر من اربد، عين تمشي، ولقوا هناك ريف وانعام ربي وحنطه وخير. قيضوا عنده هكالسنه مِقِيض طيب لما جا الصفري عاد شرقوا راجعين نكس وربعوا بديرتهم عقبما تكيلوا. ومن هكاليوم صارت رفقة حلوه هم وهالشيخ من بني صخر. قال ابن قدران: انا ابهدي على رفيقنا الاول، شيخ بني صخر، وتوكلوا على الله خلونا نغرب يم الغربيه، يم رفيقنا الاول نقيّض عنده، هالحين ريف ورغيف عنده، نكتال من الديره واباعرنا تربع ويطيب حلالنا هالسنه. قالوا: على كيفك. وخلى جماعته ورواه وقال: امشوا على اثرنا. هذا ابن محمود عيّى لا ينهج غرب، تيامن للعراق، وهذولا نووا يغربون. واركب ابن قدران مع له ركب معهم هَدُو ذلولين وجمل حر، ضروبه. وحوّلوا عليهم، على بني صخر، ابن قدران واللي معه حدري الزرقا بشنق العِمري. يوم ألفوا على الشيخ راعي الشلاله ونوخوا عنده يا والله هذا شيخٍ شايخ جديد غير هذاك، رفيقهم الاول، هذاك هافي وهذا بناخيٍ له شاخ مكانه. يا مار الشيخ الاول ما باقٍ على اثره الا بنت له حيه وحاضره. استقبلهم الشيخ أول نوبه وانطوه الهدو وحيّى بهم ورحب بهم، قال: مقبول هدوكم وحياكم الله ولا يكون الا الخير، القمرا قدامكم والظلما قفوكم ونصحبكم، بس انشا الله خلوكم مطمئنين.

Desert again. How to escape from our dilemma? What course shall we decide on?" For seven nights they remained locked in consultation, assisted by seven experts in tribal law. At last, Ibn Gidrān cut the knot: "We have no choice but to bypass them. Let's follow the direction taken by the Sirḥān and continue beyond their land toward the borders of Jordan. Let us send a present to Banū Ṣakhr." The old men howled, "May God curse your father! How could you think of venturing into the precincts of the Sirḥān after your onslaught against them? These inhospitable wastes are haunted by the hyenas of Mghērā, that kind of people. What a preposterous idea!"[17] Ibn Gidrān was adamant. "We must bring our animals to a place where they can pasture in safety amid plenty. For that purpose, Jordan is the only feasible option."[18]

Some years before, Ibn Gidrān and his tribe had trekked west to spend the hot season as the guests of a shaykh near al-Shallālah, down from Irbid. There was running water, a profusion of plant growth on land blessed by plentiful rains at the Lord's behest, and barley. All the creature comforts! Having spent a delightful summer, they went home at the approach of fall to pasture their camels in their own tribal land, having stocked up on all their needs. Ever since, they had maintained cordial relations with the shaykh of Banū Ṣakhr. Ibn Gidrān said, "I will send a present to our old friend and he will give us permission to stay over the summer. Food and grazing aplenty. We'll replenish our supplies while our camels graze to their hearts' desire and grow layers of fat to last them for a year." The others said, "Do as you see fit." He left the main body of his people behind, telling them to follow in his traces. Ibn Maḥmūd refused to go west and turned toward Iraq, while the others continued on their westward journey. Ibn Gidrān, accompanied by a few of his men, rode ahead with the presents: two female riding camels and a pedigree stud camel. They dismounted at Banū Ṣakhr's camp at the lower end of al-Zarqā region, toward the settlement of al-ʿUmarī. On arrival at the shaykh at al-Shallālah, they kneeled their camels, only to discover that a new shaykh had replaced their former friend. The old shaykh was gone and the present one was his successor. The daughter of the old one was still around, alive and well. It was the first time for the new shaykh to receive them. He graciously acknowledged receipt of the presents and spoke warm words of welcome: "Your present is accepted with pleasure. You are my guests in God's safekeeping. You will enjoy your time with us. You have come in moonlight and left darkness behind. From now on, you are our friends. Please, God willing, consider yourselves in complete security." 1.9

قالوا عرب الشيخ: هذي لقمة جتنا من نجد وخل الرِّفقات، خلنا نتقوّى ١٠،١
بهم. ودربكوا على الشيخ من هنا ومن هنا وهو يهس معهم بالطمع. يوم اخذوا ما ادري ليلتين او هن ثلاث، قالوا: والله انتم أكرمتونا وانطيتونا انشا الله الوِثَق ونبي نرجع لاهلنا نجيبهم نقداهم للديرة هذي، نبي نعانق اهلنا بها القيظ، نبي ننكس نسنّعهم. اهلهم حولِه، على اثرهم. قال: لا، حنا نزعج لاهلكم لهم دليل يجيبهم من يطلعون الوادي يما يجون بهذا. ذَلّ ابن قدران، اشْتَكّ يوم قال لهم انتم امتنوعوا يالرِكب عندنا ونرسل لاهلكم. بهالحكي هذا يا مار نوره، بنت الشيخ الاول، تسمع وعرفت بخطتهم، هم شابٍّ لهم الشيخ ومتراكين على لهم سجادة، منزلهم، وهي البنت قفوهم من تحت الذرى. وهي تسيّل القربة من بين أوزار القَشّ، يعني انتبهوا، تراهم سِيّلوا الما من تحتكم، تراهم باقوكم. يوم راعوا العيال يا مار الما يوم درج من تحت الفراش، الما يْتَلَسّن من تحت السجاده. وقم يابن قدران يقهقر الما بالباكوره ويحكي ويسولف لما رضعته الارض، واسكت واعطهم العين الرخوه ولا انطى غِيرِه، بس انه عرف الدعوى انه ملغومه، ما هي على يكونَه. إيه! تشوف ؟ قال: ما يخالف، الساعة المباركه، بس ياطويل العمر يا منُّه بغى يِمِدّ المندوب لاهلنا خلّه يَدْهَجَن الصبح اوصّيه، على اننا حنا مشينا القاع وعرفنا الطريق ونعلّمه بالمعاشي اللي هم يعشون بهن، وهو ما يعرف احوالهم والعرب مستنذره وخايف انهم يذبحون مندوبكم، يمرّن اوصيه بالامور اللي تمّنه منهم. يقوله راشد لشيخ بني صخر. قال: ما يخالف، وصه، لكن وصه وانت عندنا قاعد. مشروط

The shaykh's tribal following harbored other ideas: "This is a tasty morsel that has come our way from Najd. Forget about good companionship! Let's avail ourselves of this stroke of good luck to garner strength at their expense." Urged from all sides, the shaykh fell in with their greedy designs without demur.[19] Two or three nights later, the visitors said, "Really, we have been given a convivial reception. You have treated us very well and have inspired in us full confidence. The time has come for us to be on our way and meet our fellows so as to guide them to this district. We should rejoin them. The weather is very hot, and we have to make sure that they do not lose their way." Their fellows were not very far behind; they were on their tracks. "No need," the shaykh said. "We'll send a guide to meet your people and bring them from the end of the valley there behind you to this place." His words struck fear into the heart of Ibn Gidrān. It aroused his suspicion, being told to stay and wait while their host's men went and met his people. That kind of talk. The discussion had been overheard by Nūrah, the daughter of the old shaykh: she knew about her fellow tribespeople's nefarious designs. The shaykh lit a fire, and they made themselves comfortable while seated on his tent's majlis carpet. She was close by, hidden behind the tent's partition. The girl poured water from a skin so that it ran in a little rill from under the gear stacked outside. That was a sign: Pay attention, they are wetting the ground under your feet! Treachery is in the air! Ibn Gidrān and his companions took notice when water came dribbling in from under the carpet and collected in little pools. Ibn Gidrān stopped the flow by scraping the earth with the staff he held in his hand, keeping up the conversation and telling stories until the water had seeped into the ground. Then he stopped talking and with an amiable mien listened to his host, as if he had no inkling that something was up. But he was acutely aware of the other's duplicity. He sensed that a trap was being laid. The situation was becoming dangerous. "No matter, this is a blessed hour, only listen, may God grant you a long life! In the morning, before he sets out, let your envoy drop by. We'd like to give him some advice. We have traveled those empty plains. We know their route and the locations where they have halted for the night. He doesn't know what state of mind they are in. They are tense and sharply alert to any danger. I am afraid they might kill the envoy as he draws near before he has had a chance to speak. Let me explain and advise him on the kind of precautions he should take." In these terms Rāshid spoke to the shaykh of Banū Ṣakhr. "That's fine with me," the other said, "but you should do so while sitting here in our 1.10

له جذع أو جذعه هالنجاب اللي ينحرهم يجيبهم، قالوا: بس انت هاتهم، بغوهم، يبون يقطعون قِرْنيّاهم.

١١،١ يوم جا الصبح يا مير هو زاهبٍ المنجوب على هكالذلول. قال: عاد وصّوه باللي بانفسكم. قالوا: مير ما من وصاة حنا نوصيك بس بنفسك انت يالمرسال. خذ دربيلك معك والى شفت السلف على بعد زِلّ عن وجهه، اكمن بلك محل يغيّبك والبد عن السلف لين ما يتعداك، السلف معه جهّيل ومتعرضين قومان ونخاف يغيرون عليك ولا يريع بك الفكر يذبحونك قبل ما ياخذون علومك – هم ما يبونه يعانق السلف أول لأن السلف مشتهينٍ التغريبه – وليا فات السلف وشفت المظاهير تر قدامهن شايبين كل على له رحول، على زوامل الرويّ، وكل معه له فرس يقوده، ترهم يصيرون بين السلف والمظاهير بالعاده، يقدّون المظاهير، رجال عاقلين، لا يجيك لك جاهل يطخك أو يحسبونك قوماني، ترى الراي والامر عند هالشايبين، هم اللي ياخذون علمك زين والحكية لهم، الى منك جيتهم قل العيال طيبين ونخبر جمل البيت الاوضح رِدِي قل لهم يبادلون الجملين الاملح والاوضح للبيت – يعني يهجّون ويمشون الليل والنهار – وقل لهم ان الامور جت على مرماعكم وعلى ما تشتهون – ما همب اول هذولاك الشيبان، ابوه وعمُّه، ينصحونهم يقولون لا تنهجون، من راس ما همب مشتهين التغريبه، يبون يجلدون بديارهم؟ – وقل لهم يفارعون وادي النسلي – يعني انسلّوا بخِفْيه، امصْقُوا – وينطونا روحهم ويزيدون عليق الخيل من حب سلخط – سلخط ديرةٍ عندهم بالاردن، وهذولا يبيهم يفهمون يعني احبسوا الرجال هذا اللي جاكم

place." The envoy had been promised a four-year-old camel as a reward for his mission. Greedy to lay hands on an easy haul of plunder, they were determined to bring in the travelers by any means. They wanted to strip them bare.[20]

In the morning, the envoy stood at the ready, a bag of provisions for the road slung over his mount's back. "Now it is time to tell him what's on your mind!" They said, "Listen, envoy, it is not for us to issue instructions, but we are concerned for your safety. Take binoculars along, and as soon as you espy their vanguard in the distance, slip aside and hide. Stay out of their way and crouch, making yourself invisible until they have passed by. Among them are rash youngsters impatient to take on enemies, and they might not hold back. Do not doubt for a second that they'll kill you before you've said a word." In truth, they did not want him to contact the vanguard first because those riders had set their mind on this westward journey, come what may. And they continued: "Once the vanguard has passed and you see the train of pack camels coming, you'll notice that they are preceded by two old men, each on a camel of the kind used to transport water from the well. Also, each of them leads a mare by a rope, trotting alongside.[21] Usually, they ride between the vanguard in front and the train of pack camels that follows. They set the pace for the camel train with the tribe's chattels, women, and children. They have a shrewd understanding, unlike the rash brats who attack without thinking twice on the assumption that you are an enemy. Command and power of decision are in the hands of these graybeards. They'll listen carefully to what you have to say and will discuss matters with you. Tell them that we are doing fine and that we know that the white camel carrying the big tent is faltering: they should put that burden by turns on the black camel and the white one." That is, they must hurry, marching strenuously day and night, without pause. "Then tell them that things are as they expected and desired." Weren't the graybeards, his father and uncle, the ones who had advised against this undertaking? They were reluctant to embark on this westward journey and would rather have remained in their tribal land. "After that, tell them to go up Wādī n-Naslī." That is, *insallū*, meaning "slink off,"before anyone takes notice, stealthily. Forget about the appointment with us and make yourselves scarce! "Let them do so for our sake, and let them fill the horses' feedbags with an ample amount of grain of Salkhaṭ, *ḥabb Salkhaṭ*." That is, grain from a district in Jordan. But what they wanted the graybeards to understand was that they should put the messenger in chains; not *ḥabb Salkhaṭ* but *ḥabs al-khaṭ*: arrest (*ḥabs*) the 1.11

معه الخط، سنع لغز (حب سلخط = حبس الخط) - وخوذوا نزع الطماميع كيلكم، لأن الديرة به خير وبه نعمه - يعني انهزموا، خوذوا بس الخفيف من شيلكم، لا يعثركم الشيل، خففوا على البل لاجل تنهزمون.

١٢،١ واخرز على هالعلم يالشمالي. وهو يتلوّز بهالعلم. حطوا الذلة بقلبه وكل محل يدَزْبِل به. يوم راعى يا مير هذاك زومة السلف الصبح هو هذاك مثل الحير وهو يجي بهكالرسم وهو ينوخ الذلول وهو يقعد عنده يما تعدوا السلف. يوم اخذ الى هذولاك اللي هو ياصف له اهل الركاب والمظاهير وراهم وهو يعانقهم. قال: ابشروا انه غرا وسرا، ريف وصديق وبالطريق، وهذا وما وصّونن به رجاجيلكم. قالوا: وش وصّوك؟ قال: يقولون كان البيت متلحلح الجمل الاوضح اللي هو عليه يحطونه على الرحول الملحا ويفارعون وادي النسلي علينا، الله الله بالممشا، عن هه وهه. قالوا: هذا اللي وصاك؟ قال: هذا اللي وصّانن وهذي هالسعدونيه ام السعادين، عباة ما يلبسونه كود الشيخان اول. وسعدونيتين معه. والى مير هذا، من تحت هذا حاكّه لما بغت تنقعر من يمين، وهذيك مثله. قال: انا عباتي هاللون، يقوله حدى الشيبان. قال: وانا عباتي هاللون. يوم علمهم بالوصاة لْقِطوا الشيبان حبّهم، الشيبان يفهمون، يعرفون المتّقي. قالوا: الله يبشرك بالخير، جاي جاي يا حبيبي، جاي جاي بها الروض. وهم ينوّخون به وطخّه يا حديهم بالمِحْجان مع الجبهه ليا الدم سايل. وش علمكم؟ قالوا: ما من عِلْم، ما من خلاف. واطرحوه وصكوا حديد الفرس به وهم يجيبونه ويكتفونه واجظعوا المسامة عليه والرويّ ملايا. تبرزوا هناك عنه. قال واحد لواحد: وش

carrier of the letter (*al-khaṭṭ*). "Let them take a minimum of provisions and travel lightly as raiders do, because the land here has plentiful stocks to answer our every need." That is, make your escape as fast as you can and discard all unnecessary items! Don't be weighed down with heavy loads and make the camels run at their hottest pace!

The envoy from the north committed this advisory firmly to memory. He clung to the message with unwavering determination. They had successfully instilled fear in his heart. He went on his way, every now and then taking his binoculars to scan the horizon. Come morning, there was the vanguard, looming up in the distance like a garden dense with palm trees, surging forward toward him at an impetuous pace.[22] At a prominence in the terrain, he had his camel kneel down and kept it out of view until the vanguard had passed by. After a while, he caught sight of the riders, followed by the camel train in their wake as it had been described to him, and he rode up to meet them. "Good news!" he cried. "Your fellows are having a wonderful time. A warm welcome and great hospitality are waiting for you down the road! They asked me to convey to you a spoken message." "Let us hear the words they entrusted to you." He said, "They told me that your camping equipment chafes the back of the white camel. Let the white and the black camels carry the load by turns. Steer the camels up Wādi n-Naslī toward us. They must take that route and not any other course." "That is all the advice they entrusted to you?" "Yes, that's the message. They also handed me these two fine cloaks for you." *Siʿdūniyyah* is a kind of cloak reserved for shaykhs, persons of dignity. But how come this one has been sewn up from the hem below on the right side, and why are they so wrinkled at that spot? Both cloaks looked that way. One graybeard turned to the other: "What is this? Is yours the same?" Yes, it was. They pondered the message, and the penny dropped. They grasped the hidden meaning and told the envoy, "May God bring you happy news. Come here, here, here, our dearest. Alight here, in this valley!" They made him kneel his mount, and one of them hit him with his riding stick over the forehead, drawing blood from the gash. "What's wrong with you?" he cried. "Nothing in particular," they said. "Nothing serious." They threw him down and shackled him in iron chains used for horses. Thus manacled, he was made to lie under a pack saddle piled high with large skins full of water.[23] They walked out of his earshot and deliberated. One asked the other, "What do you make of all this?" "Look," the other said, "our men are held captive, and they have marked us for plunder. The black camel is the night and

1.12

بَه. قال: بَه رجاجيلنا مربوطين وحنا ماخوذين والرحول الملحا الليل والجمل الاوضح النهار. يبينا بالليل نهجّ قفو. ووادي النسلي النِيرِه. وحكة العباة يعني يبون يدقّوننا، يذبحوننا، يبون يِهْفوننا.

السلف على وجههم ما جوهم، اهلهم. وهم يدربلون السلف قالوا: اهلنا ١٣،١
وكاد جاهم بلا. وهم ينكسون يوم راعوا يا والله هذولاك العرب نازلين والى شيبانهم عندهم هالربيط رابطينه. هاه؟ وش الامر؟ قالوا الشيبان: الامر دياركم لعن ابوكم، نبي ننحاش، باكر حنا قاضبين اثرنا نبي نتيامن مع جْنِبة هالوادي ونجازل الوادي مجازل وكل عقلة نوازنه نشربه باليسرى وحنا مشرّقين. يوم جا من باكر وهم يسحبون. وهم يشرّقون بخويهم هذا الربيط. وليا منهم وازنوا هالعقله، مثل ما تقول ميقوع، شربوا منه. ويجون الهوجا ام كور بِجْنِبة الوادي من غرب ويِرْدونَه. يوم شربوا من الهوجا، الهوجا هاللي يم ديار عنزة فوق، قالوا: عاد انت ياللحية الغانمه جبت لنا العلم وكثّر خيرك وهذي ذلولك وزهابك وماك ومرعاك اركب ودوّر هَلَك. وليا جيت شيخكم سلم لنا عليه حق نزلتنا عليه وعنوتنا يمه يطلق العيال هاللي عنده يخليهم يجون، يرخص لهم، حنا هالحين تعنّزنا لديارنا ولا حناب بايقين نذبحك حنا، ولا حناب قاضبينك، وكان شيخكم يبي يذبح ضيوفه يذبحهم وبكيفه، وكان هو يبينا ترنا لنا قرية يقال له موقق، غربي حايل، ما تروح عن محله، ترو وْعَدُه موقق، كان هو يبينا ترنا ما نتعداه، لِلّه يما يجينا انشا الله المطر والربيع والخير. وانحاشوا لياما جوا موقق، ديار شمر بالغوطه، موقق ديرة للغفيلة قبيلة الرمال، هكالحين هي ملك للرمال لكن خلّوَه للغفيلة الباقين وطلعوا يم جبه. يوم وصلوا قالوا اهل موقق: وين ابن قدران؟ قالوا: ممسوك وبداله هذولا.

العيال كلما نشدهم الامير: وين دووا العرب؟ وش ابطى بهم؟ متي يجون؟ ١٤،١
قالوا: العرب ريّضين تَوّهم ياطويل العمر، جايين من ديار بعيده وحلالهم ردي

the white one is the day. He wants us to make a run for it, back to where we came from, all night long. Wādī n-Naslī is the way to disappear from their sight and make our escape. The cloaks sewn up the wrong way mean that they will pounce and make short work of us. They'll kill us, wipe us out."[24]

Meanwhile, the vanguard had kept up an unrelenting pace. At some point, they started wondering why the others were lagging so far behind. They looked through their binoculars and decided something was wrong. They retraced their steps. To their astonishment, they found their folks dismounted and the graybeards in the company of a manacled prisoner. "What's going on?" they asked. The graybeards replied, "This is what's going on. We are going back home, God's curse on your fathers! It is cut and run for us. Tomorrow at dawn, we turn tail and retrace our steps, keeping to the right side of this valley. We'll take it in stages, drawing water from every desert well on our left as we move east."[25] At dawn they pulled out, heading east. The fettered envoy was taken along. They drank and filled their skins from each water hole on their way, such as Mēgūʿ, and al-Hōjā Umm Kūr on the western side of the valley, upcountry in the tribal marches of ʿAnazah. There the prisoner was told, "Well, good young man, you have been so kind to bring us the message. We can't thank you enough. Here, you may take your riding camel, victuals, water, fodder. You are free to ride out and rejoin your people. Convey our greetings to your shaykh and the respects we owe him for the time spent at his place, the one we were heading for. Tell him to release our men and allow them to rejoin us with his permission. We are going home. We are not a treacherous lot, disposed to kill you or prolong your captivity. If your shaykh has a mind to slaughter his guests, let him do so by all means. It's up to him. In case he is looking for us, tell him we are at a village called Mōgag, west of Ḥā'il. He is most welcome in Mōgag. We are staying there until, God willing, the rains arrive and the time comes to move to the spring pastures and enjoy the good life." They sped off without halting until they reached Mōgag, their settlement in the tribal land of Shammar, situated in al-Ghūṭah oasis. At that time, Mōgag was settled by the Ghfēlah, a division that includes the Rmāl, but the latter left the other groups of the Ghfēlah and instead headed for Jubbah.[26] On their return, people asked why Ibn Gidrān was not with them. "He's being held captive," they said. "These are the ones who made it back." 1.13

Up north, the shaykh turned to Ibn Gidrān and his men. "Where have they gone? Why does it take them so long?" "They ride at a leisurely pace; may God 1.14

وعلى مهلهم دوبهم يمشون. يوم فات سبع ليال، قالوا: يا معزّب الرحمان، أهلنا بنجد هالحين، مير بكيفك تطلقنا والا تخلّينا. قال: كيف؟ قالوا: بس توكّل على الله، أهلنا هجّوا. يوم اخذوا لهم مده يا والله هذا المرسال يصاطغ على مطيته جاي لحاله. أطلقوه الرمال، يوم ابعدوا اطلقوه وجا. قالوا: هاه؟ وين العرب؟ قال: والله العرب حالوا من الوادي، اقفوا، من الوادي اقفوا، ما خلّونَن إلا بالهوجا ام كور. وعلمهم باللي صار عليه، قال: والله الربع عْمَلوا بي هاك وعملوا بي هاك وكرّمونن، ما ضرّونن بشي، ويوم جوا ديارهم ارسلونن جاي. قالوا: ليش يابن قدران تعمل هاك؟ قال: والله انا عندكم والوصاة مكشوفه، علمت مرسالكم وانتم تسمعون. قال الشيخ: حنا اسمنا اللي بقنا وخسرنا مير يا عيال دوّروا اهلكم، اسمكم اللي ذقتوا ملحتنا، لكم المهرّبات، روحوا. وهم يركبون عليهن العيال وهم يجونك مروّحين. ولا يجون اهلهم الا بموقق. عاد حدى الربع، العيال، ابن قدران يوصف يعني ممشاهم من حولتهم من التيم يما جوا الغربيه ويوصف عمل الشيخ معهم يوم يبوق بهم وتسييلة نوره للما وحربهم مع السرحان. وقصيدهم بهكالدور هذاك يعني مثل طَوْي الهلالات، يعني تخالط هي وايا قصيد الهلالات الا شي:

زاعن من الزبيـــــدي ظعونٍ تِقـَلّلت   صـبح ليـل تنصى المغـارف صبوره ١٥،١

يعني يغرفون الما اللي هم وردوا عليه، من كثرهم الما قل عليهم وليلةٍ كلَّه ليا الصبح وهم يغرفون غرف، يموحون.

كم خفـرة تلثى وهي مـا تظـللت   تجـل الزمـل من فوق عـالي ظهوره

تلثى: تمشي، تتعب. تجل الزمل تسوقه.

prolong your life. They are coming, but they traveled a long distance and their animals are worn out. Therefore, expect them to move very slowly. They can barely walk at all." After seven nights, they called on him: "Dear host of our Merciful Lord, our companions have reached Najd by now. Do as you like; let us go or keep us here." "How come?" he said. "Forget it, our people have made a run for it." After some more time, the envoy came staggering in, his mount swaying with fatigue. He came alone. He had been released by the Rmāl once they had reached safety. "What happened? Where are those people?" "Well, they turned away from the valley and went home. They released me once they had reached al-Hōjā Umm Kūr." And he gave an account of what happened and how he was treated: "They were generous with me and did not hurt me in the least. From their tribal lands, they let me go." "Why did you do this, Ibn Gidrān?" they asked. "Come on now," he said. "I gave my advice openly. You were listening when I informed your envoy." At that, the shaykh felt compelled to confess: "We have only ourselves to blame for losing out on account of our dishonest conduct. Now, fellows, you are free to go and rejoin your kinfolk. You tasted our salt, and accordingly you are granted the customary three days to make your escape.[27] Go!" They rode off and made it to their folks back home in Mōgag. Ibn Gidrān described the adventures of their odyssey, starting the year before at al-Tayyim: their trek to the western region, the way they were treated by the shaykh and his perfidy, how Nūrah sent a rill of water their way as a sign of warning, and the episode of warfare with the Sirḥān. Back then, poets still composed in the meter of the ancients, the style of the Banū Hilāl.[28] Most of these verses are enmeshed with similar Banū Hilāl poetry.[29]

They surged from al-Zubaydī, a laden camel train, 1.15
from well to well, scooping up water, night and day.[30]

—They descended into the well to scoop up water from the bottom: because they were so many, the water level had fallen. They kept scooping up the water from the bottom all night until morning.

No shade for the tribe's maiden, hard at work:
riding her mount, she goads the camel herds;

—"Hard at work" means "she walks, exerts herself, driving the camels to and from the well."[31]

من تشرق ياما تغيب وهي ما تعللت   تجرّ الردا من عقب اظلة خدوره
عشية عشّينا بسحّا وشيقر   والاطوا ومسحوب الرشا مع جروره

هذي كله موارد.

وعشية عشينا بخشع عذفا   والعصر جفّلنا جوازي بقوره

خشع عذفا جو بحد النفود من غاد.

وعشية عشينا قاعة انبطٍ والغضا   بصف طيقان تلاعط نغوره

انبط بحد اللبة، ابرق مُوْخْر النفود كله غضا، طيقان يعني جيلان، النغور بهن ملح هن يتبارقن وانت تبرى لهن تشوفهن بيض هن هذولنك.

وعشية عشينا نقرةٍ كوهبت بنا   جينا لنا دارٍ كفى الله شروره

ديرة السرحان.

جينا سراحين على الكود والكدى   كد جذبوا جدّانهم من قبوره

يعتزون بجدودهم.

وزاموا علينا بجمع كالرحى   وراحن بهم جفل الظبا من قفوره
وانَخْنا واناخوا وعقّلنا وعقلوا   والكل منا عيشته من دروره
وسقنا عليهم لابن محمود هجمه   شقْحٍ تشادي للشواشا وبوره

يعني انهن وُضْح.

No time to chat, she toils from dawn to sunset,
hither and thither, torn from her tent's luxury.[32]
At evening we made a halt at Saḥḥā and Shēgir,
al-Aṭwā, pulling well ropes with all our might;

—These are all water holes.[33]

One more stage to the rim of Khath' 'Adhfā;
startling roaming oryx herds late afternoon.

—Khath' 'Adhfā is a well at the edge of the Nafūd on the other side of the sands.

A night at dense *ghaḍā* bushes of Anbaṭ's vale,
lines of cliffs, white salt gleaming and aglitter.[34]

—Anbaṭ is on the periphery of al-Labbah at the back side of the Nafūd, a rocky outcrop with a sand-covered base in an area with a dense growth of *ghaḍā* bushes. "Lines of cliffs" (*ṭīgān*) are steep bluffs; "salt gleaming and aglitter" (*al-nghūr*): they are crusted with salt that glitters; they are white if you look at those formations in passing.

A night down the slope to a wide depression:
that land, may God spare us from its evils!

—"that land": the land of the Sirḥān tribe.

Battling the Sirḥān, such a grinding slog:
war cries raised ancestors from graves.

—Their battle cries invoked the names of their forefathers.

They rushed at us, a wall of churning waves
crashing down while gazelles dashed for cover.
Mounts hobbled, pitched battles were fought
by warriors fed on milk from camel udders.
We pushed on, Ibn Maḥmūd's herd our shield:
pinkish-white camels, fur a silvery shine.

—He means *wuḍḥ*; that is, "white camels."

كلّ السيف وانثنى عود القنا   وسيف ابن قدران بعياة اموره
على يدي من عميرة محفظ   وايا غلام يا تكامل شروره
وزاعوا وزعنا على صوب دربهم   يما عدّيناهم مع قهاميز قوره
وكم من سميح الوجه غمقٍ صوابه   عيى على دعاثير المداوي ذروره
كله لعيني ذيب بايت القوى   يفرح بلقوانا مقاوي طيوره
ونمنا بليل ونومنا على حَوَل   وراحوا قبلانا قبل حزة فجوره
ووردنا مع ساقتهم على جال ملكهم   غبطانه تشادي لكِتّف نسوره
واخذنا سبع اجبةٍ بين شور ومشتور   وسنّدنا والشيبان شوره بزوره
وركبنا حِرّتين واستجنبنا حِرّه   يَبْرى لهن حِرٍّ صديقك بكوره

الحرتين والحر يبونهن هدو.

وعنزنا شيخٍ على راس مرقب   وراحت شغاغيله تدَنْدِن قدوره

على راس مرقب يعني انه نازلٍ بمكان الشيخ الاول، آخذٍ بنته. تدندن قدوره يسعون بالضيفه والذبيحه.

حمّاي للمفالي ياوَيّ عذره   تطرق نظيرك مع مثاني عذوره
وحيَّى بنا ورحّب بنا وكِد فرح بنا   والشيخ ما اعطانا صماصيم شَوره
يوم جا وقت المديد قلنا نتيسّر   قال استريحوا عن توالي حروره
نزعج لاهلكم منجوب يجيبهم   دليلة يِقْدَى السَهل عن وعوره

Swords swished till blunted, lance shafts tilted;
Ibn Gidrān's sword gained vigor from smiting:
Held in the iron grip of ʿAmīrah's scion,
his panache wreaks havoc in enemy ranks.[35]
Hot on the heels of fleeing masses,
chased beyond flat-topped mounds:
Fine gentlemen nursing deep wounds,
no match for a quack's healing powders.[36]
Our fight served starving wolves a feast,
lavish banquet for ravenous birds of prey.
A night of broken sleep, tossing and turning;
at dawn our onrush scattered them like chaff,
Snapping at a camel train in retreat:
palanquins like shoulders of hulking vultures.
Seven days' deliberation spent huddling:
upcountry we rode, graybeards grudgingly.
We sent two noble camels; another trotted beside,
steered by a friend astride a pedigree stud,

—The two purebred she-camels and the pedigree stud are the presents they intend to give.

Headed for a shaykh encamped on heights
amid the din of rattling pots and banging trays.

—"On heights": he means that he is lodged at the station of the former shaykh; he married his predecessor's daughter. "Rattling pots": they put themselves out to give a hospitable reception to guests and slaughter an animal to treat them to a roast.

Herds graze his fiefdom of green meadows:
you'd rub your eyes at verdure so lush!
He greeted, bade welcome, showed delight:
dark truth masked by affable demeanor.
We took leave: "We'll fence for ourselves."
"Easy!" he said. "Stay until heat abates!
Our envoy rides to meet your fellows,
to guide them past impassable terrain."

وانْتَـلّ قـلبي مـن فوادي وانـكوى   كـد وكِّدَتْ لي بنت الاجواد نوره

اللي دفقت الما من تحتهم.

وصّيت منجوبُه وكاس البِنّ بايدي   وخـرزْت له خـرز مقـلّبات سيوره

كاس البن فنجال القهوه، يتقهوى هو، شَفّ له شفّه وحده وبقى به شفّتين، يعني انه ما تلعثم، دبّر هالتدبير وعطى هالراي والفنجال بيده، ما يعوق، بساع. مقلّبات سيوره يعني حكيت حكيٍ ما هو على وجهه.

قلت اعمد الشيبان واكمن عن السَلَف   اهـل عيــــاد تِتّليها مهوره
قل توه جت لكم ياشايبين الرضا   عـروس تَوّه تــــروّك عـطوره
يفـارعون وادى النسـلّي عـلينا   قوايله مع ليـــلها مع عصوره
ويضرب قعود الزينة على عين ثَفْنته   يـامـا يـكنهب بـيعوالي ظهوره

على عين ثفنته يعني انكسوا قفو، الثفنة ثفنة رجل البعير من قفو، قعود بنت لهم ما تْعَدَى على له جمل أوضح عجل ممشاوه، ما تعدى تمشي قفو السلف.

وخوذوا نـزع الطـماميع كَيـلكم   ياما يخاشرن بيحصيد الشويمة غموره

الشويمة فلاحة بموقق.

وزيـدوا عليق الخيل من حَبّ سَلْخَط   متــــاع وقتٍ عن توالي دهوره
ياخذون من زينـات المشاريب ورده   ووردة مـن الهوجـــا وكوره
يامـا حـلى بالعصـر هيضات زوبع   نِـدّر حـرارٍ مـن مواكـر وكوره

My heart tensed up, stung by red-hot iron,
my fears abetted by Nūrah, a worthy girl.

—The girl spilled water that came trickling from under their carpet.

Amiable, coffee cup in hand, I gave advice,
threading the needle with upside-down words.

—He held an earless porcelain coffee cup and took one sip, leaving the other two sips for later. That is, he did not fumble but kept his relaxed composure while plotting his strategy and formulating his reply, cup in hand. He gave no hint of being taken aback, not for a moment. "Threading the needle with upside-down words": that is, the message he conveyed lay concealed beneath the words' surface and had to be deciphered.

"Head for the graybeards, stay shy of the vanguard:
warlike cavalry men, thoroughbred mares and foals.
Say, 'Graybeards both, rejoice at my glad tidings:
a bride coiffed with a perfume-sprinkled mane!'
Come to us, ride up through Wādī n-Naslī
through midday heat, day and night, unflagging;
Hit the palanquin-bearing camel's stifle joints
to make it turn, loads swaying on its back!

—Hit them right on the stifle joints at the back side of the camel's legs to make it turn. He speaks of the male camel carrying the damsel hidden inside her litter. The fast-paced white male follows closely behind the armed vanguard.[37]

Take just bare necessities, as light as raiders,
till your mounts are fed al-Shwēmah's harvest;

—Al-Shwēmah are sown fields at Mōgag.

Fill up horses' nosebags with Salkhaṭ grain,
food to shield them from raging famine;
Quench thirst with water from drinkable wells,
sweet drafts hoisted up from Hōjā Umm Kūr."
Sheer delight, to watch Zōbaʿ strut and prance,
Peregrines, hatched in nests at soaring heights.[38]

مشيّخة الرعيان زورٍ عن العدا   كم قالةٍ غدوا به من بعد المناحي وزوره
ويامـا حَلى بالقيظ مِقْطان موقق   يا اصْفَرّ عِرْجود القنا من بكوره
ديارٍ لنا ما هي ديارٍ لغيرنا   ياما حَلى توقيفنا بيحيوره
ونلوذ بالغوطة عن واهج اللوى   يا قلّطوا من عند بَقْعا سبوره
ولنا بدَمْثات المباريك منزل   لى صار ما قوّادها من خبوره

Zōbaʿ herdsmen, shaykh-like, scorn the enemy:
what with feats of arms, they're held in awe.[39]
Midsummer's sojourn at Mōgag is a dream;
dates ripen in palm trees' yellow bunches;
Our tribal land and home! Ours, no one else's!
What bliss to luxuriate in heavenly gardens!
Al-Ghūṭah shelters when hot winds lash the dunes:
camp is readied by scouts sent ahead from Bagʿā.
Camels' soft couching grounds are our home,
sandy labyrinths open to crack cameleers alone.

شايع يذبح ابن قدران ويشيخ بالرمال

كثيرة سوالف شايع وانا قاضبه اول لكن ما اتميزز منَه هالحين. هذا ولد عمُّه ١،٢
راشد ابن قدران، دسم المواعين راشد، شاخ وتشازروا هو واياوه على الشيخه.
شايع الامسح، جد هالرمال هذولا، جد الجارد، طلع جذع حي. امسح ما له عين.
حدى عيونه ما من عين. قبل شايع كان راشد ابن قدران هو الشيخ. شايع طلع
رجال طيب ويركبن، ان قلت انه مالود بليلة القدر فهو مالود بليلة القدر على
سوالف يسولفونهن عنه والا ما حضرته. وحسدوه القدران وصاروا تقل اللي
ما يغلونه بالحيل. واستهوت له بنت عمه كعيب الظبي، باسنانه، بنت شخَص
ولا دونه دون ولا يبي غيره وهي ما تبي غيره، وملّك عليه. يا مار ما معه صمايل،
حلال. مَلّك على المره وراح يدوّر مرازق الله والبنت اجلدت عند هَلَه، أخذه ولا
جاه، حِيّيرةٍ لُه يعني. وهو يجي يمشي مْفَيّضٍ العراق يبي لاجل طراقي شمر يركب
معَه يطلع. وفيّض مع سيب العراق، من قرايا هالعراق، ليا راعي هكالذلول الملحا
هالولد المِشْكل، ولدٍ نَظِر يمشي مع الجادة خلاوي، امير يعارضُه: وين ياولد؟ قال:
والله ودي اخاويك. قال: حياك الله، اركب. واركب شايع معه. يوم اقبلوا على
لهم قرية ولا هي كبيره. وهو ينوّخ، غيوب الشمس. يا مير اخذ هكالدرقه وسيف
ولبس الدرقه. قال: ياولد، انت ياخويّي! قال: آه. قال: الى طْلَعَت نجمة الصبح
وانا ما جيتك فانت هالذلول وما عليه تروه لك، دور الديرة اللي تبي. عقّل الذلول
انت ياشايع، معه له دبوس، وهو يجيك قاطرُه، يتليه، يتلي خويُّه، ما يدري وشو

Shāyiʿ Slays Ibn Gidrān and Becomes Shaykh of the Rmāl

The stories about Shāyiʿ are many. I knew them well in my younger years, but by now my grasp has become less sure. One of his cousins, Rāshid ibn Gidrān, known as "Rāshid of the Fat-Laden Platters," was the tribe's shaykh.[40] The two of them clashed in a bitter contest for leadership. Shāyiʿ is considered the ancestor of the Rmāl tribe, the forefather of the Jārid branch.[41] He was an energetic and strong young man.[42] Amsaḥ, his nickname, means that he had only one eye. One of his eye sockets was empty. Before Shāyiʿ, the tribe's leader was Rāshid ibn Gidrān. Shāyiʿ was a good-natured and vigorous person. It is possible that he was born on the Night of Destiny, as he was according to the many stories about him. I cannot tell. I wasn't there to witness those events. He was envied by the clansmen of al-Gidrān; they were not much taken with him, truth be told. He and his cousin, Kʿēb al-Ẓabiy, fell in love. She was about his age, an attractive girl. There was no question of anyone else: he was her only choice, and for him it was the same. He concluded a marriage contract but was without means: he did not own property. The marriage formalities done, he traveled in search of an income that God would provide to him. The girl stayed behind with her clan and waited for him. He took her as his wife, but the marriage was not consummated. He had reserved her for himself, as was his right as a cousin. He journeyed down the road to Iraq in the hope that another traveler of the Shammar tribe would offer him a ride on his camel. He went down to the lowlands of Iraq and the villages there.[43] On his way, he encountered a young man of handsome appearance and pleasant attitude, riding a black she-camel, all alone by himself on the sandy track. The young man turned to him. "Where are you going, boy?" Shāyiʿ replied, "By God, I would like to accompany you!" "You are most welcome," the young man said. "Mount with me!" Traveling together, they came to a small village. As sunset approached, his companion made the camel kneel and dismounted. Taking shield and sword, he said, "Listen, my boy, my little brother!" "Yes?" "If I have not returned at the twinkle of the morning star, it means the riding camel and her accoutrements are yours.[44] Feel free to take her anywhere you 2.1

يبي يْعَمَل. يوم هوى بالقصر، قصر هالقرية يا مير يوم عانقه هكالعباد اللي كبر هالاوضه. يا ميريوم دلّوا يتعالبون بهالسيوف وهالدرق. تعالبوا، تعالبوا، تعالبوا. يوم انه طلعت النجمة وهم يتضاربون. شايع عندهم بس انه متّقي ولا دريوا به. يا ميريوم ان العباد وَلَى خويه، خوي شايع. قال الخوي: ما عندي من اولاد الحلال والي. قال شايع: عندك خويك، كل ما تبي خويك الى حاضر. وهو يضرب العبد مع راسه بالدبوس يا خْلاق الدرع هاويات بدماغه ليا ناتقات عيونه مقابل. اطلع خويه. قال: انهج هات الذلول. وانهج شايع وجب الذلول. يوم جا الى هالبنت واقفة بمكانه. قال: يابنت ما عينتي خويٍّ لي بهذا؟ قالت: انا خويك. قال: ما انتي خويّي، انتي مرة وخويّي رجل. قالت: نوّخ، نوّخ واعلمك. نوّخ. قالت: انا خويك، هذا العبد هاللي حنا ذبحنا، هذا عبد لابوي ويبي ياخذن وذبح ابوي وذبح اخوتي وانحشت وآخذ اختي عقبي وجايبة ولدين منه وجيت ادوّر القضا بابوي واخوتي وقاضان الله وذبحت حتي عياله، حتي عيال اختي ذبحتهم معه، ما ابي له طنوٍ عندي. وهالحين الله انطاك هالقصر وامارته وكله لك وخزونه، وانا ابيك. قال: انا قفوي لي والدين ما اقدر. قالت: وش يعوزك؟ قال: ابي سيفك هذا ودرقتك وذلولك. وخوذيهن وانطيهن اياوه، وهو يرجع لاهله.

قال يوم الله جاب لي هالسلاح وهالذلول انا ابغزي، اترزّق الله. ويغزي ومعه ٢،٢
له له ربع يداورون درّابة الشام، درابة الشام أهل الدروب، اللي يقطّعون الدروب، الدروب أول على بعارين تْخبر. ويتولّجهم هكالجذع، دغيري، يبي يغزي معهم، ما لامُّه غيره. وتلحقهم امه قالت: يا شايع ولدي فْتَنن يبي يغزي ولا والله اودعته يغزي الا معك، لكن تروه وداعة لك من رقبتي برقبتك. قال: الله يستر الحال،

like." Shāyiʿ fettered the camel and, armed with an iron rod, stealthily went after his travel companion. He wondered what he was up to. On arrival at the village's castle, his friend was stopped by a black slave, a fellow as big as this room. They skirmished with sword and shield, challenging each other with feints and probing attacks. At the appearance of the morning star, they were still at their game. They were not aware that Shāyiʿ was watching, hidden in a corner. When the slave was about to overwhelm his friend, Shāyiʿ's companion called out, "Is there no one here, not any good man?" Shāyiʿ spoke up: "Whenever you need your friend, see, he is at the ready!" Hardly had he said so than with his iron rod he struck the slave on the head. It was an awesome blow. The metal rings of the slave's coat of mail spilled onto the ground, together with his brains. The eyeballs were yanked out and fell down in front.[45] He had saved his friend. "Go!" the other said. "Get the riding camel!" Shāyiʿ went to fetch the animal. On his return, he found a girl in the place of his friend: she stood exactly where he had left him. "Hey girl!" he said. "Did you happen to see my companion somewhere around here?" "I am your companion," she replied.[46] "You are not!" he said. "You are a woman and my friend is a man." "Kneel the camel; make it lie down! Then I will tell you." He obeyed, and she explained: "Truly, I am your companion. The slave we killed was my father's servant. He desired me as his wife. He murdered my father and my brothers, but I made my escape. Instead, he took my sister as his wife and had two sons by her. I came to avenge my father and brothers. God granted me revenge: I even killed his children. I have slain the children he had by my sister. I don't want anyone left thirsting for my blood. So it happened that God threw this castle into your lap, with its domains and treasures: it is all yours. And I would like to have you as my husband." He said, "Where I come from, I have two parents to take care of. I really can't." "Is there anything you need?" "I'd like to have your sword, shield, and riding camel." She made him a present of those.

As he turned back, aiming to rejoin his family, it occurred to him: "Now that 2.2
God has bestowed on me these arms and a riding camel, I might as well go raiding and capture booty. Hopefully, I'll provision myself with goods granted to me at God's pleasure." He attached himself to a band of highway robbers preying on travelers who plied the road to Syria, mostly wayfarers who crossed the desert on camelback. Another fellow imposed himself on them, joining them all of a sudden without asking. He had a mind to go raiding. He was his mother's only child, and she came panting after them, beseeching him, "O Shāyiʿ,

أنا وهو ودّعينا الله. ويلقون لهم ربع وياخذونهم وينحرون بغداد يبون يجلبون فودهم بسوق بغداد. يوم جوا بغداد قام شايع يْتِدَغّف ببغداد من هنا ومن هنا يتصيد ويتطمّع هو وخويه. اثريه مزيون خويه يوم جا له سوق من اسواق بغداد وشافته له مغنّاه ساحره، وهي تغمز له وينهج يمّه واسقته، سحرته وغيّبِتُه عنده. هذا شايع نكس ولا لقى خويه، افخت شايع خويه. وين خوينا؟ قالوا: والله ما ندري وين خوينا دوّروا، دوروا، يوم تلّيّشوا، كلّوا خوياوه، قال: مير روحوا انا ما ادري وش عذري عند امه، ما مات اقول مات واقول ضيعت خوي يعني ما توافق، مير روحوا وانا والله ابدور خويّي. يقوله شايع. لا! قال: والله ما اقدر أواجه امه اللي وصّتن عليه، ما اقدر أواجهَه، اما اذبح والا اجيبه. وياخذ طال عمرك من الحول الى الحول وهو يوقّف عند هالناس، عند اللي يبخصون وعند اللي يعرفون وعند اللي ينقضون وعند اللي يقمرون وعند اللي يخطّون خطوط، عند جميع اللي لهم صلة بالسوالف هذي، هاللي يتكهّنون. تشوف؟ وقام يفيض بغداد غربٍ شرق يدوره. وبالبلايس وبالبلايس ويدور ويدور. وياخذ سبع سنين وهو يدوره على موجب وصاة هالمرة له.

ويا هو بيّن عينه عورا ما من عين، مسحا، من جابته امه وهو عور. قال له هكالرجال: انت يا بو عين، وش انت يا هذا؟ هاللي بس تدوّر بهالاسواق ببغداد، والله ما ندري وش انت. قال: انا خوي لي غدى. قال: وش لونه؟ قال: هاللون وهاللون جنسه. قال: ابْشِر به. قال: ابشر بالبشاره. قال: شْفُه خويك تروه بها العماره. بهالعماره؟ قال: ايه. ويداور الحيله ما يدري وش يعَمل. قال: يا جا الضحى، قبل الظهر، والناس باشغاله، ان لقيت شي والا صيده والا داب والا شي ٣،٢

this son of mine has been pestering me for permission to go raiding.[47] By God, I have granted him his wish, on condition that he'd be in your care, under your responsibility. I swear that he is no longer in my hands and has been entrusted to you, in your safekeeping."[48] He said, "May God extend His protection to us. Ask God to keep both of us in His safekeeping." They despoiled some travelers and made for Baghdad to sell their plunder at the market. Once in the city, Shāyiʿ and his companion began exploring all its nooks and crannies in search of opportunities for gain. In one of the city's streets, his friend, a handsome young lad, attracted the attention of a seductive sorceress. She gave him the eye and he walked over to her. She poured him a drink, a magic potion, and he vanished. Shāyiʿ retraced his steps looking for his friend, but he was nowhere to be found. Where had he gone? No one remembered having seen him. They continued to search for him to the point of exhaustion. He told his tired comrades, "You'd better go your own way. As for myself, how can I possibly face his mother? What excuse can I offer her? Telling her that he may or may not have died? Or saying that I have lost her son, my companion? That is not a proper way to acquit myself. In any case, you should go and look after your own business. I cannot give up my search." Thus, Shāyiʿ bade farewell to his comrades. "No!" He steeled himself. "It is out of the question for me to apprise his mother of such uncertain news. She has entrusted him to me, into my safekeeping. I cannot bring myself to fob her off with such stories. I'd rather be killed or die than fail to find him and deliver him safely back to his mother." For years, may your life be long, he kept mingling with people. He sought the opinion of experts in such matters: those familiar with the art of casting a spell and the techniques of tricksters and soothsayers. Anyone who might provide him with a lead for his quest. Even fortune tellers were consulted. For this purpose, he crisscrossed Baghdad from west to east. He employed public announcers as a way of gathering information from as many people as possible. He searched and searched. Seven years he spent scouring the city so as to honor the trust the boy's mother had placed in him.

No one would overlook him. As a person with only one eye, his defect at 2.3
birth, he stood out wherever he went. One day a man came up to him. "Hey you, one-eyed fellow, what's the matter? All day long, we see you pacing up and down the streets of Baghdad. We're wondering who you are." "My friend went missing," he said. "What does he look like?" He gave a detailed description. "Don't worry," the other said. "It will be all right." "A reward for good

تجيبه تهيض عليك الوغدان وتهيض عليك الحريم، يعني لو تشوف غديه ينزل هو وايا خويته اللي خْذِته يتفرّجون عليك، والناس باشغاله، اللي بفلاحتُه واللي بدكانُه واللي... يقول وهو يجيك يدوّر ويصيد له غزال صغير. ويطبّ وصط المدينة ويقوم يبيعه. والى مير اهل هالمدينة هذولا ما يعرفون الغزال، ما يدرون وشّو. وهي تغدي لك هالناس اطواف عليه، تغدي عليه ضول، وكل يسومه. يتفرّجون ويسومون. وعيّى يبيع. لا بشوي ولا بكثير. ويقول به هاك على هذا ويقول به هاك على الوغد هذاك، وتصيح هالوغدان وهالحريم. ما دري الا يوم طلعت هكالمغناه من العماره، يوم طلعت من العمارة وهي تجيك يم ظول هالناس اللي عند هالغزال تبي تشوفه. ليا مير هذا خويُّه يوم طلع باثرَه يتليَه مثل وجه الرخله. يوم طبّ هو واياه، قال: فلان؟ يا مير ما يدري وشوا. وينط الى هو بحلقَه. والى معه القديمي. قال: اقول؟ قالت: آه. قال: انقضي عنه، والله يان ما نقضتي عنه والله العظيم الا هالساعه اني لاقطّعك ألف قطعه، كل شجرة احط عليه قطعه. قالت: ياولد، خف الله بنفسك، ارق جاي انت واياوه وهالساعة انقض عنه. وهو يرقى معه وهي تعطيه عاد والله ما ادري وشو الدوا اللي نقض عنه. فلان؟ قال: نعم. قال: تعرفن؟ قال: نعم، انت شايع. قال: متى علمك بي؟ قال: امس. قال: انقضي عنه. حط هكالشبرية بصرصور اذنه ويبطّه بالشبريه قال: ما نقضتي عنه، انقضي عنه. وهي تنقض عنه. وثلاث نقضات اللي تنقض عنه يما صحى. يوم جا الركايب، ذلوله وذلول خويه، يا مير غاديات ست ركاب، كل هالوقوت وهو يدوّر خويه ببغداد هن توالدن. وينطي الرجال اربع، اللي علّمه به، وثنتين له هو وايًا خويه.

news," he replied. "Look, your friend is lodged in that building." "In that building?" "Yes!" Shāyiʿ needed advice, a ruse to rescue his friend, but he did not know how to go about it. "In the morning, before noon, while people are at work, bring some attraction with you: a gazelle, a snake, another animal," the man explained. "As long as it arouses the curiosity of children. If they come, the women will come. Perhaps you'll spot him in the crowd if he comes down from the building at the invitation of his female warden to let him have a look at what is going on. It must be at a time when people are at work with their crops, shops, and so on." Shāyiʿ did as he was told. He went for a hunt, caught a little gazelle, and offered it for sale in town. City dwellers were not familiar with gazelles, and the curious flocked to gape at the animal. As soon as a sizable crowd had gathered, the bargaining started. Some of the onlookers made a bid for the animal, but he turned down all offers, big or small. He engaged with the old and the young, made the kids and women cry out in excitement. All of a sudden, a beautiful woman emerged from the building and walked straight into the crowd that was enthralled by the gazelle. And there he was, his friend. She had taken him along and he followed her as if deprived of his mental powers, like a lamb. As soon as he was close, Shāyiʿ asked, "Hey, is it you, so-and-so?" No reply—he was bereft of speech. The next moment, Shāyiʿ lunged at her and took her by the throat while brandishing a dagger in her face. "Listen!" "What?" she replied. "Break the spell you put on him! God Almighty, if you don't do it here and now, I will cut you into a thousand pieces. I will dangle a piece of you from every tree." "My boy," she said, "don't you stand in fear of God? Come upstairs with me, and there I will break the spell." They climbed the stairs, and she administered a spell-breaking concoction. "Hey you, are you so-and-so?" Shāyiʿ asked the boy. "Yes," he said. "Do you know me?" "Yes. You are Shāyiʿ." "Since when have you known me?" "Yesterday," he said. Again, he turned to her. "Now break the spell for once and for all," he said, as he put the blade of the dagger to her earlobe and pricked it. "You still haven't lifted the spell!" And now she did so, three times, until finally his friend woke up. In the meantime, his camel and his friend's mount had multiplied their numbers. There were six of them. During the time they spent in Baghdad, they had produced offspring. Four camels went to the man who had pointed out the building and given advice on how to go about it. The two remaining ones were mounts for their own use, and they went their separate ways.

٤،٢ قام جاب له حاج تومّر بهم يبي يدلّهم، دليلة لهم من العراق على اباعر. يوم جاب طال عمرك الحاج وهو ينوّخ بهم بصف قنا عند ضلعٍ غربٍ من قنا يقال له ضبع. قال: عشّوا بهذا والى عشيتوا حنا انشا الله جايينكم بخير، أنا أبويق على العرب هذولا، يوم وازن اهله. يوم عشوا الحاج خلاهم يما ناموا وهو يجيك ساري يم قنا. هله عِلْمُه بهم يم قنا مبطي، له سات سنه. يوم جا هكالعجوز بله خربوش مع شنق العرب قَعد عنده جابت له له عيش يا مير هكالرقوص ولعب ودمام. قال: يا عمتي هالرقوص واللعوب وشّي؟ قالت: يا وليدي لا بلاك الله هذي مرة شايع يقولون مات وخَذاه ابن قدران وهي هذي صوتٍ ترفعه وصوتٍ تهبّطه هاللي اسمع حسه مع الحريم زافّاته، تصيح تقول تبي رجله شايع ناهج للعراق ومشيّعين عليه انه ميت وهاللي غُصِبَوَه الليلة وهاللي هالضول عندهم، اللعب على عرسهم والعيش اللي انت تاكل منه من عيشهم جابوه لي.

٥،٢ ثاري راشد ابن قدران من الزود الله لا يبلانا، الامير، الشيخ، طلب البنت وعيّت البنت، قالت ما زال شايع حي، ما جانا علمه، والله ما آخذ جميع رجل. وهم واياه وهم واياه وعيّي، قالت: والله انا ما جا علم شايع، وما دام علم شايع ما جا ما آخذ الرجاجيل، كان هو حي هو رجلي وان كان هو مات ما ابي الرجال غيره، ابد. يوم عيت كل هالوقوت واشرطوا القدران لهكالصلبي، قالوا: نشرط لك لِقِي من البل وغيّب لك عشرة ايام وعقب عشرة ايام تعال وليا مِنّنا نشدناك نقول من اين انت جاي على مسمع الانثى قل جيت من هالعراق، ترانا نبي نسعلك نقول ما عينت واحد، رجال ما له الا عين وحده، مسحا عينه ما له الا عين، اما ذْكِر لك أو شي وقل كان هو شايع الامسح ابن رمال قولة راح، هفى، على سمع

Shāyiʿ happened upon a group of pilgrims who stood in need of camel transport and a desert pilot to bring them from Iraq to Mecca. He agreed to be their guide. In the vicinity of Gnā, he dismounted at a mountainous outcrop west of the settlement, called Ḍabʿ. "Have dinner here," he told the pilgrims, "and after you have finished your meal, God willing, I will rejoin you. I must go for some urgent business with those people over there." They were not far from his kinfolk. After dinner, when they had bedded down for the night, he went to see his relatives. Six years had passed since the last time he had been in Gnā. The first person he encountered on his way was an old woman. She lived alone in a little black tent, at some remove from the other inhabitants.[49] He sat down with her and she brought him food. To his surprise, he heard the sound of dancing songs, merrymaking, and drums. "Auntie, what is going on there?" "My dear boy," she said, "may God spare you from misery, it is for the wife of Shāyiʿ. Now that her husband is no more, as they say, she has been chosen by Ibn Gidrān to become his wife." Indeed, he recognized her voice in the screams and wails that came drifting in as waves of sound. "It is her voice you hear through the shrill ululating of women who accompany her in the bridal procession. She screams that she wants her own man back—Shāyiʿ, who went to Iraq and who, as rumor has it, died while there: a rumor spread by those who coerced her into this wedding night, the rejoicing crowd, the wedding festivities. The food you've been served comes from the wedding buffet; it was brought to me." 2.4

Rāshid ibn Gidrān's despotism knew no bounds, with the liberties he took as the tribal chief, the shaykh. He had proposed to the girl and she refused, saying, "As long as Shāyiʿ is alive and I have no news from him, I will not marry any other man." She was under constant pressure: they kept insisting and she rejected their offers out of hand. Time and again she repeated, "I have not received any news about Shāyiʿ. As long as I have no definite proof about his fate, I am not interested in other men. If he is alive, he is my man. And if he is dead, I do not want any other man. Never!" As her recalcitrance showed no sign of relenting, al-Gidrān's henchmen enlisted the help of a member of a pariah tribe, a *ṣlubī*:[50] "You'll get a young she-camel if you make yourself scarce for ten days. After that interval, show yourself among us. We'll ask you, 'From where you did you come?' Within hearing distance of the women, you'll say, 'I have come from Iraq.' The next question will be: 'Haven't you seen someone, a man with only one eye, someone with one eye missing? Did you 2.5

الانثى. وانهج طال عمرك ويوم جلسوا بالليل وجاهم الصلبي، قالوا: من اين انت جاي ياللحية الغانمه؟ قال: والله جيت من هالعراق. قالوا: ولا عيّنت رجّال امسح ما له الا عين؟ اما ذكر لك عند احد او شفته؟ قال: اسمه شايع؟ قالوا: شايع. قال: امسح ما له عين؟ قالوا: ما له عين. قال: شايع الامسح اللي ما له عين هذاك راح، راح العام بالعراق، هفى، ذبح. قالوا: عنك؟ قال اي بالله عني، يا عميمي والله اني مع حفارة قبره. يقوله على سماع الانثى. واذبحوا ضحيته قباله. كذب بكذب.

وهم يصلّبون عليّه. قالوا: شايع اللي انتي ترجين هاللي راح وحنا نبيك غصب ٦،٢
عليك. قال ابن قدران: ياالله ملكوا لي. وملّك عليّه وهم بقنا، قبل تطلع ام اقلبان هاللي وراه. وعرس على المرة يابن قدران، مرة شايع، حاجر عليه، هكالليله اللي وافقت تيّة شايع. صارت تحويلة شايع على ابن قدران وجماعته ليلة دخلة ابن قدران على مرة شايع. وهو يستدير وهو يثكب ويعدي على البيت يوم انه سرت الناس ويلوّذ على اوزار القش ويلبد برواق البيت، بشنق الحجرة، الحجرة اول يعملونه بشنق المراح مَحْجَر على قِنّ على ظُلّه هكالحين ويطوونه تقل غرفه. وهو يجي تحت الظلة وهو يلبد. يقول انا كان هو عرس من خاطره وهي راضيه ولا تنيّهت ولا قالت انا مرة شايع أو خف الله أو يمنى او يسرى، أنا ما عندي معارضه، مرة بداله مره، وان كان هي صاحت والدعوى غصب انا ما انا حيٍّ حياتين. يقولون ان هذا راي شايع.

perchance hear about someone with such a face?' Your answer should be: 'If you mean Shāyiʿ al-Amsaḥ ibn Rmāl, yes, the word is, he has passed away. He perished.' Say it loud enough for the women to hear it clearly!" He disappeared as instructed, and one night the *ṣlubī* turned up in their assembly. "Where did you come from, good man?" "By God, I came from Iraq." "Didn't you see someone with one eye missing, a one-eyed man? Did someone mention him to you or did you see him?" "Is his name Shāyiʿ?" "Yes, Shāyiʿ." "Amsaḥ who has only one eye?" "One eye missing, yes." "Well, this Shāyiʿ al-Amsaḥ, the one-eyed man, God rest his soul, last year he passed away in Iraq. He lost his life; he was killed." "No!" they said. "Yes, unfortunately. Very sad. I tell you, my uncle, truth is, I was one of the gravediggers at the place where he was laid to rest." He made sure to articulate clearly, audible to the women in their compartment behind the partition. In his presence, they slaughtered an animal, as is customary on the occasion of someone's decease. All lies, damned lies!

From that moment they piled the pressure on her, saying, "This Shāyiʿ **2.6**
person on whom you have pinned your hopes, he's gone. Now we shall have you willy-nilly, no matter what you say." "Come on," Ibn Gidrān admonished them, "let's go through the wedding proceedings right away." The formalities were done in Gnā, the place before you reach Umm al-Gilbān. Ibn Gidrān married her, the wife of Shāyiʿ, the girl reserved for him. These events coincided with Shāyiʿ's arrival. Shāyiʿ dismounted from his camel close to the whereabouts of Ibn Gidrān and his fellows. That night had been set for the consummation of Ibn Gidrān's marriage with the wife of Shāyiʿ. He made a circling movement and hurried to the tent, running fast, as soon as the revelers of the wedding party had withdrawn and left the couple alone. He hid himself beneath the objects piled in heaps against the tent's sidewalls. He lay down to listen with his ear glued to the tent cloth—next to the marriage room, so to speak. In those days, they pitched a small marriage tent at the far end of the camp. It was constructed like a lady's camel litter: long curved poles over which a cover of cloth was hung and decked out with carpets to make it look like a room. He crawled under the poles and lay there in hiding. He thought: "If he wants to marry her and she accepts, without sobbing and crying, 'I am Shāyiʿ's wife' or, 'Don't you fear God?' and the like, I will not object. For every woman, there is another woman. But if she starts screaming and she is taken by force, well, you only live once." It is said that these were Shāyiʿ's thoughts as he deliberated.

يقول يا مار هكالعجوز ايوم قامت تعفط بخشمه: وشي هالريحه اللي انتشي؟ ٧،٢
حنا يما ان عندنا داب والا شايع جاي بهالديره. قالوا اسكتي الله ياخذ وجهك وش يدريك انتي. وذللوَه واسكتي. النسوان جابن العروس حطّنّه بالحجرة وهو يلّوذ عليه ابن قدران هايجٍ مثل قعود عقيل واقفن النسوان عنهم بحجالهم. قالت: يابن قدران خف الله بنفسك، ادخل على الله دِخْلِه، لا تاطا محارم ولد عمك، ياشين انا بذمّة شايع ما ادري لو يجي شايع باكر، ادخل على الله دِخْله. قال: شايع مات الله لا يرحم ابوك انتي وشايع، يا هالحين تحرّثين عظام شايع، انتي تبين تحيي لك ميت، ذبحَن ضحاياوه وخلص، مير قربي جاي. واقضب قصته واجضعه. وتفارست هي واياوه ويوم بغى ياليّه، بغى يطْرَحه لعمل الرجل بالمره قالت: شايع يا رجالي ولا لي رجالٍ غيرك واويحي واحلالاة يا شايع. قال: ليا ذْلان ما طاب خاطرك من شايع. وهو يصفقه يا هي واقعه، انت يا بن قدران.

يا شايعٍ عنده وهي ما هي دارية بُه، معه النافعي، قديمية اسمه النافعي. وهو ٨،٢
يثكب عليه مع الرواق قال: ياما عندك والله من شايع، خيال الوضحا شايع. سج الرجال بهكالشبرية يا هاوية الى النصاب، وقدُّه الى مثل السباح مصرانه بالارض. اذبحه واقرطه بشنق الحجره وهو ينام هو واياه، يجلد هو واياه يما أصبحوا. قال عاد يوم اصبحوا: انا ابي انهج يم خوياي ونبي نحج ويجرّون جنازتهم كيفهم به، علميهم به، انا ابنهج يم خوياي. العرب هكالحين كود الامير يقعد ويشب الصبح ويقود الدبش يم له جهة، ذالين من القوم. هكاليوم ما حصل يقعد. صوّتوا صوتوا يا مير لله. قالوا: يا كعيب الظبي؟ قالت: ويش؟ قالوا: وين الامير، رجلك؟ قالت: هكاللي شفُه يجرجرنّه هكالكلاب. قال: كيف؟ من جاوه؟ قالت:

It is told of the same old woman that she turned up her nose and sniffed the air. "What is this smell wafting in our direction? Is it a snake or is it Shāyiʿ who has come back?" "Shut up!" they said. "May God take away your face! What makes you think so?" The harsh scolding reduced her to silence. The tribe's women escorted the bride to the marriage tent. Ibn Gidrān joined her in a state of wild excitement, rutting like a male camel of the ʿGēl traders. The women quickly withdrew, their anklets clanging. "Ibn Gidrān, stand in fear of God!" she cried out. "Put yourself under God's protection! Do not violate the sacred rights of your fellow tribesman. What horror! I am bound by honor in marriage to Shāyiʿ. Who knows, he may come tomorrow. Seek God's protection!" "Shāyiʿ is long dead," he replied. "May God not have mercy on your father, you and your Shāyiʿ! Even now you are still raking Shāyiʿ's bones? You want to bring the dead back to life? The sacrificial sheep was slaughtered, and that's the end of it. The story is over and done. Come here, I want you close." He grabbed her by the hair and made her turn on her back. They struggled, fought, and clawed until he overcame her resistance and pushed her down. As he laid her down, ready to do the job a man does on a woman, she screamed, "O Shāyiʿ, my man! You are my man and my only man. O woe is me! O darling Shāyiʿ!" "Still the same story! Haven't you come to your senses! Still Shāyiʿ!" And Ibn Gidrān hit her hard, knocking her flat to the ground. 2.7

She had no inkling that Shāyiʿ was so close by. He pulled out his dagger and leapt into the room. "Here is your Shāyiʿ! The white she-camel's knight, Shāyiʿ!" He tore into his foe, plunging the dagger into his body up to the hilt and ripping the blade down through his underbelly so that the intestines spilled onto the ground.[51] He slaughtered him and tossed his remains outside, next to the tent. Then he went to sleep with her. He stayed until the morning. "I must go now to the rendezvous with the people whose guide I am," he told her, "and help them complete their pilgrimage. Let them bury him whatever way they like. You tell them. Now I must go to see my people." At that time, it was customary for the chief to get up and light a fire while the animals were being herded out of the camp. At night the livestock were kept nearby for fear of robbers. That morning, there was no perceptible movement. They called and called to no response.[52] "Kʿēb al-Ẓabiy!" "What's the matter?" "Where is your husband?" "There." She pointed. "Where the dogs are pulling and tearing at his flesh." "How can that be? Who came to him?" "My real man came, the one you've declared dead.[53] You were lying to make me marry your chief. He came and killed him. If you 2.8

جاوه رجلي الصقّ اللي أنتم تقولون مات، ثاريه ما مات تكذبون علي تبون تجوّزون ولدكم، جا وذبحه مير دونكم جنازتكم صوتوا لهالرجاجيل يقبرونه. وهم يتهايقون، يوم تهايقوا يا مار هو مشيِّشٍ مثل القعود الأوضح. جرّوه عاد وقْلَعوه.

شايع أدى الحاج ورجع وشاخ بالعرب، شاخ بالرمال. والى هم هافين القدران قبل مذبوحين، صارت عليهم ذبحة قبل ولا باقي على اثرهم الا الامير اللي ذبح شايع وشيبان اثنين، منديل والثاني نسيت اسمه، ويصيرون عند شايع ويحسن بهم شايع ويعيْشُهم. هو اقرب ما لهم، صاروا عنده. وقوموا يتدغّفونه يبون يذبحونه، حديهم شايب عمى معه له موس ويتدغّف شايع يبي يذبحه، وينزح شايع ويبعد عنه. قام الشايب يتلمس شايع ويتهمّاوه بالليل ويداوره معه له سكين مغيّبَه، الشايب، يبي يتقاضى لولده. وهو يعرف له شايع ويجنب عنه. وكل ما اوجسه جايب له عشاوه أو غداوه أو جايب له ما، يا معه له موس يسنّه يبي يقضب شايع يبي يلوطه. وكل ليلة يتدغفه هاللون وذاك داريٍ به. قال: ياعميمي عيّن خير، ما انت حول هالامور، وانا ولدك، وكل ليلة ترْن اشوفك، تعمل هاللون وهاللون، واليوم انا عوض عيالك، ولدك وطا محارمي وانجبرت اني افعل هالفعل، وهالحين لو تبي تذبحن من يبقى؟ ما من الا الله ثم انا وانت، مير خلن اعيِّشك ما زولك حي. ٩،٢

تراكى هو واياوه هكالمرّه على هكالمركى يعمل له القهوه وعنده، عند المركي ويصب له. وهو يقعد يسولف على شايع يبيه يسهي مع السوالف ويبي يتمكّن من الحاسون، السكين، صفّاطيه يبي يضربه بَه. استحس به شايع وهو يخلّي له الهدوم، الفروه والعباة على مكانهن وهو يسلّ روحه وهو يصير بهذاك، تِبَرَّز، وهو يقعد يبي يراعي وش يعمل. وجينا من هاناك ورحنا من هاناك وقلنا هاللون وعَملنا هاللون ياولدي. ويزحف يقول هاك يما تمكن من السكين وهو يتوازن له وهو ١٠،٢

wish to inter him, go ahead. Call your men to take his corpse and bury him." They craned their necks to have a good look at the cadaver. There he lay, stone dead and torn to pieces like a slaughtered white male camel. They dragged the body away, removing him from the scene.[54]

2.9 Shāyiʿ accompanied the pilgrims to their destination. On his return, he became the tribe's chief, the shaykh of the Rmāl. The lineage of al-Gidrān was on the brink of extinction.[55] There had been killings before. The chief slain by Shāyiʿ was the last one alive, except for two graybeards. One was named Mandīl. I forget the name of the second old man. They were being looked after by Shāyiʿ: he took good care of them and provided them with meals. They were around wherever he was. Yet they were biding their time, waiting for the right moment to kill him. One of them, who was blind, carried a sharp knife under his clothes, always on the lookout for an opportunity to stab him to death. Shāyiʿ was careful not to let him come too close. The graybeard was fumbling for the razor-sharp knife hidden under his cloak, ready to pounce if he found it. The old man could only think of avenging his son's death.[56] Shāyiʿ was aware of his designs and evaded him. Whenever he saw Shāyiʿ bringing supper or lunch or water, the old man groped for his well-whetted knife. His obsessive desire was to grab Shāyiʿ and slit his throat. Every night he was lurking, waiting for a chance. The other knew it: "Uncle of mine, keep safe. These things are not for you. I am your son. Every night you are trying to get at me. Don't you know that I have come in the place of your children. Your son trespassed on my womenfolk. I had no choice but to act the way I did. And now you want to kill me! Who will remain? No one. There is only God, you, and me. Let me take care of you for the duration of your life."

2.10 They were not sitting far apart. They shared one camel saddle as an armrest between them, while he prepared coffee and poured him a cup. The old man told long-winded stories in order to distract Shāyiʿ and meanwhile fumbled to get a good grip on the knife. He wanted to stab him with a lock knife. Shāyiʿ was aware of what he was up to. While sitting there, he quietly slipped out of his clothes, his fur coat and robe, and stole away to another part of the room. Moving away and aside, he sat down to watch the old man going about his scheme. The other continued his tale: "We came from there and we went from there; we said this and we did that, my boy." As he kept talking, the old man slid forward, took hold of the knife, moved closer to the side, and drew the knife. And he stabbed, right in the fur coat and the robe. "I left it at your side

يسجه، يا مير بالفروه والعباه. قال شايع: مْشَطّرَه لك يا عمي. شاف انه عرف نيته ولا عاد له حيله. وهو يرتكي نكس على الشداد وهو يدلي يتمثل الشايب. تمثل على بيتهم وعلى خيلهم وعلى جيشهم، يبكي على عزهم اللي هفى قبل. لكن ان دينهم تقل وسط، هم القدران. شايع تِقي:

١١،٢ قال ابن قدران بيوت يولّفها   كما الدنانير بين عَدٍّ ونقّاد
الله من دارٍ خلت عقب سكنه   ما بقى الا البوم والبِيض الارياد

يشبه شايع على البوم والبيض الارياد البنات.

الله على فَهدْةٍ سودٍ مدامعه   تجيب الظبي على القرنين كدّادِ
الله على بيت طوال كسّره   مرفوع العِمْدان مطموغ الاوتاد
الله على صفرانٍ طوال معارفه   لها على الخيل سرداد ومرداد
والله على ملحانٍ شيب محاقبه   لها مع القاع دفلاج وفداد
والله على قروة تفيض وتمتلي   مثل الثغب المنقاد بين البوادي
والله على طفلة تظفي جداه دون قُرباه   وهي عن درب المناقيد صداد

١٢،٢ يوم خلص رد عليه شايع قال:

١ قال ابن مرداس بيوت يولفها   كما سَدْي الخام بين مبرم وغزال
على الله حوال يدبرها   رفع الهكيع وهدة الشامخ العالي
ما ينفعك جيلك الاول   الي هفى جيلك التالي
ولا ينفعك زاد كليته امس   هذاك يصبح بطنك منه خالي

for you, Uncle." He understood that Shāyiʿ had intuited his intentions. His ruse having failed, he was at his wits' end. The graybeard slumped back against the saddle's cushion, broken and dejected, and began to recite verses. He spoke about their house, horses, riding camels. He shed tears as he remembered their days of pride and decline.[57] The Gidrān clansmen were lukewarm in their performance of religious duties. However, Shāyiʿ was devout.[58]

Gidrān crafted verses with consummate skill, **2.11**
tinkling gold coins counted in market shops.
God pity an abode desolate and forsaken,
but for owls and orphaned damsels.

—He compares Shāyiʿ to an ominous owl; "orphaned damsels" are the tribe's girls.

God pity cheetahs, tear ducts streaked black,
hunters of gazelle for thick-tressed girls.
God's mercy on lofty houses of woven hair,
raised high on poles, pitched with iron pegs.
O God, I miss my long-maned white mare,
warhorse deft at the charge and turn.
O God, I miss black camels, shoulders gray,
speeding over plains at a steady trot.
O God, I miss food trays overflowing with fat
like a gully's streamlet teeming with Bedouin.
O God, I miss a girl a cut above her peers:
perfectly polished, impeccable of conduct.

When he had finished his declamation, Shāyiʿ riposted: **2.12**

Ibn Mirdās crafts verses like an artisan
weaving cloth with loom and spindle.
God's wisdom steers the universe,
elevates down-and-outs, humbles power.
Ancestors stand helpless, give no succor,
if progeny slides down slopes of decline.[59]
Yesterday's provisions are of little avail,
don't fill empty stomachs the following day.

عـــلـيــك بالصِقّ والصوم والصخــا   والصلاة عند الموت هن خير الاعمال
والعي عي الى مـن يبــــــــــلش   والسيل ما ينحاوه الا جروش الجال
ولا تعيل ولا تميل ولا تنسى الجميـل   ولا تغفــــــــــر زلّات من عــال
وكـل يا شـاب عــــــاب   وصـار بـالبيـت رحـال ونـزال
وحنا يا ركبنـا تجض الهجـن منا   كمـا تجض من الارشـاة محـال
والى ارخينـا محازمـنا مشـن بالهون   والى كربناها غدى للجيش ملمـال
تـلقى سودان الروس تجِفّ بنـــــا   كمـا العذارى تحف بسيدها الغالي

سودان الروس الرجال.

يقول افْرِك الغرابة ومت، الشايب العمى. وهو يثور يمه شايع وهو ينهض راسه ١٣،٢
يا مير ما به روح، ميت وتجيب مرة اخو راشد ولد سموه محمد. وتحمل كعيب الظبي وتجيب ولد سموه على جده عميره. وقال: يالرمال، أمر وقضى وقدر، ابن عمي وطا محارمي وانجبرت وذبحته وهالحين لا تقطعون جثيمة القدران، هالوليد اللي بقي خلوه يبقى، اجحدوا هالسالفه، وانا ابعتبر نفسي ابوه والله اني ما اجعله الا مثل ولدي. وربّوا الولدين مع بعض وعيشوا لما ارشدوا ما دري احد. يوم تمرجلوا غدوا جذعان صار عميره ولد شايع يمشي مع البل جنّاب وهذاك ياخذ الفهدات ويمشي يباري للعرب على هكالذلول ويطرح من هالصيد ويجيب. الي رحلت العرب رحّل امه معهم وركب ذلوله وجنّب، معه له فهده، وكل يوم محمّلٍ ذلوله صيد وليا صاد هالصيد جاب له له عنز وسحب شواه اللي ببطنه ودخّل به شحمه وكبد وقلب من هالصيد، وخلّه ويا حوّل قال: يايمّه اديّها لعمّي، حقه. وهذي حالتهم.

Abide by rules of truth, fasting, and liberality;
gain praise by saying prayers for the dead.[60]
Obstinacy is not broken until put to the test:
sheer rock makes torrents change course.
Don't trespass or wangle; repay benefactors;
don't forgive wrongdoers' vile violations![61]
Infirmity strengthens from youth to senility:
a graybeard's travels and travails are at home.
Our camels shake with tension if we ride,
as well ropes drawn taut over pulley rollers.
If we unbuckle and relax, our mounts trot at ease;
if we tighten, they get flustered.
Shammar's black heads serve us well,[62]
as women tend to a lord with tender care.

—The "black heads" refer to the men with their long dark hair.

It is said that the blind old man clasped his hands around the knob of the saddle and died. Shāyiʿ jumped up and rushed at him but too late: his soul had left him. He was dead. Rāshid's brother had a son called Muḥammad. Kʿēb al-Ẓabiy gave birth to a son named ʿAmīrah after his ancestor.[63] Shāyiʿ said, "Look here, men of al-Rmāl, what happened was foreordained. Let bygones be bygones. I had no choice but to slay a kinsman who violated my marital rights. Let's stop hacking into the corpse of al-Gidrān. This boy who has survived, let him live. Forget the story. I consider myself like his father. By God, I will treat him as if he were my own son." The two boys grew up together, and until they reached the age of discernment they were not aware of any difference between them. When they had grown strong and were on the verge of manhood, ʿAmīrah, Shāyiʿ's son, accompanied the camels to pasture as the herd's armed guard. The other youngster took their cheetahs hunting at some distance parallel to the Bedouin camel train.[64] Any game he killed, he donated to the group. On migrations, their mother traveled in her camel-borne litter chair, while he covered the caravan's flanks riding his mount, together with his cheetah. No day passed without him feasting them on meat of game. If he captured a gazelle, he stuffed its intestines with its fat, liver, and heart, dismounted at his mother's place, and said, "Mother, give this to my uncle. It is for him—a special delicacy!" This was their life. 2.13

١٤،٢ ويتخانق رماليٍّ هو وايا شايع. ويزعل على شايع. يوم رحلوا العرب وجوا المنزل وهو يقوم يتلقّف للّيد (= للوليد)، الرمالي. وينكس الولد محمّل ذلوله معه بارووده وجاك منكف والعرب رحيل. ويجي له هالرمالي المقرود، يعترض له قال له الولد: ما عينت الشيوخ هم قدام والا قفو والا وين نزلوا؟ وين دَووا الشيوخ قال: هم الشيوخ الجديدين أو العتيقين؟ وهو يصطغ عليه قال: وشم الشيوخ العتيقين ووشم الشيوخ الجديدين؟ يقوله انت يالولد. قال: القديمين اهلك اول والجديدين شايع وجماعته. قال: وشلون صيفته؟ قال: صيفته الامارة لكم انتم. قال: وش اودعَه تنهج منا؟ قال: ابوك مات موت وعمك راشد ذبحه شايع وجدك مات جزع انه ذبحه شايع ولا تْقيضي بُه. وقص عليه السالفه كله. قال: ما تقيضي به؟ قال: لا. يوم توكّد وهو ينوّخ الذلول وحط بدال العنز تيس، وحط بالتيس وانتم بكرامه فِرث. يوم حوّل قال: يايمّه ادّي حق عمّي. وهي تاخذه ما بدِقّت به (= ما لاحظت) وهي تِدّيه. يوم ركّد الصيد وخذى قراميش الخلا، الغزاي، البارود والقربة وحطّهن على الذلول، قال: من جانا جاوه الله. يقوله شايع يوم ركّدت التيس. قالت: ما ادري. قال: يا جيتيه سلم لي عليه وخليه يتنانن معي له وصاة ابوصيه. يوم جت ياهو مقشمط القراميش على ذلوله وثاني رِكْبته على الشداد، يبي يركب. قالت: ياوليدي وين تبي؟ قال: ابجيب صيد لي بقى بمقناصي اليوم واجي هالحين. قالت: عمك يقول اتنُه يبي يوصيك. قال: اجي هالحين ويا جيت يوصينن. واركب الذلول. وايت وصر ورا الدبش يا مير عميرة، ولد شايع، جناب مع الدبش، وهو يدهجه، يوم جاوه قال: ابا الثواريات راشد، واضربه يا ذابحه، اعد على عميره ولد شايع مع البل واذبحه. يوم ذبحه وهو ينحاش وهو يجي جبه

One of the Rmāl quarreled with Shāyiʿ and harbored a grudge against him. Once, when the Bedouin pitched their camp for the night, this tribesman contrived to casually come face to face with the boy, as if by chance. The boy was making his way back to the Bedouin, armed with his flintlock on a camel carrying his loads. On running into this nasty member of the Rmāl, the boy asked him, "Haven't you seen the shaykhs? Are they ahead or back there? Where have they put up their camp? Which direction should I take to join the shaykhs?" "What do you mean?" the other said. "The new shaykhs or the ones from before, the old shaykhs?" The boy asked, "Who are those, the old shaykhs and the new shaykhs?" He said, "The shaykhs of old are your folks, those from before. The new ones are Shāyiʿ and his group." "So how did he acquire his title?" He said, "The title of the tribe's shaykh belongs to you." "And what is the reason we lost the title?" "Your father died a natural death. Your uncle Rāshid was murdered by Shāyiʿ and your grandfather died from anguish that your father's murder would go unavenged." Then he told him the entire story. The boy asked, "So his death was not avenged?" "No, it wasn't." Now that he knew the true story, the boy couched his camel and took a billy goat instead of a gazelle. He stuffed the slaughtered goat—pardon the expression—with the undigested remains of food in the animal's intestines and stomach. He alighted at the camp and said, "Mother, this is for my uncle." She took it without taking a closer look and prepared it for consumption. He left the game he had hunted stacked in a pile and collected the necessities that a desert traveler, a raider, takes with him, such as gunpowder, weapon, and waterskin, and slung them on the camel's back. "Whoever brought this, may God give him what he deserves!" Shāyiʿ said when she had put the billy goat in front of him. "I have no knowledge of it," she said. "Go and see him to convey my greetings and tell him to wait for me. I'd like to impart a piece of advice to him." She found him all set for departure with his fully equipped camel. He stood at the ready, knee bowed against the saddle and about to vault onto his mount's back. "My boy, where are you going?" He said, "I want to shoot some more game. I haven't finished hunting yet. I'll be back forthwith." She said, "Your uncle wishes to speak to you and give you some counsel." "I'll be back soon; his advice can wait." And off he rode. At the far end of the camel herd, he met ʿAmīrah, Shāyiʿ's son, who kept an eye on the animals. He fell upon the unsuspecting boy, shouting, "This is the revenge for Rāshid!" as he struck and slew him.[65] Then he fled to Jubbah to seek out a craftsman who specialized in 2.14

ويجي صانع يزيّن الاشِدّه اسمه عِيد وياخذ منه شداد وقربه وهو يحطهن على ذلوله وانحش هو وعيد النجّار، جلوا وطبّوا على بَقْعا ومن بقعا النية انهم اشملوا للعراق ما يِدْرَى وين دووا. هاللي يقولون اغدي القدران هاللي طلعوا تالي اغديهم عيال له وقصد الولد، قال:

١٥،٢ قال ابن قدرانٍ بنفسٍ رفيعه   عينٍ للضعيف صخيف
أداور الحيلات وانا محمد   ربيت بالحقران وانا شريف
يا عيد يالنجار زيّن لفاطري   ثمان عياد وسرهن لطيف

عيد من الصناع اهل جبه، أهل جبة على وقت عميره، صناعهم.

على ملحانٍ مثل دالوبة الرشا   على مثل ناعور القليب تقيف
يا بركت بيمنهل فرجلت به   براطمه كاللزا لهن رشيف
ياكن ضْباب الباب ملقى عضوده   ودفه لمنجور الشداد صخيف
والله ما ابي عليها مع السلف   ولا ابيها بين الاظعان تقيف
أبيه ليا خلى الدناوي خويه   أنسف على عالي قراه رديف
أبي عليها هفة قدام السلف   ولا اخليه بين الظعون تقيف
العنك يا رجل نسي دَين عمه   يا عاد عفيف ورباوه نظيف
يا عاد هذاة بالمربط سلاله   تلاوي مجدولٍ عباوه رصيف

سلاله الذلول، والرصيف الحبل.

manufacturing wooden camel saddles.[66] He fastened one of the saddles and a waterskin to the camel's back and they made their escape together, he and ʿĪd, the carpenter. First, they took refuge in Bagʿā and from there proceeded north toward Iraq. Their final destination is unknown. Some say that perhaps the Gidrān, the ones who emerged on the scene later, are his children. As he went, the young man composed a poem, saying:

These are the words of proud Ibn Gidrān, 2.15
    tenderhearted to the poor and oppressed.
Muḥammad I am, artful in my designs,
    raised in indignity, though of noble birth.
O ʿĪd the carpenter, craft a saddle for my camel,
    eight wooden pieces, bound by leather thongs!

—ʿĪd was an artisan from Jubbah. At the time of ʿAmīrah, Jubbah was famous for their craft.

Black, she speeds like a well pulley's ropes;
    her neck towers up like its wheel's supports.[67]
Couched at a rich source, she savors the flow:
    her lips lap up the water gushing like a garden basin.
Muscles bulge at the joints like bolts on gates;
    her soft flanks cushion the saddle's fittings.
By God, with her I don't want her to swagger up front
    or sidle up for a chat at the ladies' litters.
No! If villains forsake travel companions,
    I invite a fellow to ride with me behind.
She storms ahead to outrun the vanguard;
    far from me to loiter with women at the rear![68]
Damn you! Failing to avenge an uncle
    while passing for upright and well-bred!
At the stable a full-blood is waiting,
    twisting its head and chafing at the lead.[69]

—By "full-blood" he means his purebred riding camel. "The lead" is the rope for steering it.

ويا عـاد هـذا الشعـر كاسٍ عوارضي   ورمـحي مـن ريش النعـام يغـيف
جـانن مـنك يا شـايع النـبا فـتوى   وانـــا عـلى فـتواك حفـيف
يا عاد ما انت لاقيني على صوب ملعب   ولا ادور مـن زينـاتهـن وصـيف
أصفّ الخطـا من بين غـالي مـذاهبي   أصف الخطـا مـن بينهـن وأقـيف
حـنا العتيقـين والجـديـدين غـيرنا   حنا كما كوكب تاتي دلاوه ذريف
ذبح عـمي وانـا باللفـــــاع   وعيشتي من قهارير الصدور عطيف

اللفاع المهاد.

ذبحت بابا الدسما دسم المواعين راشد   لى هبّـت النكـبا بـدورٍ عنـيف
مـدمي خشوم انفوس من شمّـخ الذرى   لى صـار ما بالمـرزمـات عطـيف

١٦،٢ قال شايع: من جانا الله لا يجي بخته؟ قالوا: جاكم الفهادي. قال: الله يجعلكم انشا الله ما تكثرون مع العرب. ولا والله كثروا من هكالدعوة ليا هالحين، عَقْبهم هالحين بس رجال واحد. كل حمايل الرمال غدت زْجال هالحين، كل رجل قفوه له عرب، وهم انقطعوا، بس على رجال رجالـــ.

Braided tresses tumble down my temples;
ostrich feathers adorn my spear's shaft.
I was summoned: "Shāyiʿ will tell you!"
Dead set I am against all your notions!
You don't ache to meet me in combat,
nor do I seek to impress fancy girls;
I strive for a conscience immaculate,
impurities washed out: standing tall!
We are true chiefs of old, the others parvenue;
we are zodiac signs, harbingers of rain.[70]
My uncle was slain when I was in swaddling,
fed with milk straight from camel udders.

—The covering, *al-lfāʿ*, is the swaddling.

You slew Rāshid, hero of fat-dripping platters;[71]
at times of want, lashed by icy northern winds,
His axes' blades ran red with the blood
of yearning camel mothers whose milk has gone dry.[72]

2.16 Shāyiʿ said, "From the time he came to us, our luck ran out." "The cheetahs were upon you," they said. He cursed Ibn Gidrān's branch: "May God not let them prosper or increase in numbers!" That is what happened. Only one of them is still alive. By contrast, all forefathers of the Rmāl grew into full-fledged tribes. Each man is backed up by an entire tribe, while their branch came to extinction, but for a very few of them.

شايع عند راعي بقعا

شايع الامسح يوم هو قصير عند ابن مفلح الاسعدي، راعي بقعا. صار قصير عنده واكرمه وردّ له خيله من المستّت، اطلب المستت اللي نهب خيل شايع ولحقه بخشم ناظر وذبحه واخذ منه الخيل وردّهن على شايع حسب القِصْرِهِ. وقال شايع: ١،٣

قال ابن مرداس فتى الجود شايع   حداني زماني والحمول ثقال ٢،٣
ذبحت عدواني وطفيت نارهم   والدم من ضرب المهنّد سال
وانا زبنت لمن كان يحمي جوانبه   كعّام لمن تاه الطريق وعال
معيّش الخِطّار في ليلة الدجا   ان جَوه جوعا والركاب هزال
سعد زعيم والسواعد هل الوفا   تفخر به اجيال وبعد اجيال
أجاد واعطاني من جواده سلاله   وايضا عطاني من الغيد جلال
ارخص بهن زيزوم الغانمين ابن مِفْلِح   من الغرس مطويٍّ عليه ظلال
وانا شفاتي غلمة نعتزي بهم   ربعي سنادي مطوّعة العيّال
على عوص الانضا والرمك مسرجينهن   ومن فوقهن عود القنا ورجال
يقودهن المصطور سعد الحسيني   الاسعدي عِرْب الجدود وخال
وظعونهم كما المزون يا ركّزت   من الشبط جوعا والمكيل شمال
شتّوا بخَبّ الحمض أيضا وربّعوا   والريم عنهم عن مربّه جال

Shāyiʿ Sojourns with the Chief of Bagʿā

Shāyiʿ stayed as a guest of Ibn Mifliḥ al-Asʿadī, the chief of Bagʿā. Shāyiʿ lived under his protection and was treated very well. His host saw to it that horses seized from him by al-Msattit were retrieved.[73] The chief rode in pursuit of the robber and slew him at Khashm Nāẓir. He restored the horses to their owner, Shāyiʿ, his protected neighbor, as demanded by hallowed custom. On that occasion, Shāyiʿ recited: 3.1

Hear verse by Ibn Mirdās, noble Shāyiʿ, 3.2
hard-bitten and burdened by Fate:
I slew my foes, doused their fires,
blood spattering from my blades.
My refuge is an uncompromising lord,
the scourge of miscreants gone astray;
In dark of night a haven for travelers,
famished and weary, mounts emaciated.
Lucky chief, undergirded by bonds of loyalty,
tower of pride built through generations.
A purebred steed he bestowed on me;
gifted me a grove of majestic palms.
Ibn Mifliḥ, fortune's redoubt, is liberal
with the fruit of gardens enveloped in shade.
I long for fellows, united by common descent,
with the aim of bringing troublemakers to heel.
They ride rugged camels, saddle horses,
the quivering shafts of their long lances aloft;
Troops led by undaunted Saʿd al-Ḥusaynī
al-Asʿadī, both parents pure Arabian blood.[74]
His camel trains move like heavy cumulus clouds
to stock up north against February's famished cold.
Winter and spring, we graze at Khabb al-Ḥamḍ,
sending gazelles bounding from pristine haunts:

عــدي بشــامخ البــنا قصــر مــارد　　مــن الذل مــا دَبّت عــلي نمــالــ
وان كــان بالجــيران جــارٍ مــدلّل　　فجــار ابن حــتروش ربى بــدلالــ
سقى الله دار سكنهــا العــتيــبي　　سقــاه مــن نوّ الثــريا خيــالــ
ولي بــين اجــا والنِفْــد مسكن　　عندل لها القلب من بِدّ الخلايق مالــ
والحي لا بــدّه عــلى الحي عــايــد　　بتــدبــير مــن هو شــرّف الاميــالــ

As if high and dry on turrets of Mārid's castle,[75]
  not the tiniest ant of fear crept up my sleeves.
If ever neighbors were cosseted and coddled,
  guests in Ibn Ḥatrūsh's embrace are the ones.[76]
God, shower the ʿUtaybī's homeland with rain, 15
  in buckets from the Pleiades' autumnal clouds.[77]
My lands stretch from Ajā to the dunes,
  a fair beauty to hold all hearts in thrall.[78]
Surely one day kin must rejoin their kin,
  by decree of the Lord of Mecca's holy places.

شـايع يْعَـيّي يـدفع الودي للشريـف

الشريف يادا الناس هكالحين، كأنه حاكمٍ الجبل والديار اللي حوله وشايع منتزحٍ ١،٤
شويّ، ما ادري بجبّه والا حوله. شايع عيّى لا يدفع الودي. وحارب الشريف. والشريف عاد بالتالي حاربوه كل سنجارة اللي بهذا وعبده وتغلبوا عليه. بس ان القصيدة هذي به اشكال بين عبدة وسنجاره متخالفين على به لَه بيت. وانا ما احب اقوله. وفيه اللي يقول:

ألى ياخوي دورّ لعيـني الدوا   يم صنعـا وهـيضـات سوقـه ٢،٤
ألى ياخوي ارتحل فوق ملحا   ملحا وكن الشب غاشٍ شدوقـه
فكّرت بالدنيا وناظـرت ما به   ما طـير بـرٍّ سـالمٍ من طقوقـه
ألى ياعين من يحري ويذري ويلتقي   وياخذ من الربع الحماقا حقوقـه
ألى ياعين من يـدمح الى شـاف زلّه   زلّة صـديقٍ ما نشـد عن مـروقـه
عشـير صعـلوكٍ قليـل نيـاقـه   وعـدوّ مـالٍ كـثّر البخـل نوقـه

السديري وسالم ابن طواله قرّروا انه لشايع وابن وريك من الاسلم يقول ٣،٤
لقيته مكتوبة عندي لي بورقة قديمة من جدي منسوبة لشايع ولكن الناس من عام الاول وجاي يقولون اغديه لفلان من اهل بقعا واللي يقول انه لفلان من حدري حايل واحد يقول انه لابن مويجد من عبده، وسالم ابن طواله يقول وشي افعال ابن مويجد اللي هو عامل، علمونن بهن؟ ما لقوا عاد اللي يصرّف. قال هذي لشايع معروفـه.

Shāyiʿ Refuses to Pay Tribute to the Sharif of Mecca

In those days, the Sharif of Mecca used to take tribute from people. He acted as if he were the ruler of the Mountain and its surrounding areas.[79] At the time, Shāyiʿ was staying in an outlying place, at Jubbah or thereabouts. Shāyiʿ refused to pay: he was hostile to the sharif. At some point, all of the Sinjārah division in this region, as well as the ʿAbdah, rose in revolt and prevailed over him. However, the ʿAbdah and the Sinjārah are at loggerheads over one verse of this poem, and therefore I will omit it from my recitation. These are some of the verses: 4.1

My friend, go and search my eye's cure; 4.2
go and comb Ṣanaa's uproarious markets!
Yes, my friend, ride a dark camel,
bluish-black, its jaws white as if crusted with salt.
I pondered the world, held it up to view:
no small bird abroad averts its blows.
Yes, my eye! Surmise, shield, confront![80]
Wrestle your rights from stupid rabble!
Yes, my eye! Overlook inadvertent slips. 5
Don't question a friend's follies.[81]
Be kind to vagabonds, poor in camels;
be an implacable foe of misers rich in herds.[82]

Al-Sudayrī and Sālim ibn Ṭwālah maintain that Shāyiʿ is the poet.[83] Ibn Wreyk of al-Aslam avers that he possesses a version attributed to Shāyiʿ, written on an old sheet inherited from his grandfather. But from early on down to today, people have said that perhaps it was composed by a poet from Bagʿā. Others assert that it was composed by someone who lived to Ḥāyil's east. Yet another person holds to the view that the verses stem from Ibn Mwējid of ʿAbdah, to which Sālim ibn Ṭwālah retorted, "Does anyone know what famous deeds were performed by Ibn Mwējid? Tell me if you do!" No one came forward in response to the challenge. He said, "This is a piece by Shāyiʿ; it is common knowledge."[84] 4.3

حرب شايع والشريف

١٠٥ شايع الامسح عاصر الحميدي الجربا. هو يوم شاخ صارت الرجال كله تِرِدّ لُه، معه فَتْل وعِزْف وياصل العدو. هكالوقت امحل الجبل هذا وساقوا شمر يبون الحجاز، مربّع الحجاز. وطلب منهم الشريف، شعثا ونعامه. الشعثا والنعامه من البل الخيار واللي على حد الخيار. ووافقوا وجوا رجال الشريف يسربون من البل شعثا ونعامه. يا مار فيه العَجَرّش، من العجارشه هذولا فرّيس، اخوات شلوى، هذا قبل شويش. العجرّش عنده له قصيرة صخريه، من بني صخر، وشافوا نياقه يا كلهن مغاتير. نَقْوه. كِلّهِن خيار. اللي يجمعون السبي، الحلال هذا، قالوا: يا عم هذي كلها شعثا ونعامه. قال: قَطْع يارميح، نياق الصخريه، ما منهن عقلا، ما يبقى منهن العود. رميح هذا هو اللي يجمع الودي للشريف وهم يقطعونهن كلهن وهي تصيح الصخريه قالت: وين العجرش! ويجيهم العجرش، قال: ياجماعه، هذولي نياقي خوذوهن الله وامانه كلهن، اما قصيرتي ما تاخذون نياقه. قالوا: رح وراك بس. ياناس، يا ! قالوا: ابدا، هذولن للشريف، هذولي اللي يصلحن، كلهن شعثا ونعامه، انطَه انت نياقك. وهو يلكد على رميح، على كبير السرية، وهو يلهبه بالسيف يا راسه بوزنه. وكل كبارهم، الكبار يذبحهم وهي تهِجّ شمر، تِطِقّ، تهج لدياره. يوم جوا ديارهم ويرزقهم الله بامطار وصيوف وربعوا. الشريف عقبما

Shāyiʿ's War against the Sharif

Shāyiʿ al-Amsaḥ was a contemporary of al-Ḥmēdī al-Jarbā.[85] When he became shaykh, all tribesmen took their cue from him. He was cunning and wise, and enemies were not safe from him. In that time, the Mountain suffered from severe drought. Shammar packed up and drove their herds toward the pastures of the Hijaz. The sharif demanded from them "Shaʿthā and Naʿāmah"—that is, the pick of camels or quite good ones.[86] They accepted, and the sharif's officers came to survey the herds and make their choice. One of the Shammar clans was the ʿAjarrash. The ʿAjarrash were first-class warriors. This was before Shwēsh al-ʿAjarrash.[87] Brothers of Shalwā![88] A woman of the Banū Ṣakhr tribe had put herself under the protection of the ʿAjarrash. Her camels, pure white ones, the cream of the crop without exception, drew the attention of the tax inspectors. The collectors of livestock told their boss, "We can't choose; all of them are Shaʿthā and Naʿāmah." "No two ways about it, Rmēḥ!" he said. "None of this woman's camels remains hobbled where it is.[89] Take them all! Don't leave any of them behind!"[90] Rmēḥ was the name of the sharif's tax collector. They unfettered and rounded up the entire herd of white camels. The woman of Banū Ṣakhr was screaming, "Where is the chief of al-ʿAjarrash?" Al-ʿAjarrash came and said, "Listen, men, if you take my camels all, you won't hear a murmur of protest, be assured of that. But keep your hands off the camels of this lady, my neighbor." They wouldn't hear of it: "Get out of our way!" Good grief! "Impossible!" they said. "These will be dispatched to the sharif; they fit the bill to perfection. All of them are Shaʿthā and Naʿāmah. If you like, give your camels to her in compensation!" Al-ʿAjarrash spurred his mount and galloped at Rmēḥ, the leader of the band of tax collectors, swooshed his sword, and there lay his head on the ground, severed. There was no stopping him: in his fury, he cut the entire group to pieces. Shammar fled to their tribal lands. They took to their heels as fast as they could. God came to their aid by sending plentiful rains that allowed them to graze their animals on the pastures of spring and early summer. When the sharif learned what had happened, he said, "By God, I have no choice but to go after them. I must launch a punitive raid against Shammar." 5.1

جا هله، قال: والله ما لي عنهم الا اغزي على شمر، انا لازم اغزيهم. قال ابوه: لا تغزي على شمر، طِع شَوري، لا توازيهم بديارهم، انتم اخطيتوا عليهم. قال: والله ما لي عنهم. وهو يجيك.

٢،٥ هام الدواسر وهَجّوا عنه. يا بوجهه ابن حميد، يوم شافه ابن حميد هَجّ عنه وزبَن الضِلع. وتياسروا لعقلة الصقور دون المدينة، وهم يهجون عنه. ترى هالكلام على وقت ذهاب العيينه. قالوا: العيينة ذهبوا هله يا محمد الشريف ولكن اغديك ما دام قرّبت لهم تغزيهم وتسباه. ونزل البدايع بالخرج معه هل الحجاز، قوم ما تحصى. واخذ بالخرج له مده. ووفدت عاد عليه الناس اللي تخاف منه من الحضر والبدو، وفدوا عليه اللي هو اصحب واللي هو وِدى واللي هي اِخِذ. وسباهم يوم ان الله اوزاهم صار زود نَقْصٍ عليهم. اخذهم، اخذ القوم. فتّش البيوت واخذ الذهب والدبش. عاث بوادي حنيفه لأنه اذهبه الوهم قبله. وجاك يم الوشم وينزل البرّه. وهم يافدون عليه هل الوشم. قالوا: وين تبي؟ قال: ابي شمر. قال ابن جعيثن من شعار هل الوشم، قال: انا اشير عليك لا تسنّد يم شمر تَرْهم ياخذونك، ما هم مثل هالناس اللي انت فعلت بهم هالفعل، هذي صميمة عربان وفرسان تراهم ياخذونك. قال: انا ما ارجع الا من معان، من شمر ابي معان، اي ابرّد القبايل، ابي بني صخر وهالدنيا هذي كله اللي ما يِصِحبن اباخذه. وجاك يبي شمر بهذا. جوا الاسلم، اول ما جوا الاسلم، اهل سَلْمى، واهل سلمى سدّوا عليه الارياع، ارياع جبال سلمى، وجنّبهم. واستَنْذروا به يا عبده ريّسهم ابن علي. ونوّخُوا له يا عبده يوم استضام ابن علي، حْمَلَت عليه هل الحجاز وزِمِل، وارسل لشمر وهم على

His father tried to dissuade him: "Stay away from them, take my advice! Don't bear down on them in their tribal district. You were the ones who started the trouble by committing a wrong." "No," he said, "I have no other choice."

First, he hovered around the lands of the Dawāsir, but they fled. Then he set course to Ibn Ḥmēd, but as soon as the shaykh spotted them, he was off and withdrew to mountainous terrain.[91] Next, he veered to the left and marched on ʿUqlat al-Ṣuqūr, a place on the way to Medina. Again, the population quickly pulled out. These events took place when al-ʿUyaynah had gone to ruin. They said, "The people of al-ʿUyaynah have deserted their town, Muḥammad al-Sharīf, but since you happen to be in the area, why not raid the town and take whatever plunder we find?"[92] He and his big army from the Hijaz put up quarters in al-Badāyiʿ at al-Kharj. He remained there for a while to receive delegations from the cowed population: some from sedentary communities, others Bedouin. Some sought to ally themselves with him; others came with presents by way of tribute; and still others came to plead for the return of goods that had been confiscated from them. He shook them down, seeing that they were hard-pressed. By coming forward, they only added to their losses. He stripped people of their possessions. He searched their dwellings and looted their gold and animals. He marauded through Wādī Ḥanīfah, where the population had been decimated by cholera. He marched to al-Washm and pitched his camp at al-Barrah. The people of al-Washm called on him and asked where he intended to go. On learning that his destination was the tribe of Shammar, one of the poets of al-Washm, Ibn Juʿaythin, said, "I would advise against proceeding upcountry toward Shammar. You risk incurring severe losses. They are unlike the people you have encountered and dealt with on your way so far. They are hardcore, belligerent Arabian tribal fighters, and they will overwhelm you."[93] He said, "I'll go ahead and march as far as Maʿān. From Shammar I'll continue to Maʿān. Don't worry, I am going to take the tribes there down a peg, Banū Ṣakhr and the rest. Those unwilling to pay fealty will be made to cough up, whether they like it or not." He made his move toward Shammar, and the first division of that tribe that he reached were members of al-Aslam, the inhabitants of Salmā Mountain. They had blocked the roads through the passes, and he left them aside, but they had sent a warning to Ibn ʿAlī, the chief of ʿAbdah.[94] At his call, fellow tribesmen rallied to the cause. Ibn ʿAlī took fright at the approach of the army from the Hijaz and asked Shammar tribesmen at Mōgag for help.[95] His appeal was rebuffed: "No, we won't. We aren't your 5.2

موقق. قالوا: ما ننهج يمك، حنا ما حنا ذبايح لك يا بن علي، انزل علينا ونفكك كان انت خايف، اما عاد اننا نبي نجرّد نصادم الشريف هناك ويصير الفخر لك. يقوله الحميدي الجربا وشايع الامسح واللي عاد حاضر على وقتهم.

٣،٥ وهج يابن علي وازبن على شمر بموقق. يا هذا الشريف باثره. وارسل الشريف لشايع، قال: نبي الودي. قال: كيف تادانا، حنا منك وانت منا! ولا يوخذ الودي الا على الصلبه. قال: الا تدّون الودي والا ترو عليكم مجرود النقا. قالوا: عرب شايع خلنا نِدّي له، هذا حاكم ما ينتحارش، خلنا ننطيه طْلِبُه ونسلم منه، هذا الحاكم مثل الجبل هكاللي ان وقع عليك دقّك وان وقعت عليه دقك. قال: ما اطيعكم. ونكّس المراسيل قال: كان هو مقلّط عليه لا يوخرّ. وهم يتكاونون هم وعبده بتلعة عند موقق. تسعين يوم وهم منوّخين عبده. يوم ضاقت محايلهم عبدة وهم يفزّعون زوبع، الصايح كله، وهي تجي فزوع. فزّع يا شيخ عبده لشايع. ويجونهم فزعه ويعرضون عندهم. وينوّخون الجرود بلهم زبارة بين الشريف وبين العرب، قوم شايع. قالوا عبده لحريمهم: سَوّن يالحريم طعام وكل خُبْرة حطوا عنده صحن، كرامة لهم. وهن يسون الحريم وكلٍّ تجيب له صحن. يوم جن الاولات صحونهن على روسهن وكل من يجن يبن يحطن عنده الصحون قالوا فِتِن للخبرة الثانيه يما فاتنّهم كلهم. وهن ينكسن بصحونهن، يعيّون لا ياكلون، زعالى انهم ما وَلوا الشريف. نكسن الحريم كلهن عليهن صحونهن به طعام. قالوا: وش علم هالعرب، وش علمكن نكستن بالزاد؟ قالن: عيّوا، جينا لنا رجال طنايا. هاللي جابت لشمر الطنايا، هي هذي. قالوا: الصايح طنايا، ابشروا انشا الله بالعز. وهم يْسَمّون الطنايا من هكاليوم إلي اليوم.

sacrificial lambs, Ibn ʿAlī! You may come and stay with us. We'll look after you if you're terrified. But no mistake, we'll prepare for war and meet in battle with the sharif out there, and you may claim the victory if you like." Thus spoke al-Ḥmedī al-Jarbā and Shāyiʿ al-Amsaḥ and the other chiefs at the time.

Ibn ʿAlī heeded their words and sought refuge in Mōgag, with the sharif on his tail. The sharif sent a message to Shāyiʿ, demanding that he pay tribute. He replied, "Have things gone to your head? How dare you presume to impose tribute on us? We are your fellows and you are one of us.[96] Tribute is levied from *ṣlubis* and their ilk." The sharif insisted, brandishing a threat: "You'd better pay up or we'll declare war and deal with you as we see fit." Shāyiʿ's fellow tribesmen entreated him: "Let's comply! We are in no position to stand up against a ruler's power. Let's pay up and be safe! A ruler is like a mountain: you're crushed, whether he falls on you or you fall on him." He said, "I don't want to hear this kind of talk," and he sent the envoys back. "Let him come sooner rather than later, if he likes," he challenged them. Battle between the sharif and ʿAbdah was joined at a mountain gully near Mōgag. There were ninety days of infantry warfare.[97] When the tide of war ran against the ʿAbdah, they called for assistance from the Zōbaʿ, the entire division of Ṣāyiḥ.[98] The auxiliaries came. The chief of the ʿAbdah also called for help from Shāyiʿ. On arrival, the fresh troops held a parade with war dances, and then the men of Shāyiʿ deployed to a low sand hill that stood between the sharif and the populated area. The men of the ʿAbdah told their women: "Prepare food and bring a tray to each group of fighters in token of our appreciation!" The women did as they were told; each prepared a tray with food. When the first arrived at the front, balancing the trays on their heads, and made to set the trays down on the ground before them, the fighters told them to pass them by and take the tray to the next group, and there the women heard the same: they all sent them on to the next. Bewildered, they returned with their full trays. The men refused to eat: they were chafing at the bit, impatient to defeat the sharif. The women came home with the food untouched and were asked what was wrong. Why didn't the men want to have any of it? The women said, "They were adamant in their refusal to eat. The men were *ṭanāyā*, swollen with anger." That is how the nickname of Shammar became "swollen with anger," *al-Ṭanāyā*. They said, "The men of Ṣāyiḥ are swollen with anger. Brighten up, victory is in store for you!" From that day on, they have been called "swollen with anger."[99] 5.3

٤،٥ قالوا انتم يا عبده لكم من صلاة الظهر الي ما تغيب الشمس وحنا يالصايح لنا من الصبح يا صلاة الظهر. وهم لك يتلاقون وتصير المجاولة على الشريف وهم يشلّعونه. تجاولوا بهالتلعة اللي شنق موقق. وهو الله يكسرهم. كسروهم وانتصروا قوم شايع، شمر، عليهم. ويِهْوُونُه مع شعيب بيض، شعيب طويل مع ايمنهم ضلع ومع ايسرهم ضلع. وهو لك ينقصم الشريف على الصايح. خْذَوا العْبِدات ثلاث خيل. شايع وقومه عيّوا لا ياخذونهن. وصارن عند العبدات قطعة خيل مرابط من خيل الشريف. وبَيص عبد الشريف فارس تحَوما عند عمه اول نَوبه وضربه العجرّش من الثابت بالسيف يا قاطع يده. وهو يلحقه نوبه قال: يا عمي ما معي سيف. قال: انطوه بعد سيف بيده الاخرى. والخيل تشلع بهم. وهو ياخذ السيف بيده هذيك. يوم رد عليه نوبه يومي بيده هذيك وهو يضربه بعد من هانا. قال: حتّ الرحَمان وانا اخو شلوى. وهو يضربه يا مير طافحة بيده هي وسيفه. وهو يلحقهم العبد يعض الرسن بافمه. قال: بيص يا ولدي. قال: يا عمي جتك قوم ما تعرف بَيص، شوف لون يديّيي هه، العذر لله ثم لك. واركبوا عليهم يا زوبع واللي عاد معهم واكسروا الشريف وخوذوه. يقول الشريف:

٥،٥ قال الشريف من حليات الامثال ... برّقت بالدنيا وانا قبل فاكر
يامل عين للشريف محمد ... تهلهل دمعها من قبة الراس حادر
جرّينا السبايا من الطايف والحرم ... وشلنا وحلنا يم وادي الدواسر
وصفقناهن باليمنى على ابن حميد وانتحى ... وقفّى وانحى عن ملاقانا مخاير
وصفقناهن باليسرى على الصقور وانتحوا ... وقفوا وعرفوا به حمر النواظر
وصفقناهن على الديرة اللي اسمها باسم اهلها ... كرام اللحى بايام حرّ المساعر

اللي هي سلمى واسم اهلها الاسلم.

Taking the lead, the Ṣāyiḥ fighters proposed to the ʿAbdah: "You do the fighting from the time of noon prayers until sunset, and we, the Ṣāyiḥ, from dawn until noon prayers." They did battle until the tide of war ran against the sharif. They dislodged him. They skirmished and squared off in the gully on one side of Mōgag and broke the sharif's ranks. The men of the Shāyiʿ, Shammar, gained the upper hand in the battle. They chased him down the valley of Bīḍ, a long, drawn-out valley between two steep mountainsides. The sharif broke his teeth on the Ṣāyiḥ. The troops of the ʿAbdah took three of his horses, but Shāyiʿ and his men found it beneath them to do so.[100] The ʿAbdah ended up being the only ones with a few horses from the fabled stables of the sharif. The sharif had a bodyguard on horseback, a black slave called Bēṣ. In a joust, al-ʿAjarrash of the Thābit tribe swung his sword and hacked off his hand. The slave galloped back to his master: "Uncle of mine, I have no sword!" He was given another sword by the sharif. The enemy cavalry was hot on their heels. And he dashed off at furious speed, the sword in his sound hand, the blade raised high and ready to swoop down. The other cried, "Damn it in the name of the Merciful, I am the brother of Shalwā!" and struck an awesome blow that sent the slave's hand flying, sword and all.[101] The slave grabbed the horse's reins between his teeth and made it back. "My God, Bēṣ, my poor boy!" "Master, let me tell you, you've met your match. These men don't give a hoot about Bēṣ. Look what happened to my hands: bloody stumps! I offer my excuses to God and then to you."[102] Zōbaʿ and the others charged and smashed into the troops of the sharif. They routed his army. In defeat, the sharif expressed his feelings: 5.4

The sharif composed these exquisite verses: 5.5
I weighed up the world, pondering it over.
Poor Sharif Muḥammad cries out his eyes:
tears burst forth and run down in streams.
Cavalry trotted from al-Ṭāʾif and holy Mecca,
traveling long and far to Wādi al-Dawāsir.
Right they veered, made for timid Ibn Ḥmēd,
scaring off the coward's pants: he darted away.
Swinging left, we sent al-Ṣuqūr bolting,
frantic, terrified by our blood-tinged stare.
Our steeds steered to land named for a tribe,
noble entertainers in times of scalding heat.

—He means Salmā Mountain and its inhabitants, al-Aslam tribe.

وكد دوجن بنا ببلاد شمر   بديار مرذين العدو بالمناسر
ومنهم صفقناهن على ديار عبده   حنا واياهم بين وارد وصادر
وفاضوا مع شعيب بيض وفضنا باثرهم   ولجوا والتجوا في طمان المغاتر
وتطاردن باللغف في حد موقق   وطيّر حْذاهن عجّهن بالاكادر
ومناخنا لعبده تسعين ليله   بالتعلة الليّا حصاها جفادر
ولو ندّنا هوش السناعيس قطر   تقطير دغلوب نشّت عنه المغادر
وضاقت محايلهم وللعز فزّعوا   ياما وطونا بالحذا والكنادر

فزعوا لربع شايع وللجربا.

ياما لقت له سربة زوبعيه   قِبٍّ يلاوي صرعهن كل نادر
جونا على الطوعات عيال المحمد   من فوق طفقات المهار العنابر
يذودنا طلق اليمين محمد   يشعث بتالينا والعجّ طاير
يا وردوهن كالشياهين خِفّق   يا صدروهن كاللقاح الصوادر
عليهن من ولد الغفيلي سربه   وساع الطعون ومدركين المفاخر
عليهن ذيب الخيل شايع يقودهم   لهم علوم بالجدود الاكابر
عفية بني عمي وجادوا رفاقتي   أركوا بكبدي حاميات المخاطر
وعيال ثابت يوم وردوا وسبّلوا   دكّاتهم بالهوش دكة عساكر
يا مكرمين الضيف يا ويل ضدهم   كرام اللحى بايام حر المساعر
ما تشوف ضرب سيوفهم بيظهورنا   مثل حشاك المزن من نَوّ ماطر

Our troopers made for the home of Shammar,
dogged warriors who wear enemies down.
We headed for the lands of ʿAbdah division;
sallying forward, we clashed, back and forth.
Pushed by us, they poured into defiles of Bīḍ,
seeking shelter inside Ṭimān al-Maghātir.
Cavalry raced and chased in Mōgag's gorges,
palls of dust thrown up by hooves and boots.
Ninety nights long we fought pitched battles,
hemmed in by cliffs of a boulder-strewn gully.[103]
If it were al-Sanāʿīs alone, we'd drain them,
like a puddle left by dried-out pools of rain.[104]
Pressed hard and desperate, they cried out,
rallied, hooves and boots trampling us!

—They rushed to the assistance of Shāyiʿ and al-Jarbā.

Time and again, Zōbaʿ horses came charging,
broad-chested, reins pulled by noble falcons.
Muḥammad's boys attacked us, riding mares,
fleet thoroughbreds skimming over ground.[105]
Liberal-handed Muḥammad kept us at bay;
wreaked havoc at our rear in whirling dust.
Fast on the wing as falcons pounce on prey;
in retreat, ambled like sated pregnant camels.
Squadrons mounted by al-Ghfēlah's pick:
their thrusts' gashes open gates of fame.
Shāyiʿ, cavalry's wolf, leads to glory,
goaded by ancestors' legendary feats.
Bravo, cousins! My kinsmen did well!
You pressed red hot irons against my liver![106]
Rushing forward, undaunted scions of Thābit
smote and struck like soldiers of an army.[107]
Lavish entertainers of guests, enemy's bane,
noble entertainers in times of scalding heat.[108]
See how their swords cut up our backs:
blood spouts as rain from brimming clouds;

ما تشوف جثي الخيل من حر ضربهم   هشيم سمر جابه السيل حادر
حلوا بتالينا وانقاد سرحهم   وايدي بيص قطّعن بُحَدّ شاطر
قطع يديه الفارس اخو شلوى   حر الحرار اللي عريب المواكر
صكّوا علينا سربتين تذودنا   هذا مورّدها وهذاك شاهر
زوبع وعبدة يا تصافوا بينهم   ضديدهم ضاقت عليه المعابر
وصاحت علينا سربة فاضليه   ضديدهم ضاقت عليه المعابر

فاضليه من المفضل من عبده

صاحوا علينا صيحة تِرْمِل النسا   خَذَوا نوادى الخيل والقبس ثاير
خذوا نوادي خيلنا واقرشوا بنا   ورحنا على الطوعات والكون عابر
ورحنا بغلب والسبايا تذودنا   هذا موردها وهذاك شاهر
والخيل بالفرسان قامت تذودنا   ومن دوّر العيلات هذاك خاسر
علنا عليهم عيلة من خَطانا   وانا على ما دبر الله صابر
وردّوا علينا خيلنا عقب قوه   شيمة عرب من مكرمين القصاير
رحنا وخلينا شيوخنا بديار شمر   خلينا حوشان وعقيل وجابر
هذا وصلى الله على سيد الملا   عدد ما كبر بروس المنابر

٦،٥ ردوا عليهم خيلهم عقب ما ولوهم. قالوا انت الشريف وهذي خيلك. ما اخذوا منهم شين. وذبح من الاشراف ثلاثة، هذي سمرا حوشان هاللي دون المختلف، ذبح به حوشان الشريف.

Butchered horses lie there belly up,
stiff-limbed as dead wood swept up by torrents.
They fell on us, drove the rear like sheep;
a blade flashed; off flew the hand of Bēṣ:
Hands severed by Shalwā's dashing brother,
hatched in a nest of pure Arabian peregrines.[109]
Two squads closed in, stopped us in our tracks,
pounced by turns, and as fast shot up again:
If Zōbaʿ and ʿAbdah make common cause,
enemy plots are wrecked and founder.
Fāḍiliyyah's squadron shouted battle cries,
gave no quarter to foes scurrying away:

—By Fāḍiliyyah he means the Mufaḍḍal branch of the ʿAbdah tribe of Shammar.

Shouts herald grief and widowhood,
steeds snatched in clouds of swirling dust.
Robbed of our fabled racers, we conceded,
turned back, defeated, tail between legs,
Crestfallen, beset on all sides by cavalry:
wave upon wave, leaping and pulling back.
Thwarted by desert knights at every move:
so trespassers receive their just deserts.
Weren't we the ones who did wrong by them?
As for me, in submission I await God's decree.
Magnanimous victors, they returned my racers,
as behooves noble and bounteous Arab hosts.
Our shaykhs stayed behind, slain in Shammar land:
we bade farewell to Ḥōshān, ʿUqayl, and Jābir.
God bless the Prophet, humanity's foremost,
as often as calls for prayers are sounded.

Generous in victory, they returned the horses, saying, "You are the sharif and these horses are yours." They did not divest him of any of his possessions. Three of the sharifs were slain in battle: hence the name Samrā Ḥōshān, a rocky outcrop on the way to al-Mukhtalif; that is the place where Sharif Ḥōshān met his end.[110] 5.6

جماعته يستمحنونه يبونه يجوز عن الكرم

شايع ما قِضَب هْبِشُه وكَرَم به، ما قضب من بعير انطاوه والا ذبحه والا باعه والا راح. أبد، يوم يجي الربيع والصيف يكسب ويجيب كسبُه ويحذيه وينطيه. ويوم يجي رْحَلة الناس من الما بالصفري يا والله هلكان ما عنده شين، ما حاشت يده نَقّده. ويجمعون له ربعه رِحله ويرحلّونه. ويغزي ويجيب اكثر من المال الاول. وهذا عَمْلُه. والزمان الاول ما من شي الا نْهابه، هذا ياخذ من هذا. الرجل يمسي غني ويصبح فقري. خْذِتُه لُه قوم. قالوا ربعه حنا ابلشنا هالفيد هذا، شايع هذا ابلشنا، نجمع له كل سنة رحلة وياكل الرحلة وياكل اللي غيره، حنا نبي نرحل ونخليه على جُبّه واغديه يبقّي لنفسه، ما حناب معطينه من شان يشوف عازة الدنيا غديه يَنْكل. قالوا: انت اذهبتنا كل يوم نجمع لك اباعر ولا نَبْدِق (نشوف، نلاحظ، ندري) الا انت مفرّقه. وهم يرحلون ويخلونه. قال: ياهل جبه، الكلبان يا جماعتي، ابيكم ترحلّونن على معاويدكم بهالنازية القبليه، ورا الغوطه، جبل اسمه غوطه بشنق جبه، على الخَلّ. صار على مِطّرَق القرا. ١،٦

يبي يعاندهم، يبي يعاند جماعته. وهو يرحل وهو يصير على الخل ويجلد ما معه الا ولده وحريمه ثنتين، عقيلة مرته من الفداغه وكعيب الظبي بنت عمه. ونزل بام لحم هاللي بيننا وبين قنا، نزل، عندُه صقَارِه وعنده له جمل يروّي عليه. وهو يدلّي ٢،٦

Shāyiʿ's Fellows Put His Generosity to the Test

Whatever income or gain came Shāyiʿ's way was promptly consumed in splendid outlays lavished on his guests. Any camels he acquired were given away, slaughtered for sumptuous dinners, or sold, or they somehow disappeared. Without exception. In springtime and early summer, he'd go raiding and return with stolen camels, only to make presents of them or casually let others have them. In autumn, when it was time to pack up and leave the wells, he was hamstrung, completely destitute. He had spent his all. It would fall to his fellows to collect pack camels for him so he could join their migration. And he'd go raiding again and bring home even more animals than before. These were his habits. It was the way of things in the days of old. The only way to make a living was to go on a plundering expedition. One man would take from the other. You would go to sleep rich and wake up a pauper: despoiled of everything by enemy tribesmen. Shāyiʿ's fellows said, "This irksome man only causes us trouble. This Shāyiʿ gives us headaches. It is the same story every year: we collect pack camels for him and he expends them on meals that are consumed by him and others. This time, let's travel and leave him behind in Jubbah, letting him fend for himself. We won't give him anything. That will teach him how things work in the real world. Perhaps he will come to his senses." They told him, "You are ruining us. Time and again, we must collect camels for you, only to find out that you have frittered away what we gave for your upkeep!" They went on their journey and left him behind.[111] He said, "Hey, folks of Jubbah, al-Kalbān, my fellow clansmen![112] Give me a hand: let me have some of your camels, the ones you use for irrigation! I need those to carry my chattels to that sandy hillock to our southwest." He meant a sandy outcrop behind al-Ghūṭah, which was a mountain near Jubbah, on the way through the sands, slap up against the path linking the villages. 6.1

An obstinate person, he had a mind to push back against his fellow tribesmen. He traveled down that track, accompanied only by his son and his two wives: ʿGēlah, his wife of the Fidāghah tribe, and Kʿēb al-Ẓabiy, his cousin. They put up camp at Umm Laḥm, a place between here and Gnā. He brought 6.2

يقنص. وكل ليله خمس ظبا، ست ظبا، سبع ظبا، ويجيبهن ويكرم بهن لهالضيفان، على الخل، خل حايل، من جبه. قالوا: نبي نْغَرْبله، نبي نغربله اغدي الله يهداوه يجي معنا. ويركبون اهل عشر ويوم قرّبوا عنده وهم يغيّبونهن بهكالنازية، وهم يخلون قَشّهم عليهن، قشاطهم وملابسهم، وهم يجون بس بطروق الثياب، وعليهم غِدِر، مطر وبرد. وهم يجونه رِجِل، كلٍّ آخذٍ معه له عليقة بيده كنهم رجليه. يوم جا العشا وهم يلوّذون عليه. ولده على البعير ناهج يجيب مانٍ ما ادري يم جبه والا يم قنا مير يخَمر على الما هو، ما يجي يمه. قال: يا لله حيهم، يا هلا يا هلا، وابرك الساعات، الساعة المباركه اللي جابتكم. قالوا: الله يحييك، والله حنا مقصَّل، غزينا وحوّلنا العواجي وخذى جيشنا وجينا على رجلينا. الله يحييكم.

شبّ النار. والى مَير ما عنده ما يِقْرِيهم. العْشَيّ اللي عاد الله قاسمه آكله هو ٣،٦
والحريّم. صوّت لعقيلة شنق، قال: اقول. قالت: آه. قال: ابي اذبحك وابي اطبخ من لحمك وابي اعشي هذولا، هذولا جايين هلكى. يبي اغديَه تِطلِع كان عندَه شين، ما من شين هكالحين، ماهو هالوقت هذا لِلّه الحمد قالت: واوه والله لاصيح. قال: اقعدي، اقعدي، ما انا ذابحك انتي ابذبح كعيب الظبي بنت عمي. صوّت لكعيب الظبي، بنت عمه، ابعد به شنق، قال: والله انا قلت لعقيله وبغت تصيح والا هي الحْم منك فلكن ابذبحك انتي وابعشي هالربع. قالت: انا ما اذبح، انا عارفة كل دعاويك، فلكن ان كان الربع هذولا ضيوف فانا عندي لهم عشا، وان كان ما همب ضيوف فهو استمحان وعشاهم نعرفه. قال: وشلون كان ما

his hunting falcons and a camel for fetching water. Much of his time was spent on hunting. Each night, he'd come home with five, six, seven gazelles. They'd consume the meat and treat their guests to it, the ones who traveled the road from Jubbah to Ḥāyil. His fellow tribesmen said, "Let's play a trick on him and confound him. Who knows, it may convince him to mend his ways, and then we'll have the benefit of enjoying his company again." They rode out, ten men on ten riding camels. Not far from where he had pitched his tent, they halted and couched the camels, invisible from where he was behind a sandy hillock. They did not unload. All luggage was left on the backs of their mounts, their gear and clothes. Then they walked up to him, dressed only in their long shirts, even though they had traveled in foul weather. It was rainy and cold. Each of them carried a sack of the sort used by travelers on foot. Around dinnertime, they appeared at his tent, seeking shelter from the inclement weather. His son had gone out with the camel to fetch water, in the direction of Jubbah or Gnā. He would not return that evening, and would spend the night at that distant well. Shāyiʿ gave them a warm welcome, shouting enthusiastically, "God's welcome to you! Most welcome, most welcome! This is the most fortunate of hours! How blessed is the moment that brought you to us!" They replied, "God's greetings to you. Truth is, we are completely down-and-out. We went raiding, but al-ʿAwājī intercepted us and despoiled us of our riding camels. For that reason, we came on foot."[113] "You are most welcome."

He lit a fire. The problem was, he did not have any food to prepare and serve them. That night, he and his wives had already consumed the meager supper allotted to them by God. He called ʿGēlah aside. "Listen!" "What?" "I have a mind to slaughter you and cook your flesh to set before those folks as dinner. They came as tramps, destitute and on the brink of perdition." He said so in order to find out if perchance she had a cache of food for her own usage.[114] He stood with empty hands. At this point he was really hard up. Those times were not as we live today, praise God. "Awawaw, by God, I am going to scream!" "Calm down!" he said. "Just have a seat. I am not going to slaughter you. I will cut the throat of Kʿēb al-Ẓabiy, my cousin." Then he called Kʿēb al-Ẓabiy, his cousin, and took her aside some distance, and said, "Well, I told ʿGēlah but she was going to scream, and therefore, though she is meatier than you are, I will slaughter you and serve your flesh as supper to my guests." She said, "I am not going to be slaughtered. I know you and your ways. If those folks are guests, I have some food to serve them for dinner. And if they are not guests and have 6.3

همب ضيوف؟ قالت: كان هم على ركاب تراوه استمحان، اذبح حدى ركايبهم. قال: وش يعرّفن كان هم ضيوف والا استمحان؟ قالت: حِطّ حَطَب على النار، جب لك غمر حطب من هالصليخ وحطه على النار وخلهم يثورون، كان هم يوم يثورون يا مير قدومهم متسفّطه ومتعكرشات من قفو ترهم على ركاب وركابهم حولنا، يبون يغربلونك ويستمحنونك، دوّر ركايبهم واذبحهن وعشّهم من ركابهم، وان كان هديماتهم سمحات ومِلْس فهي بيانة انهم رِجل ووجهك علينا وانا عندي لهم عشا.

٤،٦ ادهج الحطب وخذ هكالغمر حطه على النار. يوم رمى حزمة الحطب على النار وشبّه وقبّت النار، قال: ضفّوا النار، ضفوا النار عن هالبرد وعن هالغدر، تِشَلهبوا. يوم ثاروا يتصخّنون إلى مير متعكرشات هدومهم من قَفُو، ولا هن مبتلّات من المطر، توّهم محوّلين من مراكبهن، من الاشدّه. اقعدوا اقعدوا الله يستر عليكم. قال: حديكم يسوي القهوة لخوياوه. وهم يقلط حديهم يحمل القهوة وهو يلوّذ على الحريم، قال: خِذِن زبلانكن وسلاحكن. وياخذ هو هكالنافعية، قدَيمي ويطلع مع شنق البيت ويجي مع اثرهم، وهن يجن وراوه. ويقص اثرهم يوم جا يا مير هذولي عشر ركاب كلهن معقّلينهن بهكالنازيه. عاد هو بالليل شوف الرجّال بالنهار، وبالنهار شوف طير وهو ما له الا عين وحده. يجيك مع اثرهم يا والله هن هذولن هن يتجرّرن عشر ركاب. وعقد ارسانهن باذنابهن واشكمهن وحط كل وحدة شكيمته بعِكْرته ويذبحهن. كل العشر ذبّحهن، من خوفه لا يَطْنَى

come to put you to the test, in that case you know about their supper." "What do you mean? Why shouldn't they be guests?" "If they came riding on mounts, it is a test. Slaughter one of their camels!" "How can I find out whether they are guests or have come to put me to the test?" "Throw wood on the fire! Bring an armful of dry kindling, throw it on the fire, and make them get to their feet. When they stand up, look and see if the back side of their long shirts is crinkled and shows folds. If so, it means that they have been riding and their mounts must be somewhere nearby. In that case, their visit is for the purpose of confounding you and seeing how you deal with the situation. Go and search for their mounts, slaughter them, and serve them up as their dinner. If their clothes are smooth and even on the back, it means that they have come as wayfarers on foot. We are honor bound to receive such guests, and I will prepare something to eat for them."

He did as she said. He took an armful of wood and threw the entire bundle on the fire, kindling that made the flames shoot up. "Draw near to the fire; sit close to it!" he called. "It is horribly cold and wet out there. Give your body a nice little toasting!" As they scrambled to their feet to warm themselves, he saw that their clothes were crinkled from behind. Also, they were not soaking wet from the rain. They must have clambered down from their mounts and their saddles only a short time before. "Sit down, sit down, may God protect you! Let one of you prepare coffee for the company!" One of them volunteered to prepare coffee, and Shāyiʿ withdrew to his wives, saying, "Get pails and kitchen utensils!" He grabbed a dagger, a large, razor-sharp one, and walked away with it from the side of the tent, following the traces of their footsteps. The women came with him. Lo and behold, where the tracks ended, they found ten hobbled riding camels at that sandy hillock. He was known for his ability to see at night as if it were day, and in daylight his vision was as good as that of a falcon, though he was a one-eyed person.[115] There they were, at the end of the traces of the visitors' footsteps, ten riding camels ruminating calmly. He tied their reins to their tails, muzzled their snouts, and fastened the muzzles under their tails, and he slaughtered them. All ten of them. He was afraid that if he killed only one, and not the rest, that camel's owner would be furious. For that reason, the place where he slaughtered the mounts, halfway between Jubbah and Gnā, is called Umm Laḥm, "Mother of Meat," down to the present day. He removed the entrails, hearts, livers, and kidneys. He put them in pails, carried them to the tent, and returned to his guests. He had covered the carcasses with brushwood 6.4

واحد لو ذبح مطيته وخلى الباقيات. الي هالحين يسمونه ام لحم، المكان اللي ذبح به ركايبهم، بالمنصفه بين جبه وقنا. يوم ذبحهن وهو يِظهر شواياهن وقلوبهن وكبودهن وكلاهن وهو يحطهن بالزبلان وهو يجيبهن ويقلب عليهم. حط حطب على مذابحهن عن السباع وعن الحصانيا. وهو يجيبهن قال: اطبخنهن على كبرهن، على عدلهن، لا تقطّعنهن. وهن يطبخنهن وهو يجي وهو يتقهوى عندهم ويتعلل هو واياهم.

٥،٦ يوم انه انتهى العشا وهي تِطِقّ الذرا وهو يقلطه لهم. قال: سمّوا، سمّوا الله يحييكم، افلحوا يا عيال، افلحوا الله يزيّن دربكم، سموا الله يحييكم ونتعذركم باللي قصرنا به، والله يالربع جيتونا بهالليل وهذا الميسور. قالوا: مير ما قصرت. وش معك يا فلان؟ قال: كِلوه. وانت يا فلان؟ يقوله هكالشايب بهم، قال: قلب. ومن لمس هاللون ليا هذا قلب، ليا هذي كلوه، قال: يالعن قلب امكم وابوكم هذولي قلوب ركابكم، من اين لهم القلوب. يا معهم لهم صانع، صانع على له جمل. يقول ان الصانع انه طقع يوم قالوا هذا قلب جملك، يقولونه. قالوا: وشّن هذولي؟ قال: هذولي ركابكم عشيتكم منهن والى جا الصبح ادهجوهن وكل ياخذ له منسر ونعول من جلودهن. وهم يفرّون. يوم جوا الركايب يا مير ما تجي هكالجيه، عشر ركابهم مجدّخات، حتي غطيانهم، الفرا، أخذهن ومخَلٍّي بس الاشدة عليهن عضو. وهم ينحاشون لاهلهم رجل يما جوا اهلهم وهم يجمعون لهم زمل ويجونه وهم يرحّلونه. قالوا ما بك حيله. ويَسِفْرون لحمهن اهل قنا واهل جُبّه.

٦،٦ وقصد عاد هالقصيده:

١ يقول ابن مرداس فتى الجود شايع اشوم كما حِرّ المراقب شام
اشوم عن السِفْلى وانزل بالعلى وانا بالعلى من سابق وقدام
ولو كل من بغى العلى ينزل بهن تِلْقَى بها فروخ الدجاج نيام
انا من هل الجبلين من روس شمر عن الودي عاصي ما علي حكام

to keep predators and foxes away. Then he told his wives, "Cook them whole in one piece, as they are. Do not cut them up." They started cooking, while he joined his visitors, drinking coffee and making conversation.

6.5 When she beat the flap of the tent as a sign that the food was ready, he went to fetch it and set it out before his guests: "In the name of God, start eating! Welcome in the name of God! Enjoy the food, fellows! Enjoy it, may God ease your path! In the name of God, start eating! Our apologies if we have fallen short in what we owe you. By God, men, you came to us at night, and we can only give you what is available." They replied, "Why, you have not fallen short! What is it that you have, so-and-so?" "Kidneys," he answered. "And what about you?" asked one graybeard of their group. "Heart," he replied. Whatever their hands touched was a heart, then a kidney, and so on. "God damn the heart of your mother and father!" he cried. "These are the hearts of your mounts. From where else would he have gotten those hearts?" Now, one of them was an artisan, a workman riding a male camel. It is said that this artisan let out a fart when told that he was eating his camel's heart.[116] "What are these?" they asked their host. "These are your camel mounts, which I have served you as dinner. Tomorrow morning, go to the place where you left them. There are plenty of chunks of meat for you to take along, and you may cut yourselves sandals from their skins." They hurried off. As they came to the place where they had left their mounts—may you be spared such a horrific scene!—there were ten mounts, completely cut up; even their fur coverings had been taken away. The only thing left on the carcasses were the wooden saddle frames. They fled as fast as they could on foot until they reached their people. Without further ado, they began collecting pack camels to help Shāyiʿ on his way. They said, "You are impossible. We are powerless against you." Their camels' meat was distributed among the people of Gnā and Jubbah.

6.6 On that occasion, he composed a poem:

1 This is the song of Ibn Mirdās, generous Shāyiʿ:
up I soar, noble falcon deft on the wing.
I soar away from the contemptible below:
my abode is lofty heights, now as of old.
If all who aspire to those heights there alight,
they'd be crowded with poultry, fast asleep.
I'm from the Two Mountains, Shammar chief:
free of rulers, dead set against paying tribute.

اعته يستمحنونه يبونه يجوز عن الكرم.

يا جانن علم من الشريف تركته   اقول علمك يالشريف خمام
ما اناب خطو الشبر اعيش بالمنى   يا فات عام يرتجي له عام
حنا قدايمنا تعيّي بحقنا   وحنا للعَيّ العنيد كُعام
وحنا هل المعروف والمجد والفخر   وحنا للجمع الثقيل زْقام
وحنا غفيلات واصلنا بعالي العلى   لنا في تاريخ الجدود مقام
وحنا هل المنسب عريبٍ ساسنا   هواشم من ترثة الاكرام
حنا ليا جانا العيا من ضديدنا   نسقيه من كاس الحمام غرام
يلومونن الانذال لا كِثِر خيرهم   يلومونن ومِثْبِعِينَن ملام
يقولون خَلّ الضيف لا تِعْتِني به   يبون الرِدَى يَبْني علي سنام
وحلفت ما ابقي حلال لوارث   ولا احِطّ بين الصَقّتَين اقسام

الصفتين الوارث والعاصب، يعني ما ابقّي حلال للورثه يتنازعون عليه.

حْذَى مهرةٍ صفرا ولَدْنٍ من القنا   كما سابح طَبّ البحور وعام
ونوبيةٍ ما تَمْرَح الليل كِلّه   لها عند هجعة الناس مقام

الدَلّه.

ترو هذاة الغي يا داير الغَوَى   رد على التالي وهن حوام
يا بنت عمّار وياخت معمّر   يابنت اجاويد ونَسْل كرام
لا تلطّمين البيت من يمّ جارنا   زادٍ بلا جار علي حرام

Put on notice by the sharif, I spurn his call,
saying, "Your notice, Sharif, is a piece of shit."
I'm no bumbler, hooked on wishful thinking:
"If not this year, then perhaps the year after."
Unyielding, our ancestors stood up for their rights;
we subdue the obstinate who refuse to bend.
We are paragons of goodness, glory, and pride;
our cudgels hit enemy bands on the snout.
Ghfēlah is our tribe, from the highest ranks:
tall we stand on foundations laid by ancestors!
Arabian pedigree, pure from its very roots:
Hashemites, heirs to high-minded nobility.[117]
If inveterate enemies seek to hold us up,
our cup pours them a drink of fated death.
Vile sluggards are blaming me: let them rot!
Damn their carping and tedious protestations,
Urging me: "Leave off, forget about your guests!"
Ugh! They want to build on me a hump of shame.
Hereby I swear, nothing I'll leave my inheritors,
nothing for my two rows to fight about,

—"My two rows"—that is, his inheritors and his kin. He means: "I am not going to leave behind anything for inheritors to wrangle about."

Except for a long-shafted lance and a sorrel mare,
like a fast-stroked swimmer cleaving the sea;[118]
And for a Nubian disdainful of taking rest:
awake all night, at the ready, as people sleep.

—"Nubian" means a coffeepot blackened on the fire.

You, desire's flunkey! Speak of infatuation:
I shield the rear with death hovering above.
Hear, daughter and sister of wealthy nobles,
daughters of lavish spenders, born to munificence!
Keep tent flaps open; don't shut neighbors out!
Food not shared by neighbors is forbidden fare,[119]

. اعته يستمحنونه يبونه يجوز عن الكرم

يا بدهم من خامة يَذْرعونها   وِيْحَطّ لي بـه مَـيزر ولثام
ويملّونَن مل العجـال شواتهم   هم بنوّ رحيلٍ وانا بنوّ مقـام

٧،٦ وقصد بعد شايع يقول:

يقول ابن مرداس فتى الجود شايع   وايا بطـل واكثر علومي قدايـم
انا كما عود القـنا زاد ذرعـه   تْعَـدي به العـدما على من يزايـم
تشوفن مع الجمع القليل وتنكرن   كما الحر مقطوم الجناحين حايـم

تنكرن يعني تخاف مني، تنحاش عني.

كم عقلة بالقيض بحنا ترابـه   ابا القيض حادينا خبيث السمايـم
ياما خذينا باكواننا من عـزبـه   تشبع بجرتنا رجالٍ هلايـم
وياما قطعنا باكوراهن من خايع   ويامـا قطعـنا من بعـاد الخرايـم
ياما قـطعنـا سهـلة مجرهـده   فوق النضا نقطع بعيـد الخرايـم
نبـذل كثير المـال لعيون زوبع   يا جوا يحظون النظـا بالهمايـم
وانا الفتى من قوم بـذّالة الصخا   واهل الصخا ما باقي إلا الذمايـم
واليوم ألى ياكثر منّانـة العطـا   ومشـاورة النسوان سود اللثايـم
لا هـلّهـم لا بلّهـم وابـل الحيـا   ولا جاضَعَتهم رادعات الوشايـم
زاعوا وخـلّون بمِشـاريق غوطـه   واعْتَـظْتهم باللي يجيب الغنايـم
تَحَيَّلَوا بي وصِرْت اطْيَب منهم حِيله   وخَلّيتهـم يمشون فوق القدايـم
عَشَّيتهم واشْبَعتهـم من ركابهـم   عشر نَظْواتٍ كل ابوهـن همـايـم

Until my shroud's measurements are taken and I,
dressed in loincloth, jaws tightly closed,
Lie abandoned in haste, like a loaf baked in hot ashes
by impatient travelers, keeping still forever.[120]

In another poem, he said: 6.7

This is a song by Ibn Mirdās, generous Shāyiʿ:
champion of famous feats celebrated of old,
He thrusts and stabs, hard as spear shafts
hurled by knights smiting defiant enemies.
Foes shrink away, terrified at seeing me in a small party,
like a sickle-shaped falcon hovering over prey.

—"Shrink away" means "be scared, run away."

We clean out many a sand-filled water hole,
lashed by blasts of poisonous summer winds.
We wage battle and capture enemy herds,
a boon for starving paupers on our heels.
Tireless, we cross countless empty plains,
forsaken tracts of remote rocky wilderness.
Resolute, we cut through barren vastness
on sinewy camels inured to desert travel.
Airily, we spend our all for Zōbaʿ's sake,
haven of travelers staggering in from far.
I am born to a line of lavish entertainers:
nobles supplanted by breeds of miserly curs.
Today's sort unashamedly trumpets any gift,[121]
doormats at black-veiled women's beck and call:
I pray, no life-restoring rain on that trash!
Tattooed beauties! Spurn their nuptial bed![122]
My tribe left me beached east of Ghūṭah;
I served up their raiding mounts to settle scores.
They plotted, but I am the better plotter:[123]
outfoxed, they tramped home on foot,
Crammed with my roast of their mounts:
ten sturdy camels, fleet desert cruisers all.

البجادي ينهب بنت شايع وشايع ينهب بنت البجادي ام القرينيه

١٫٧ البجادي هْزِبُه أبوه. نهج قال: يايبه، أنا والله خطبت بنت فلان. تقل ان البنت آه مزيونة ولكن ابوَه رِدي. قال: ويش عاد، خاطبٍ بنت شايع ابن رمال! قال الولد: والله كان انا ولدك كود آخذ بنت شايع. واركب من العارض وغرّب لديار شمر، هقوتي ديرته حول الخرج. اركب وايتك وحول عند شايع فوقٍ من جبه، بغربي جبه بْلُه مكانٍ يقولون له المربوب، هكاللي غربٍ من جبه، ضِلْعان بنفود، المرابيب. يامير لو خطب مْنُه لا هو مجوّزه، ولا يدري وش حيلته. وهو يصير فْداوي عنده، عزوبي. يسرح بالزمل، ويورد الزمل على الما، وراعي بيت، وعنده. بالشتا هم بالنفود، غضا وارطا، غابايْه (= غابات)، وارضهم به صيد. ويا مار يقنص شايع من جهه وهو يقنص من جهه. يوم يروّحون يا والله كلٍّ جايبٍ له كم ظبي والا بقر والا بْدون والا.

٢٫٧ والى البجادي على جملٍ لُه يقال له قِدّين. سِمٍّي قِدَّين ان ما يقضب شدادُه الا القد من نشاطه، بطانه وحقبه قد، ما يقضبه الا القد، والا الحبال يقطّعهن من حَمُو ركضه، الى ابترم وركض قطّع الحبال. ولا يقيّده الا مع الخيل، يحدّده بحديد مع الخيل، يحدد الجمل ويخليه مع الزمل. ما يراكضه لا فرس ولا غيره، واسمه قِدَّين. وشداده ما يْعَدَى عليه، دايم شداده عليه. قالوا: اقرط شداده. قال: والله ملهّسه انا ما يْعَدى شداده عليه، وهو صيده ناوي ينهب البنت. ومشمّله ولا يخلّي احدٍ يضرّبُه كود هو. المراد انه جا شايع، طال عمرك، ويجلد عند شايع،

Al-Bijādī Steals Shāyiʿ's Daughter and Shāyiʿ Steals al-Bijādī's Daughter, the Mother of al-Grēniyyah

When Al-Bijādī told his father that he had asked for the hand of a certain man's daughter, his father challenged him. Apparently, the girl was beautiful but her father was no good. His father mockingly said, "So what? It's as if you asked for the hand of the daughter of Shāyiʿ ibn Rmāl!" Nettled, his son said, "By God, as certain as I am your son, come what may, now I must have the daughter of Shāyiʿ as my bride." And off he rode west from al-ʿĀriḍ to the lands of Shammar. I believe his tribal district was around al-Kharj. On arrival, he dismounted at Shāyiʿ's place, west of Jubbah at a location called al-Marbūb, a string of stony hills in the area of al-Nafūd, al-Marābīb. If he asked Shāyiʿ for his daughter's hand, he would not consent to betrothing her to him. How to go about it? Shāyiʿ agreed to take him into his service, a bachelor youngster. His job was to go out with the pack camels and water them at a well. He lived in his own tent, pitched nearby.[124] In winter, they stayed in the sands of al-Nafūd, amid plentiful growth of *ghaḍā* and *irṭā* shrubs and game.[125] Shāyiʿ would go hunting in one direction and he in the other. They'd come home with gazelle, oryx, ibex, and other game. 7.1

Al-Bijādī rode a male camel, named Giddēn because its saddle girths were made not of rope but leather thongs. At great speed, ordinary ropes would snap under the strain of the animal's violent jerks and the saddle would come off. Similarly, the belly girths and the girths around the haunches were made of leather. If the camel glanced backward while running hard, ropes would snap. At rest with the tribe's pack camels, it was shackled in iron, like a horse. At full speed, Giddēn would outrun horses, any mount. It was always kept at the ready and saddled. If asked why the saddle was never taken off, he'd say that the beast had grown up that way and was accustomed to it. In truth, he kept the saddle on so as to be ready at a moment's notice to elope with the girl. Also, he had netted its crotch and would not let anyone use his stud to cover a she-camel without his permission. He stayed for some time as seasonal labor. After a while, he asked Shāyiʿ for his daughter's hand. Shāyiʿ excused himself; he did 7.2

يتعزّبُه. ويطلبه بنته، يطلب شايع بنتُه، وهو يْتَعَذّرُه شايع. وطْلبُه شايع انه يضرّب الذلول، ذلول شايع، وعيّى بالجمل. قال: كان تملّك لي على البنت والا ما أخلّي جملي يضرّب ذلولك. قال: البنت حافظة زملي ولا عندي احد، ولا ادري ويش. إيه، تَعَذّرُه. الجمل يسرح بحديده، قامت البنت نوّخت لُه الذلول وهو بحديدُه. وهو يقمز عليه ويْحَفْزَه وهي تْعَشّر الذلول. يوم روّح الجمل عرف البجادي ان جمله مضَرَّب، عرف واسكت.

٣،٧ يوم اخذ له ايامٍ عندهم خلّى البنت يما سْرَحَيْه وابعَدَيْه وهو يركب الجمل يبي يلحقه، قال شايع: وين تبي؟ قال: والله انا ماشي، اسلم عليكم، ابروح لاهلي. لا، وش معِجْلَك! قال: والله اسلم عليك، ابروّح. تحابّوا هو واياوه وتوادعوا. وهو يعقرب على بنت شايع مع الزمل، وهو يفك عن الجمل وهو ينوّخُه. قالت: وين تبي؟ قال: والله ابروّح مير جاي اسلم عليك واودعك. عِدُّه اخوٍ له هو. وهي تجيه تبي توادعه، وهو يثوّر الجمل واركب وهو ينصلّ مشعابه. قال: الحقي انطينن مشعابي. وهي تجي وامسك ايده وينتله وانْسفَه بْقَرا الجمل ويمعطُه، يَتْمِز به وهو يركبَه على الجمل وهو يحزّم قرونه بمصلاب الشداد، عليَه قرونٍ طوال، تقل حبال. وهو يحزّم قرونه بعصيان الشداد، بالظلاف، مصاليب الشداد من قَفُو. وهو يعَمَل لَه هكالحوايه على وروك البعير، اما عبايْه والا شي وقاةٍ لَه. وهو يحَزْمَه معه وْلِسْبيع. وهي تقعد تصيح: يا، يا، يا مير ماش، حرمة ولاه له حر. اشلحه، انهزم به.

٤،٧ يوم روّح الزمل ما معه احد وجا الصبح وقصّوا على أثره، يا هذا مناخ الجمل ومِرْكْبَه معه وضاربُه وفايع له مفاع. وهو يلحقهم شايع على ذلوله الوضحا. يوم لحْقُه بالخَبّ، خب السطيحه، وهو يطلع عليه مع هذاك، مع الخب. يوم لحقه بالخب، حزم، ما هو بعيدٍ عْنَه، وهو يجي وهو يبسط الجمل، قِدّين، مع الكوع،

not give his consent. For his part, Shāyiʿ asked for his female riding camel to be covered by the stud camel, but his request met with refusal. The other said, "Only on condition that you give me your daughter in marriage; otherwise, my male will not cover your riding camel." Shāyiʿ pleaded that he needed the girl to look after the pack camels and that he had no one else for that job. It was a transparent excuse. The shackled male camel would shuffle off to go grazing. The girl took her father's riding camel and kneeled it at the stud. Though shackled in iron, the male leapt on the female and impregnated her. When the stud camel returned, al-Bijādī at once knew that he had covered a she-camel but pretended ignorance.

For a few days he avoided the girl, until he saw her drive the animals out 7.3
and she had gone some distance. Then he mounted his camel to catch up with her. "Where are you going?" asked Shāyiʿ. "Well, I am leaving. I say my farewells to you. I want to go home." "No! Why this haste all of a sudden?" Shāyiʿ asked. "Really, I am saying goodbye. I am rejoining my people back home." They embraced and exchanged kisses, saying their goodbyes. With a crablike movement, he sidled up to the daughter of Shāyiʿ. He found her with the pack camels and kneeled his mount. "Where are you going?" she asked. "I am going home but wanted to say goodbye." He had become like a brother to her. She walked up to him to bid farewell. Then he mounted and let the camel raise itself, but dropped his riding stick as if by accident. He said, "Please help. Can you hand me the riding stick?" As she did so, he grabbed her hands, pulled her up, and set her down on the camel's back. He snatched her up, grabbed her. He tied her long tresses to the wooden crosspieces of the saddle's hind part. Her hair was as long as ropes. For her comfort, he made an improvised seat for her on the camel's haunches, fashioned from a cloak or similar garment by way of protection.[126] He also roped her to himself. Off they went to Sbēʿ. She sat there, screaming and crying, "*Yā yā yā*, no, no, not this!" A woman snatched by a noble falcon, powerless to resist. He seized her and ran off.

The pack camels returned without her. Next morning, her kinsmen fol- 7.4
lowed the tracks. They came to where he had kneeled his camel, grabbed her, and raced away with powerful leaps. Shāyiʿ rode in hot pursuit on his white camel. He almost caught up with them in the long spur between the sands, Khabb al-Sṭēḥah. As he drew nearer, the other had only to give his mount a slight stroke at the elbow for it to catapult forward. The distance of its leap from where it pushed off with the hind legs to where it came down on its

وهو يقمز. يوم قمز يا مير مطب رجليه عن يديه مثل بعد شنق القهوة هذي عن شنقه من هنا. يا مير ما حوله لا سما ولا ما، ما له حيله، ما يقوى يلحقه، قدَّين ما يِلْحَق. وهو ينوّخ وهو يحط على مطب يديه رجم وعلى مطب رجليه رجم، مقْمِزُه، مقمز الجمل، وهو يرجم على مطب اليدين وعلى مطب الرجلين يوم يقمز، تسمّى ام رجامه، هاللي ورا جبه، علشان شايع الامسح رِجَم على مقمز الجمل. وانكس يا شايع.

٥،٧ هذا البجادي يوم جا هله قال: وكّلي، انا والله ما انا ناهج ابوق، وكّلي وكيل ويجوّزك لي. وكلت. ملّك عليه وتجوزه غصب وساق عليَه لَه اباعر، مغاتير، بْعَبْدَه، براعْيَه وْوَسّم البل الباعج، حط الباعج على الكلوة اليسرى، وسم الرمال، ثلاث مطارق يتطاولن على الشاكلة وجههن حَدِر ويقطعهن مِطْرقٍ هاللون، يغَدي مِشْط، ومطرقين على فوقي ثفنة البعير وسم شايع يصير شاهد.

٦،٧ اثاري البنت معلمة ابوه اني ضرّبت ذلولنا جمل ضيفنا لا تجرِف عَنَه، اللي يوم تضرّبَه وهو بُه حديدُه. الذلول عشرَيْه (= عَشّرت) وجابت بَكْره ويْغَذَى البكرة، يَغذاه على امَّه ويذبح عليه ضيرٍ آخر، يبي يكِرْمَه من شان تكبر بساع. ويذبح عليَه ضير. والسنة هذيك والسنة الاخرى يذبح عليَه ضير آخر والسنة هذيك يَعسْفَه. ما عسفه الا مرمّية العظام، سنونه. يوم عْسِفَه زيّن طبعَه ويخلّيَه سنه كامله. على انُّه يعِدّ سنينَه بقصيدتُه. يوم جت السنة هذيك عْسِفَه، زين طبعه. وهو يركبه يامير بس تقول هاللون. يوم استِتَمَّيْه وهو ياخذ زهابُه ويركبه قال ابشوف كان هي يعني صارت حول مقماز ابوَه فانا ابدوّر القْضا عليَه. ويمشي عليَه ويوم اقبل على الرجوم، ما هو بعيد، مثل هالباب، يوم اقبل على الرجم، أول رجم، مضرب رجليه، يامار هي غافله وهو يْتَحَمّى لَه بالكوع وهو يرفسَه على غَفْلِه، أول تمشي بُه، يوم اقبل على الرجم وهو يرفسه وهي ترِمز مثل رمزة الظبي، وهي تنبر من وراوه يامير

forelegs was the length of this coffee place from one side to the other.[127] There was nothing he could do, "no sky and no water" as people say, meaning "nothing at all." He stood powerless. There was no way he could overtake them. Giddēn was unbeatable for speed. Shāyiʿ dismounted and built a cairn on the spot where the forelegs landed and another where the hind legs had pushed off. The location of the leap is called Mother of the Cairns, beyond Jubbah, because Shāyiʿ al-Amsaḥ built these cairns to mark the length of the stud camel's leap. Then he went home.

On arrival, al-Bijādī told the girl, "Name a person to represent you! By God, I have no intention of being dishonest. Authorize someone to marry you to me!" She did as she had been told. The contract was concluded, and he married her through force majeure. He paid her the bride-price in camels, white ones, and added a slave girl to tend to them. He branded the animals with the tribal markings of the Rmāl, called *al-bāʿij*, on the left kidney: three vertical strokes bridged by another stroke to make it look like a comb; and two strokes on the upper part of the callosities on the stifle joints of the camel's knee, the personal marking of Shāyiʿ's brand.[128] 7.5

Earlier, the girl had told her father that she succeeded in having their she-camel impregnated by the stud of their guest, even though it was shackled in iron. She cautioned him to preserve the semen and not wash it away. The she-camel became pregnant and gave birth to a female calf. He made sure that it was well fed. The young suckled its mother at will. In addition, he slaughtered another camel's calf at birth and assigned that camel as a wet nurse to the young calf. Shāyiʿ had a mind to pamper it, feeding it exceedingly well so it would grow up quickly. Each year he trained a new suckle mother whose calf was killed at birth to give her milk to his favorite. This privileged treatment continued for several years. Once she had shed her teeth, not earlier, her regime of exercise started. Her training as a riding animal completed, he granted her another year of freedom to roam pastures to her heart's content, as explained in the poem, year by year.[129] When the camel was at the peak of her strength, he started riding her. He slung his bag with victuals over her back and set out for the spot where the camel's father made his legendary leap, saying to himself, "I am going to get my revenge!" He went on his way and made for the cairns, which were not far off. The first cairn was built on the spot where the mount's hind legs pushed off. His she-camel looked placid and absent-minded. To fire her up, he rapped her knee with the riding stick, catching her unawares. 7.6

متعَدّيةٍ مقماز ابوَه، الى والله زوده على ابوَه بوعين، أبدا مقمِزَه بوعين زودَه على ابوَه، زوده على مقماز الجمل، أبد نذرعُه، يا عندي بهذا نراعي لهن. وهو يحط على مطب يديَّه رجم ومطب رجليَّه رجم وغدن اربع رجيمايْه. هذا رجوم ابوَه هاللون وهذي رجومَه هي هاللون، مع شْنِقُه، زالِفةٍ هاللون، ذراع. هن يغدن رجيمايْه، نسمّيه ام رجامِه، مقمزهن، ليا اليوم هذا، يا تاريخ هالزمان، انا وعيتهن الرجيمايه ليا عندي بهذا ومسمينَه ام رجامه هالحين، أسمَه ام رجامَه.

٧،٧ وهو يبَتِّل بوجهُه يما لفى على البجادي. يوم جا طوارفهم وحِف على العرب وامسك له رجال قال: البجادي وينه؟ قال: البجادي هو هذا وهذاك بيته والخيام هذولنك، خيام بنت ابن رمال زوجته. قال: هو آخذ بنت ابن رمال؟ قال: ايه جابه وملك عليه وعلّمته بوسم هله ووسم البل وسم اهله. ساق عليه خمس وعشرين وفرس وعبد، هكالمغاتير هذولي باسمَه هن وعبدهن وفرسهن. وهو يقعد يهدّج مع الحلال، يمين يسار، ما يبي يبيّن روحُه ولا يبي يجي الناس بْشِفَق، يبي يجيهم بليل وهو يِقَع بهاكالبل، يامار مغاتير، بيض. يوم جا يمّه يامار هذا الباعج عليَه، وسمُه، وهذا شاهدُه عليه، وهو يجي راعيه، قال: وشّي هالبل هذي، هاللي عليَه هالوسم؟ قال: هذي للبجادي ساقه على بنت ابن رمال. قال: بنت ابن رمال؟ قال: آه. قال: وين هي عنهُ؟ قال: باني لَه بيت والبل تروّح عليَه، بصفّ بيتُه، البل اللي ساقهن البجادي على بنت شايع حط عليهن وسم شايع، وسم ابوَه، سَوق. وصّف له المحل. وانهج تِمقّل البيت. يوم غابت الشمس وجا الليل، مع دِمْشة الدماس، ختّم اللمَم، لِمَم الصفره، يعني بياح الصفره اكتَم شوي، يا مار هو محاضبٍ البيوت. وهو ينوَّخ بصفّ البيت، ما هو بعيدٍ من البيت، هذا بيت البجادي وهذا بيت بنتُه، بْصَفَّه. وهو يِنْسَلّ على البنت.

٨،٧ يوم جا البنت يا مير توقِد عشاه والرجال هم هذولا بالبيت، بيت الأمير. وهو يجْيَه وهو يَنْدَه عليَه، قال: انتي فلانه؟ قالت: ايه، أنت ابوي؟ قال: اي بالله انا.

At first, she had ambled calmly toward the cairn, but at the whack she bounded forward like a gazelle. She outdid her father's leap: her legs came down two spans of outspread arms beyond the length of her father's jump. The daughter left the stud behind. Absolutely, we measured it! Again, he built cairns at the spots where the hind legs took off and where the forelegs touched down. Ever since, there stood four cairns: those of her father and, next to them, hers, spread out over a few meters as she slid to a halt. These cairns mark the location of their jumps. For that reason, it is called Mother of the Cairns until this very day, Umm Rijāmah.[130]

He kept riding hard until he arrived at the tribal homeland of al-Bijādī. 7.7
On his approach, he looked for people and accosted someone, asking for the whereabouts of al-Bijādī. The man pointed. "That is where he lives. That's his tent; and those are the tents of his wife, the daughter of Ibn Rmāl." "Did he marry the daughter of Ibn Rmāl?" "Yes. He brought her here and concluded the marriage contract. She told him the markings of her tribe and he branded those on her camels. He paid a bride-price of twenty-five camels, a mare, and a servant. Those white camels are her property." He kept pace with the slowly moving herd, alternating from one side to the other. He didn't want to show himself and meet people in the last light of day. It was his plan to enter the camp by night. He mingled with the herd, white camels all. On closer inspection, he noticed that they had been branded with the *bāʿij*, his tribal branding mark, and his own personal markings. He went to the shepherd and asked, "What are these camels and their brand mark?" "These are the camels al-Bijādī gave to the daughter of Ibn Rmāl." "The daughter of Ibn Rmāl?" "Yes." "Where are they living?" "They built a tent for her, and in the evening the camels on their return lie down close to her tent. The camels al-Bijādī gave as bride-price to the daughter of Shāyiʿ. They have been branded with his tribal markings. The markings of her father, the price al-Bijādī paid for Shāyiʿ's daughter." The shepherd having pointed out where she was staying, Shāyiʿ went there to take a closer look. It was after sundown and getting dark. At dusk, as the last light faded away and the day's curtain was about to close, he slunk past the tents and had his camel kneel not far from her place: al-Bijādī and his daughter's tents were pitched in the same row, next to each other. He tiptoed to her tent.

She was busy preparing the evening meal for the men in the tent of the 7.8
shaykh. He called softly: "Is it you?" "Yes. Is that you, Father?" "Yes, it's me!" She put her hand on his mouth. "Be quiet, don't speak!" She stepped outside

وهي تِهِد افمَه لُه بيدَه، يعني اسكت. وهي تطلع معه، وهو يسلّم عليَه. قال: وش لون الدعوى؟ أنا جاي أبيك. قالت: الدعوى لك بناخي هالحين، انا معي وغد ولا أقاضي لك انا يِبه، القْضا ما اقاضيك انا، انا خَذَن البجادي وجبت منه ولد وحامل، مير وش وقع مطيتك؟ قال: والله يا فرحة عضاديك. قالت: يقاضينَن بنتُه، بنتُه مخبّايه، وانا اعتذرت اني ما انام بها لخيام الا بنتك عندي تجسّرن، بنت له، وانا متحرّيتك تجي، كل هالمده، ليا نامت كل عين نوّخ ذلولك بهكالعواشز وانا اجيبها لك واشلَحَه مثل ما شْلَحَن. قال: وش لون تجيبينَه لي؟ قالت: اجيبه لك، بس قرّب مطيّتَك كان هي ما ترغي، تبيّن علينا، قرِّبَه بشتَق البيت من هانا وابي اجْيَه هالحين ما زال الناس غافله وابي اطلعَه لك.

٩،٧ وهي تِنْسلّ عليَه مع قاعة الرواق. قالت: يا خيّتي ابي آصل هالشجرَة وراي ومنخرعه بهالليل ابيك معي. يعني وانتم بكرامه كنّه تبي تَدْفِق الما. قالت: اذل يِدرَى بنا. قالت: لا ما يدرى بنا، هذي الرجال تَعَلّل وهالحين نجي. قالت: بس انا ما اقوى آطا. قالت: نَزْوي على رجليك هالحرير ونِهِل هالدرعه ونِنْكِس قبل تقضي الدرعه. وهي تنسلّ معَه وهي تجيبَه ويوم جوّا بشنق الشجرة يا مار هو متوَلّم ومزيّنٍ الحوايه، شايع. وهي تطلع معه، يوم شافته قالت: هالسماره وشي؟ يا مغطّيٍّ الذلول بعباته، سودا بالليل. نبي نشوف هالسماره. وهي تهزع يمّه. يوم انه جته ويمسك يده. قال: شوفي والله يا إن تكلمتي لاخلّي هالقدَيمي تهوي بمنحرك، اسكتي. واويحي. قالت: لا تقولين واويحي، هذا ابوي يبي ينهج بك مثل ما نهج بي ابوك. وهي تَتْمز هي يا هي بافْمَه، البنت، لا تصيح، وهي تتمز بافمه وهو يحطه بوروك الذلول، يركّبونه على الحوايه. وهو يدِعِس رجْلَيَّه من تحت الحقب، حقب

with him to greet him properly. He said, "How are things? I've come to get you." She said, "This is the situation. You have a new relative: I have a little son. I am of no use for the purpose of settling accounts with him.[131] My person does not cover that bill. I became al-Bijādī's wife. We have a son, and I am pregnant again. But tell me, how is your camel doing?" "By God, she is pure delight." "Fine," she said. "You should get even with him by snatching his daughter, the one who is always kept inside.[132] I've excused myself, saying I can only put up with sleeping alone in this tent if his daughter keeps me company. Otherwise, I feel alone and am afraid at night. I said so because I always expected that one day you'd be coming. That feeling stayed with me all the time. Now listen! Once everyone has gone to sleep, kneel your camel there at those boxthorn shrubs. Wait there, and I will bring her to you. Snatch her away as he did with me!" "How will you manage, bringing her to me?" "Don't worry, I'll bring her. Only lead your camel closer, so she doesn't roar and give us away. Couch her close to the side of the tent here. I'm going to fetch her right away, as people are not paying attention. I'll bring her out."

Stepping silently, she walked back and crept into the tent from under the sidewall. "Little sister," she said, "I want to go to the bushes out there but I am scared all alone by myself in the dark. Please come with me." That means, excuse me for saying so, she made it appear as if she needed to go for a pee. The girl said, "I am afraid we'll be noticed." "No, no one will see us. The men are engrossed in conversation; this is our moment." "But I can't walk barefoot." "I'll wrap your feet in this silk. Then we'll unwind this ball of wool and go back on our traces before it has wound off the spool." They went outside and furtively moved toward the bushes. Shāyiʿ stood at the ready and had finished crafting a comfortable seat on the camel's haunches. As they came walking, the girl made out a dark shape and asked, "What is that black thing over there?" He had draped his cloak over the camel and it stood out as a black blot in the dark of night. "Let's see what it is." And she veered sideways to take a look. At once, Shāyiʿ grabbed her hand and said, "Keep silent! One word and I'll plunge this dagger into your breast. Don't say anything!" "Oh, woe is me!" "Don't worry," Shāyiʿ's daughter said. "This is my father who wants to abduct you, just as your father did with me," and taking a quick step forward she closed the girl's mouth with her hand. "Don't scream!" He lifted her onto the mount's haunches and installed her on the improvised seat. He pushed her feet under the breast girth, while she kept the girl's mouth shut tight. Then he took the long tresses of her 7.9

الذلول، وهي صامّةٍ افمَه، وهو يمسك جديلة قرنه ويعقّده على غرابة الشداد مثل ما عقّد قرون بنته البجادي، بمصاليب الشداد. قال: اطلقي افمَه خلّيَه تصيح. وهي تطلق افمَه. قالت: انحش. قال: لا، ما انحاش الا تعلمين ابوَه بي، انهجي يمه تراي انا بمكاني لما تعلمينُه، انا ما اناب مثله اسرق سراقه.

١٠،٧ وهي تنهج البنت وهي تعلم رجله قالت: ابوي نهب بنتك. وهو يشب النار وهو يدلّي يصيح ويروشد ويرمي. وهي تجتمع عليه سبيع، قالوا: وش علمك؟ ثبّت! ثبّت!، ثبّت! ثبّت! قال: بنتي نْهَبه شايع الامسح. قالوا: وش نعمل بهالليل ولا نقدر نقصّه؟ قال: جيبوا كل فرسين بينهن قدر ونشِقّ قاعته ونربطه بحبال بالمعارق ونشِبّ نار به ويصيرن مردّف على الركاب ويوقدون القدور المردّف، يتعاقبون عليهن. وهم يسوّون الحيلة هذي، ارضهم نفود. وهو يفك عن الجمل هو. فك عنه الحديد وهو يركبه، وهي تركب الخيل باثره. وهم يدلّون يقصّونه، بالشعله، ضو، نار. اركضوا يا مير الشعله هذيك باثرهم، باثرهم، واغدي يالشعله، طوّلت عليهم المتيته وشايع انحاش والبجادي يساريه على الجمل، يتلقّف لمصابيحُه. الخيل نْكِسيْه والجيش نكس، بس الجمل.

١١،٧ يوم اصبح الصبح، وهو على وجهه، يمشي على طَريقُه. يوم اصبح الصبح وراعى يا مير هو هذاك قدامه، على طريقه، مشى بس على طريقُه. يوم راعى شايع يا ما طالعٍ كود أبوَه باثرُه على قِدَّين. وهو يقرّب له بعض التقريبات، خلاوه يما قرب له ادون من البيت، بيت الشعر هذا، وهو يمسح رجلُه عليَه وهي تجمح وهو يهوب الهوا بينهم. يوم قرب له النوبة الأخرى قال: ياشايع، ياشايع! قال: نعم. قال: ارتخ ابعلّمك، ابحاكيك. قال: آه، وش تبي تقول؟ قال: أقول بنتَك اخذته منك

plaited hair and tied them to the saddle knob, as al-Bijādī had tied the tresses of his daughter to the saddle's wooden crosspieces. He said, "Now take your hand off her mouth. Let her scream!" She let go of her mouth and said, "Flee!" "No," he said, "I am not going to run off. First, walk up to her father and tell him about me! Go now! I will stay put until you have informed him. I am not going to act as he did: steal her, spirit her away behind the father's back."

She walked to the tents and told her husband, "My father came and snatched away your daughter." Crying and sobbing, he lit a fire, shouted his war cry, and fired his rifle. The tribesmen of Sbēʿ came rushing to him from all directions. "What happened? Tell, tell, tell!" "My daughter was stolen by Shāyiʿ al-Amsaḥ." "What shall we do? How can we follow his traces in the dark of night?" "Bring the horses, two by two, and between each pair suspend a cooking pot and make a hole in its bottom for the ropes and fasten these to the horses.[133] Light a fire in the cauldron. Two men on each camel, one of them to keep the fire burning with wood and kindling, by turns."[134] They followed his instructions to make this stratagem work. The soil of the land was sandy. He unchained his stud camel, unlocked the iron shackles, and vaulted onto its back. The horsemen took off after him. They followed the traces in the sand with the help of their torch—the light cast by the fire of burning wood in the kettle. The riders galloped ahead, while keeping an eye on the burning torch behind. Oh torch, help us! It was a long, exhausting race. Shāyiʿ had sped off. Riding his stud camel, al-Bijādī was on his heels, straining his eyes against the first light of dawn as he tried to catch sight of him. The horsemen turned back, and so did the camel riders. Now al-Bijādī was in lone pursuit. 7.10

As dawn broke, he held to his course, riding straight ahead without interruption. Lo and behold, he spotted his man right in front of him. There he was, Shāyiʿ, her father, and al-Bijādī was catching up, riding Giddēn, his famed stud. He drew nearer and nearer, closing the gap between them. Shāyiʿ let him draw up to him, closer than the goat-hair tent you see over there! Once the other had come that close, Shāyiʿ touched his mount with a slight stroke of his foot, enough to make her leap forward with such power that he pulled away from his pursuer with lightning speed. Then he slowed down once more, allowing al-Bijādī to gain on him until he came within hearing distance. He called, "Hey Shāyiʿ, Shāyiʿ!" "Yes?" And he turned to him. Al-Bijādī pleaded, "Slow down a bit, please. I must tell you something. I want to talk to you!" "All right," he said. "What's on your mind?" He said, "Look, I eloped with your daughter. Now I am 7.11

وهي هذي مرة لي هالحين، ولا والله اني يوم أنا انحاش بَه انُّه ما ينشدن الله عْنَه إلا عقب ما جيت هلي ملّكت عليه وسقت عليَه لَه اباعر ووسّمت وسمك عليهن، هذي اول وحده، وثانيٍ اسمك اللي تقاضيت وعليك الله وامان الله انه وزت نصيبك هالحين امِلّك لك عليه وارجع على بيت بنتك وتزفّه ببيت بنتك واباعرك تروّح عليك، واسمك اللي تقاضيت هالحين، واما يعني اني جيته قبل اسوق عليه والله انه ما يسألن الله عن لحمَه اني جيته يعني او فعلت به الا عقب ما سقت عليه، وهالحين ابيك ترجع معي من شان سبيع يشوفون انك انت نسيبي، وانت نسيبٍ تبيّض الوجه.

قال: انا بالله راضي، انا بالله راضي، وانا والله بس ابي القضا. وهو يحرفَه عليه ١٢،٧
وهم يتحابّون وهم يجون يتبارون نكس. يوم جوا اهلهم، اهل البجادي، ويجيب هكالجزور ويذبحَه البجادي ويْحَجِر لُه عليَه ويدخل عليه. ويجلد عندهم يما حْمَلَيْه البنت. يوم حمليْه وهو يروح، قال: يا منه اظنت تراوه هو طلاقه، ما انا ناهج به يم ديار شمر من هانا. ويروح لحاله. وجابت ولد، جابت ناصر جد القْرِنه، هاللي تاليهم القرنة عند سبيع ليا هالحين يقال لهم القرَينيّه، هاللي بالعمّاريّه اللي بغربي شعيب الدرعيه، من عَقْبُه. أميرهم ابا الروس اللي بالعمّاريّه، هذا من عقبه. شْرِكوا يمّنا بعد بعَضهم، دَرُو، ابا الروس له فلاحة عند طلال. ايه عاد شايع يقول:

قال الغفَيلي والذي مَسّ حبلَه ... على بنت قودا من خيار الزمايل ١٣،٧
خلّيتها عامين وهي ترضع امّه ... وعامٍ بضيرين وعامين حايل
وعامٍ ترجّيته وعامٍ عسَفْتَه ... يما لفتنا بالرديفين شايل

married to her; she is my wife. Truly, when I made off with her, I acted correctly and treated her decently. Nothing that God would hold against me. After I came home, I saw to it that a marriage contract was concluded. I paid the bride-price in camels and branded them with your tribal markings. That is one. The other thing is, now that you have gotten even with me, God be with you and protect you! My daughter has fallen to you now. She is in your care. I am ready to marry her to you. Turn back to the tent of your daughter! There we will celebrate your wedding with a marriage parade, and you may take possession of the camels. You have settled accounts with me. As for any suspicion that I might have taken her as my wife before paying the bride-price: really, I can assure you that God is not going to ask me why I touched her body or did anything improper before having paid the bride-price. Please return with me, because I want the tribesmen of Sbēʿ to see with their own eyes that you are my father-in-law. You are an in-law whose good name reflects on me: you whiten my face!"

Shāyiʿ replied, "I have no problem with your suggestion. It is fine with me. 7.12
My only concern is obtaining justice and settling our accounts." He pulled the reins and made a sharp turn toward him. They embraced, kissed, and rode side by side back to the camp. Following a joyful reception by his people, al-Bijādī slaughtered a fat camel. A nuptial tent was prepared for Shāyiʿ and his young bride, and the marriage was consummated. He stayed with them until the girl was pregnant. Only then did he go on his way. Shāyiʿ said, "Once she has given birth, consider her a divorcée from that very moment. I won't take her to the tribal land of Shammar." Accordingly, he left without her. She gave birth to a boy, Nāṣir, the ancestor of the Grinah tribe, those whose offspring have remained with the Sbēʿ until today. They are called al-Grēniyyah and their native area is al-ʿAmmāriyyah, west of the valley of al-Dirʿiyyah, beyond it. Their chief is Abā al-Rūs, who lives in al-ʿAmmāriyyah. These are his descendants. Some of them moved here when they learned about their origins. Abā al-Rūs has agricultural land at Ṭalāl. Shāyiʿ commemorated these events in a poem:

Al-Ghfēlī spoke, reins held in a tight grip,[135] 7.13
    perched on a sleek daughter of finest breed:
Two years she suckled her mother's milk;
    two years a foster mother, two years freedom;
One year of coddling, one year training:
    ready she is to carry a co-rider and me!

يوم ينحاش بالبنت يعني.

جـدعيّـةٍ ما يلحق العـلص بدّه   ولا يلحق المحجان ملوى الشمايل

العلص: الولد الطويل، يعني ان الذلول طوايليّه.

يا كن يد الوضحا ليا ما نـزرتـه   يد صانعٍ يـرجى العشـا بالعـميـال
والا يـد البـذّار يا كـبّ حبّـه   بالوسـم يوم انحى سـموم القوايل
اقفت وجِرْد الخيـل ما يلحقنّـه   اقفت كما هيقٍ سريع النقـايل
نارت عن المطلب وشبابة الضوا   خيل تعادى حـاميات الشعـايل
تَسْمَع صِرير الكور تحتي وفَوقـه   كالميس ما بين الرشا والمحايل

الميس المخطر، مخطر المحاله هاللي ما مشى تسمع صريره.

شبّهتهـا بالحيـد الادنى نعـامـه   والحيـد الأقصى زايـلٍ به زوايل
يا كن بنات البدو يمشطن ذيلـه   حـدرٍ من العـرقوب غـاد فلايل
يوم البجادي عيّفن لذة الكـرى   اخـذت ثـارٍ له سنـين طوايل
انا ابن مرداس الذي شـاع ذكـره   أسقيت عدواني بكـاس الغـلايل
عيـب على مثـلي يهـدّ وينْثِـني   يا حَلّ ضرب مصقلات النحايل
أخيـف سـباع الضواري بالخـلا   ودشـاش غـبات البحور الهوايل
أنا عـزيـز الجـار ما دِسْت زَلّـه   ولا مـرة دست الخنا والفشـايل

—He means, when he rides off with the girl sitting behind him on the camel's back.

Hulks can't reach the hump of this five-year-old;
riding sticks' tips fall short of her behind.

—By "hulk," he means a strapping fellow, and from that it follows that the camel's back is very high.

White beauty! Scolded, her feet go frantic
like workers' hands begging for supper;[136]
Or like the hands of peasants sowing seeds
in fall, when the poisonous hot winds subside.[137]
She sets off faster than the fleetest mares,
races with an ostrich's burst of speed,
Outrunning pursuers armed with torches
flaming in cauldrons carried by horses.
My saddle's frame screeches madly
like wooden pulleys spinning over wells.

—By "wooden," he means axles made of rosewood that turn the wooden rollers over which the well rope runs and that make a screeching noise while turning as the bucket is hoisted up.[138]

Zipping past mountains: a fleeing ostrich,
fleeting shape whooshing by that distant peak.
Her tail: thick, as if combed by Bedouin girls;
below the hocks dangles the fluffy plume.
Years without sleep due to al-Bijādī's guile,
I savor slumber on taking sweet revenge.
Ibn Mirdās I am, renowned far and wide
for pouring foes goblets of bitter rancor.
Men such as I are loath to set out, and flinch
if warriors clash, curved swords in hand.
In wilderness, fierce predators run in fear of me;
at sea, I plunge undaunted into heaving waves.
My neighbor's rampart: I won't let him down!
Filthy deeds and betrayal are abhorrent to me.

السيف يشهد لي ويشهد لي القنا   ان جا عـدو الدار للدار صايل
وليا حكوا باخبارهم عقب حربنا   يقولون ابن مرداس راعى الفعـايل
وانا الذي عرضي نظيف عن الخنا   وانا صخي الكَفّ راعى الجمـايل
وانا من اتلى جيـل بذّالة الصخا   وهل الصخا ما باقي الا الذمـايل

My sword is my witness, my spear testifies for me
  when sworn enemies launch their attack;[139]
They testify for me about battles we fought,
  say, "Ibn Mirdās's deeds speak loud indeed!"
My honor is sparkling clean, free of blemish;
  munificent, my hands are liberal with gifts;[140]
Survivor from generations of lavish spenders,
  I am last among a bunch of sluggards.[141]

شايع عن الفضول يوم يْتِسَمّى لبّاد

تنازل شايع هو والفضول. هو رجّالٍ الى ما جازوا له العرب ومشوا على كيفه رحل وخلاهم لو هم ربعُه. نزل عند الفضول والحوال كسيفه. تْحتُه له بعيرين ومعه مْرِتُه كْعَيب الظبي بنت عمّه. نزل عليهم وجاب انثاوه وصار بْلُه خرَيبيشٍ ما هو شِين. يا مير هو مهثّلٍ روحه يبي ما يِعْرَف. هو ذالٍّ من الدموم من كثر ما يلاقي الغزوان ومن كثر ما يلاقي العدوان. جَحَد روحُه خايفٍ انه يِطْلَب، حط على عينه، عينه مسحا من الله خلقه، ما له إحِجّه، ما له حجاجٍ من هانا، ولا مضرب عين، حاطٍّ عليَه لبّادة كنَّه عينٍ تْحَتَه، حط على عينه لبّاده وسمّى روحه لبّاد، على شان ما يعرف. وش اسمك؟ اسمي لباد. ويتخيبل هو، أدْعَى روحه سِفيه. ويَذْهَج خَطْوان المرة تسوّي على الصاج يجيب له له شْوَيّ جلّة وياخذ لُه رغيف مْنَه. خِبلٍ نْذَهوه. لكن كيف هالمرة عنده صابرة عليه يوم يراعون لونَه! وذلوله دْهَنَه بْلَه ذْوا كنّه جربا وحط عليه له خْياش ونِزل بصف الأمير. ١،٨

جا بعض الاحيان يوم وِرْدت اباعر الامير ويوم بحّر ليا مير كل ما تِرِدْ مَعَه لَه بكرة وضحا حول اللقِيّه تنهج تلقّط العظام ما هي عطشانه، ان بغى يطول ظما البل والا يقصر. تلقط العظام ياما يجيبونه للما، ظما تشرب وظما ما تذوق الما. ظما ما تشرب وظما يالله تِذِبّ له طرقوع. قال لمرته كعيب الظبي: يا حلولاة يامن شد هالبكره، لا واهني والله من مَسّ حْباله يا كعيب الظبي. قالت معزّبتُه، بنت عمه: امنّا بالله، كل هالجيش وهالبل وهاللي هذا حلوه ما طاح نظرك الا ٢،٨

Shāyiʿ with the Fuḍūl, Incognito as Labbād

Shāyiʿ decided to join the Fuḍūl tribe.[142] He was that sort of man: if people were not to his liking and did not act in a way that pleased him, he packed up and left, even though they were his fellow kinsmen.[143] He was in a pitiful condition when he set up camp at al-Fuḍūl. With him he had two camels for transport and his wife, Kʿēb al-Ẓabiy, his cousin. He and his wife pitched a miserable, poor-looking tent. He did not wish to make his identity known while he was in straitened circumstances. Also, he was afraid of being spotted by someone who had reason to take blood revenge for men he had killed on his frequent raids or in encounters with enemies. He assumed a false identity for fear of falling prey to pursuers. He covered the part of his face where one eye was missing. That was as God had created him. He had no eyebrow on that side and there was no eye; the socket was empty. Therefore, he put on an eye patch to make it look as if there were an eye hidden under it. Because of the patch, he called himself Labbād, "Wearer of an eye patch." That way no one would guess who he was. "What's your name?" "My name is Labbād, the man with the eye patch." He was an imaginative person. He behaved as if he were a bit of an idiot.[144] He would walk up to a woman who was baking loaves on a sheet of metal, bring her some camel dung as fuel, and ask her for a loaf. A fool whose behavior people would ignore. They wondered how his wife could possibly put up with him and why she had married such an idiot in the first place. He smeared his riding camel with ointments as if it was suffering from mange and covered its back with sackcloth. Being a guest, he was encamped in the chief's row of tents. 8.1

When the camels of the chief came to be watered, he'd study them closely. One day his attention was caught by a young white she-camel that was about three years old. It strolled around, snatching up bones from the ground. Back from pasture, the animal did not appear thirsty at all, no matter how many days the herd had spent away from water. She'd search for bones and crunch them until she was watered at the well.[145] Sometimes, after days without water, she'd drink; at other times, she'd continue thirsting without drinking at all. 8.2

على هالبكيرة الوضحا اللي هذا لونه! قال: هذي لو تآخذ عشر ليال عن الما ما تعطش، لكن وش يجيبه لي؟ لا معي شينٍ اشريَه. قالت: اي والله؟ قال: اي. قالت: انا اجيبه لك.

عرفوا ان البكره هذي مع اباعر الامير، امير الفضول. يا مير لُه مرةٍ هو الامير. ٣،٨
قالت له مرة شايع: انا ابسيّر عليك يا خيّتي اشوف صوغك اللي جاب لك رجلك. الصوغ هكالحين طوق ومُساك، ما من صوغ، المساك اللي يحطّن بالايدين مثل المجاول. قالت: والله يابنت الحلال انا خذيتُه واعتذر انه لما يجلبون والى جلبوا جاب لي صوغ، وكل سنة تَناحَى الامور. قالت: واللي معك ولد منُه ولا شرى لك صيغه؟ والله انَّه غميضة شبابك، سيّري عليّ أوريك صوغي. وهي تلبس مكالهدوم مرة شايع، هدوم برَيسم عنده والبسي الطوق والمساك والزينة. يا هي مزيونه، زاهيتهن، زينة بليّا هدوم، وش عاد يا لَبْسَت الهدوم الزينه والصوغ. وهي تسيّر عليَه مرة الفضلي. يوم سيّرت لقِتَه حاطّةٍ المَعانق وحاطّةٍ الطوق وحاطّة المساك وحلاق الاذان والزمام. قالت: ياخيّتي أنتي مرة لبَّاد؟ قالت: آه. قالت: وهذولي لك؟ قالت: جلي ما عندك مثلهن؟ قالت: لا ما عندي شين. قالت: كيف تنقّحين لرجلك وهو ما يجيب لك مثلهن؟! ياختي انا لباد ما له الا هالجمل جاب لي هذولي وعندي اكثر بعد، عسى تلوى غناتكم، وهالحلال اللي عندكم ما لك مثلهن؟ قالت: انا جابن ابوي!! وانتي مرة لبّاد ما عنده الا هالاملحين اللي هو راكبٍ عليهن، وانا هاللي الطرش قدام البيت وقفاوه!! والله وحارمٍ عليّ ومن جذلتي جِذلِه انّه ما ينجضع على ذراعي متوسّدُه الا هو جايبهن لي. قالت: عاد ان اعتذر بالمطاريش انه ما يوجد بهالديرة الا يطرش للمدينة، ترون حنا نبيع من قراميشي، حنا علينا ضيق ظهر ونبيع من قراميشي. قالت: وش تبيعين؟ قالت:

She'd go without water for days on end and not drink, or would take no more than a few sips. He pointed her out to his wife, Kʿēb al-Ẓabiy, exclaiming how taken he was with the animal: "Ah, what a dream to trek with that camel! Lucky fellow, the rider who takes hold of her reins! My God, Kʿēb al-Ẓabiy!" His wife and cousin said, "May God help us! Here we have all these fast riding camels and wonderful herds. And you have only eyes for this lousy, scroungy white!" Calmly, he replied, "This she-camel can go for ten days without need for water.[146] But how to get her? I don't have the wherewithal to pay for her." She said, "You're sure you really want her?" "Yes, by God, really." She said, "In that case, I'll see to it that the camel becomes yours."

They knew that this young she-camel was one of the animals of the chief, the emir of al-Fuḍūl. The wife of Shāyiʿ said to the shaykh's wife, "I wish to pay you a visit, sister of mine, to admire the jewelry your husband presented you with." In those days, women wore necklaces and armlets, not gold. They'd wear the armlets around their forearms like bangles. "Look here, good girl, I married him and he excused himself, saying that he would bring these, together with other supplies, when they were going to send for them. Year after year, things get put off." "Oh, I say! You gave birth to his son and he didn't buy you any jewelry? How can that be? By God, such a shame, a young woman of such beauty! Pay me a visit and I'll show you my jewelry." The wife of Shāyiʿ dressed up nicely and elegantly. Clothes made of silk, necklace, bracelets, all kind of adornments. A natural beauty, her looks in this apparel were stunning. She was good-looking even without these attributes, let alone thus attired. When the wife of the chief of al-Fuḍūl came on her visit, she found the wife of Shāyiʿ decked out with bangles, necklace, armlets, earrings, and nose rings.[147] Astounded, she asked, "My sister! And you are supposed to be the wife of Labbād?" "Yes, indeed." "And all these are yours?" "Of course. Don't you have similar jewelry?" "No, I don't have any." "How can you primp yourself before sleeping with a man who doesn't bother to make you happy with similar ornaments? Look, sister, Labbād, though he owns no more than this camel, made me presents of all these nice things. And I have more than what I'm now wearing. Your riches might as well go to waste if in spite of such great assets you're not gifted with similar things of beauty." She said, "By the life of my father who begot me! You are married to Labbād with his two black camels, while I have entire herds in front and to the back of my dwelling! By God, I will cut off one of my forelocks as a reminder that from now on I'm no longer available as a cushion to hold him 8.3

الطوق أو المساك أو حديهن اللي تبين. قالت: والله لو تقولين باللي تقولين. قالت: اقول بالبكرة الوضحا اللي هذا لونَه.

٤،٨ يوم جا الليل وجا الفضلي يبي ينام يا هي منتفخةٍ، طَنْيانه. وش نوحك؟ يا حيفك والله يام فلان، وش امرِك؟ قالت: والله ما اكبر من امري اللي مرَة لباد كل صوغ حلوٍ عنده وكل قشٍّ حلوٍ عنده وهو على هالمِلح المتقطّعات، وانا ما عندي العُود، وهالطرش اللي هذا كثره، وش نوحي ما انا مثل كعيب الظبي مرة هالخبل اللي لَه هدوم هالبريسم عسي تِلوى غَناتك؟ والله ما تدخل فراشي الا تجيب لي مثل اللي عند مرة لباد، مرة لباد تلبس من الذهب وانا مَلطا رُقبِتي. قِل به، قل به. قالت: ابد. قال: يا بنت الحلال، حنا اول عذار وما عذار وهالحين عليك الله وامان الله يا اوّل مدينةٍ ناجدهن به الا نشريهن. قالت: هي هذي عنده تبيّعهن. قال: انهجي يمّه ويحدّونهن. قالت: يبون لهم بعير، حدى السلَع. قالت: يا كعيب الظبي، يا مرة لباد، وش تبي تنطينن؟ قالت: انطيك المساك. قالت: وش البعير اللي تبين؟ قالت: هذا رجلي يجيكم الصبح واللي هو ببي، اللي هو يرضى به ياخذه منكم. يوم جلس قال: يالباد يا بناخي عند هلك لهم سلعةٍ يبون يبيعونه واهلنا عليهم حاجةٍ منَه وتبون ثمنه بعير، يا وردت البل افطن للي تبي من هالبل واخذه، ان غرّت مير عن فحل النياق وذلولي، خذ البعير اللي انت تبي، ان بغيت جمل، ان بغيت ناقه، اللي تبي. قال: والله حنا ما حناب عاضّينكم ياجيراننا، نبي هالبكيرة الوضحا. قال: خذ بعيرٍ ينفعك، قال: هي تنفعَن. قال: خْذَه. خذاه وعسفَه وزيّن طبعه، وصارت هي الوضحا ذلوله اللي عليه العلم.

٥،٨ وينبّهون للمغزى الفضول، يوم نبّهوا بالمغزى وهو يخلّيهم يما مشوا الغزوان. يوم مشوا واقمز على البكرة ونتّفه، نتّفه، نتفه، بقّع به، ويغطّه بهكالبرغيل وخذ

in my arms until he brings me what he promised!" Shāyiʿ's wife said, "Still, he will have the excuse of the travel involved. There is no such jewelry in our district: to find it, he must journey to town. But we may sell some of my precious ornaments. My jewel box is overflowing, and therefore we are selling items of my jewelry collection."[148] "What kind is for sale?" "Necklaces, bracelets, whatever you like." "By God, name any price." "I ask for the white she-camel," and she gave a description of the animal she had in mind.

That night, the Faḍlī, the shaykh of al-Fuḍūl, wanted to sleep with her, but 8.4
he found her steaming mad, furious. "What's wrong with you? Woe to you, mother of my son, what happened to you?" She said, "By God, it upsets me that Labbād's wife has loads of nice jewelry and beautiful objects, though he owns no more than two wretched black camels. And look at me! I have nothing of the sort in spite of these large herds of yours. That's what's wrong with me! That a woman like Kʿēb al-Ẓabiy, the wife of that idiot, dresses in finery made of silk. May your riches dry up! By God, stay away from my bed until you make me a present of something similar to what Labbād's wife owns: she is wearing gold and my neck is bare of it." "Come on now, come on now, let's play a bit!" "Never!" she said. "Good girl," he said, "first of all, I apologize, though there is no reason. I take a solemn oath, God is your witness and protector, that the first town where we find such things, we'll buy one." "She is ready to sell one to us." "Walk over to them and ask for what price they are ready to part with it." "They ask for one of your camels." She went to ask: "Kʿēb al-Ẓabiy, wife of Labbād, what are you prepared to give me?" She said, "I will give you the bracelet." "And what is the camel you want in exchange?" "My husband will come to you in the morning, and it is up to him. Let him take the one he has in mind." When he had come and sat down, the Faḍlī said, "Labbād, dear brother, your family has some article you'd like to sell and our family needs it. The price you ask is a camel. Go and have a look at our animals and take the one you like best. You can take any camel except for my she-camels' stud and my personal riding camel. Take any camel that strikes your fancy, be it a male or a she-camel. It is your choice." "We don't want to rip you off, dear neighbors. All I ask for is that little white she-camel." "Why don't you take a camel that is of some use to you?" "That is the one I can use." "Then take it!" Shāyiʿ trained her until she made for a fine mount, the riding camel for which he became famous.

The Fuḍūl were summoned to join a raiding expedition. When the news 8.5
reached Shāyiʿ's ears, he waited until they had departed. As soon as they had

هكالسماد وهكالدهن ويطلاه، هي ما به جرب، بس يعني ان به جرب، ويحط عليه هكالخيشة ويشدّه بشداده ويحط عليه اجلّتّه. خلاهم يما مدّوا وهو يجي باثرهم، يتليهم، يتلي الغزو. يوم عشوا وهو يجي يبي يراعي يتمسّس الرجال، من هو اطيب الرجال علشان يخاويه. نوّخوا وقت العشا وخبّروا، هذيك خُبْره وهذي خبره وهذي خبره. يوم جا يبي يخبر عند هكالخبره وهم يسرجفونه، ياراع الجربا اقلع ماخوذتك. وخلّه بوجهَه. تجي عند هل الخبرة هذولاك ويوم جاهم سرْجَفْوه: اقلع جرباك ياراع الجربا. وهم يْدَلّون يقلّبونه بوسط هالخبر. وهو بس مخليَه بوجهه ما يقول شين. وينحر خبرة العقيد، قال: وراك وراك، شطّر جرباك بهذاك وانت حياك الله. وهو يصطغه وينحر خبرة الاخرين، ومثل. من جا قال: ياخوي ابعد جرباك عن ركابنا. وهو يْهَزَع يم الاخرين، قالوا: يسارك ياراعى الجربا لا تِعدِي ركابنا، ابعده، ابعده. وهو يجي هذولاك: يسارك، يمينك، يسارك. الثمرة تماطا هالخبر كلهم ما تلقى اللي قال يالله حيه أو نوّخَه بهذا ما يخالف.

٦،٨ واليا مير هكالثنين الواحد كبر الجمل وعلى لهم زوامل اثنين مْعَشّينٍ لحالهم وفَرْشهم اللي هم ياكلون به الخوا صفحةٍ هالكبر، وسلاحهم قْنِيٍّ معلّقينهن بعلايقهن بغرايب الاشده، يقال لهم البطحي من الفضول. البطحي شايبين واحد اخذ مره وجابت ولد واخوه ما لقى مره وهو يخليَه له وياخذه وتجيب ولد وكلهم جميع على المرة والعيال. البطحي الشيبان اجلدوا والعيال غزوا على لهم زوامل. وهو ينهج يمّهم. ما جا من خبرة: لباد وعلى جربا، الله يقلعك انت وايا جرباك. يما جا عيال البطحي قالوا: يالله حيه، يالله حيه، ياهلا، ياهلا، الحق، الحق ياراع الجربا،

gone, he rushed toward his camel and began to remove her fur, to thin it out. He plucked the hair here and there so her fur became patchy. He made a mixture of cracked wheat kernels, ashes, and fat as an ointment and smeared it on her body. She was not mangy, but he made her look as if she were. He overlaid the coating with pieces of sackcloth, fastened the wooden saddle, and put his coverings on her back. He let them head out and then followed in the raiders' tracks. On his arrival, they were eating supper. He meant to take the men's measure: to see who were the best among them in order to determine whose group he would join. At dinnertime, the raiders had dismounted and divided themselves into small groups to have supper together. He was chased away from the first group.[149] They hit at him and his camel with their sticks from both sides. "Hey, you and your mangy wretch, away with your rotten mount!" He passed by and continued to the next group. They received him with a hail of blows with their sticks. "Beat it! Get lost, you and your mangy camel. Go away!" Wherever he went, as he made his way from one group to the other, it was the same story. He let his camel move at will without saying anything in reply. He headed for the group of the raid leader. "Go back, go back! Leave your mangy mount there, away from us! Then you may join us." Without a word, he turned aside and headed for other groups. Everywhere he met with the same reception. As soon as they saw him coming: "Hey, brother, keep your mangy animal far from our mounts!" And he would turn aside to try his luck with others. "To your left, you and your mangy camel. Do not infect our camels! Away, put distance between us and yourself!" And on he'd go. "Your left!" "Your right!" In short, he trudged past all groups of eaters and found no one who welcomed him or told him to kneel his camel at their group without further ado.

At length, he stumbled on two men, one of them as big as a camel, travel- 8.6
ing on two ordinary pack camels, who were sitting alone by themselves. They had spread out their food on a big piece of leather, the kind that can be folded to serve as a water basin for camels to drink from. Their weapons were clubs with cords so they could be suspended from the knob of a camel saddle. They were called al-Baṭḥī, a family of the Fuḍūl. They were the offspring of two graybeards: one was married and had a son by his wife; and then he let his brother have his wife because no woman had been willing to marry him. His wife had intercourse with the unmarried brother. She conceived and gave birth to the brother's son. They shared in the woman and children. The old al-Baṭḥi brothers had stayed at home. The sons joined the raid on their pack camels.

قلّطه جاي، جاي. قال: ابي ابرّزَه عن الزوامل، جربا – وهي ما به جرب، مير يحسبونه جربا – قالوا: والله ما تبرك الا بينهن، نوّخه بينهن، قرّبَه، قرّبَه. قال: يالربع جربا. قالوا: ابد، حنا ان الله جاب لنا فود ياخوي نبدّلهن، ما نبيهن هن وجَرَبهن، وان عاد ما جانا فود فحالنا حالك، حنا نَطْلى، حنا مْجارْمِيّه، هاتَه بين الزوامل. قال هذا غْرِضِي. وهو يقرّبَه لهم ويجيبَه بين الزمل، وهو يسلّم عليهم. ايه، صار خويٍّ لهم. قال هذولا هم اللي وْقَعَوا على مخُّه، هم الرجال اللي يبي. صار معهم طال عمرك.

٧،٨ واعدوا بمغزاهم وإِتهْمُوا الجو اللي هم جايين يمّه بشنق هالوديان، شنق طِفّة هالعراق من جاي، غَدَوا عنه بالليل، عطشوا والدبش ما يدرون وين هو. فيه مِقْرٍ ما دلّوه القوم، مقر خفي، دوّروه ما لِقوه، بْلُه حمادةٍ بهالحماد، خارقهن الله من دون لا حفر ولا شين، ويَكْلى بالما. والمِقْر الصميد يحفظ اللي به ولا عليه عَلَم، مقرٍ خَفِيٍّ مواريه. هو ما هو بعيد عنهم المقر بس افختوه وشايع يدلّه هو وتِدِلُّه الذلول، ذلوله اول من كثر ما ينهج عليه. واهزع عليه واسقَه وروّى قربته والحق خوياوه وقصّدهم. قالوا: من اين لك هالما؟ قال: من الجو الفلاني. قالوا: ليه ما علّمتنا. قال: ما احسب انكم تبونه، هذا اخبره هكالحين انا ارعى مع لي غنم وادلّه. وهم يصوّتون للامير وهم ينكسون. قال لخوياوه: يالربع علموهم يمشون مع اثرنا انا ترونن قدامكم ولا تعلمون، بس قولة امشوا امشوا وحنا انشا الله نبي ندور الما. وهو يمشي قدامهم. قالوا: بس امشوا نبي عاد حنا ونصيبنا، يقولونه خوياوه للغزو، امشوا جاي، امشوا، امشوا. يقول وهو يمشي بهم يما جا المقر، يقول قدامهم

He ambled toward them. The other groups had scolded him and chided him away in a gruff manner: "Labbād, on a mangy mount to boot! May God uproot you and your mangy wretch!" When he came to the sons of al-Baṭḥī, he heard: "Welcome, welcome, God's guest! Come over here, be comfortable! Come closer, come here, rider of the poor mangy beast. Bring her over here, over here!" He said, "Let me kneel it a bit farther away from your camels. She suffers from mange." She wasn't mangy, but the others were made to think she was. "By God," they said, "you are not going to couch her anywhere but together with our camels. Kneel her there, in between them. Bring her close, bring her close!" "Please, fellows," he said, "she has the mange." "No matter," they said. "Brother, if God grants us booty, we will replace them with other camels. Mangy or not, it is none of our concern. And if we return empty-handed, well, in that case we are together in this: we depilate and treat them. No matter what, we stand together, as one man. Come on, couch her right here, with our camels!" He said to himself, "These are the kind of comrades I was looking for." He brought her, couched her as he had been told, and greeted them. He became their companion. They were of the sort he had been looking for, the type of friends he fancied. They stuck together.

The raiders continued, but they missed the wide basin for which they were heading. It bordered al-Wudyān, the nearest part of Iraq from here. In the dark of night they had strayed off course. The robbers were thirsty and had no inkling of where to find camel herds for the taking. They knew that somewhere around there should be a small water hole, such as are closed off by placing a big stone on it, but they looked for it in vain.[150] It was a hidden water hole. They had no clue. The water hole was located in a featureless plain of hard ground. It was a natural well created by God, not man-made, of the kind that fills with water without human intervention. It had an impermeable bottom so that water brought by rain or torrents remained and did not seep away. It was unmarked: there was no cairn on top of it, no sign of its existence. This particular hidden water hole was not far away, but they did not find it. Shāyiʿ and his riding camel knew where it was from the many times they had been there earlier.[151] He steered away from their course, headed for the water hole, and filled his waterskin. Then he rode to catch up with his comrades and pour them some of his water.[152] "Where did you find this water?" He told them from which basin it came. "Why didn't you tell us?" "I thought you had no wish to go there. I know it from the time when I was pasturing sheep and goats in the area." They 8.7

هناك، قدامهم. يا مار الى افمه مليان. وهو يخليّه تكمع به الذلول يما شربيْه، يوم شربيْه وهو يجي وهو يمسك بالرسن وهو يقعد على افمُه، حط عليه له رضمه، قعد على افمه ورجلُه تحَيْه (= تحت). يا مار هو واقف، يا مار مو هو بيّن المقر، ويحسبونه هو قاعد بهالسهله. آه؟ وين الما؟ قال:

وردنا قْطِري من عقب عشوه لا علامات ولا رجومٍ تسوّى

يقول له قطري المقر.

قاعدٍ على جباوه واخض برجلي ماوه لعيون من قرنَه يلوّى

٨،٨ نوخت القوم، لْقِتُه، ونوّخت القوم وأسقَيْه (= أسقت). يوم خلصوا رِيّه واصبحوا وقّفوا بهالديان الخاليات ما صادوا احد. وهم يجونك. قال: يالامير انا ابشير عليك. قال: آه. قال: الجو مثل البعير الميت أو الشاة الميته اللي كل طير ينزل عليه، نبي نجلد على هالما مغدّانا ونبي نحط بهالثنايا قْضوب يرقبون لنا يشوفون، واول رجالٍ يجي انشا الله نطرحه على هالما يعلّمنا عن العربان. قال: اللهم اني مطيعك. قالوا: تطيعه نخيّم على هالما لا هذي ولا هذيك. قال: بس اطيعوه، هو اللي دلنا على الما البارحه. وهم يغدّون، يوم غدّوا يا والله يوم طلع هكالطرقي والقضب من وراوه وهم يحوشونه وهم يطرحونه. البل؟ قال: البل ابشروا به، على الما الفلاني آمنينٍ غير خايفين، عِزْبةٍ ما توصف ولا تعدّ. وهم يْعَدُون. ويوم عَدوا وحْفِزَوا الجو يا والله يلعبون طهور وعروس وتضرب هالناس حَسَاسه.

went to call the raid leader and came back accompanied by the others. He told his comrades, the al-Baṭḥī brothers, "Tell them to follow in my traces. I am going to ride ahead. I'll stay in front of you, but you should act as if you are not aware of me being there. Keep shouting to them, 'Go, go! God willing, we will end up finding the water.'" He rode ahead. They called to the others, "Go, go, forward! Fortune may yet favor us!" That is what his comrades told the other raiders. "Here, this way!" In this manner, he guided them to the water hole as he rode in front of them until he came to it. It was there, ahead of them. The hole was filled with water up to the rim. He let his mount drink from it while she stood, head and lips down to the water at the rim, until she was sated. Then he took her by her halter and sat down on top of the water hole's mouth. He had placed a rock over it and took his seat on it, his legs down the water hole. But in reality, he was standing. He kept the water hole invisible. It looked as if he was sitting on the ground of the plain. "Where is the water?" He said:

> We headed for water after a night's march,
> a hidden water hole not marked by cairns;

—He called the water hole *gṭirī*.

> Sitting on top, I dangled my feet in water,
> for a beauty swinging her plaited tresses.[153]

8.8 Seeing him, the raiders dismounted, drew water, and replenished their skins. Next morning, they looked around the empty vastness: there was no one in sight. "Let me give you a piece of advice, Emir," he said. "The basin is like the corpse of a camel or sheep on which birds of prey alight in droves. Let's stay at this water hole until lunchtime and post watchmen to the lookouts at the passes on those ridges. Let them seize the first wayfarer who appears and bring him here to tell us about people's whereabouts." "Excellent idea," the emir replied. "I take your advice." The others protested: "Why do you listen to him? Why camp here at this forsaken water hole and not go some other place?" The leader silenced them. "Just obey! He is the one who guided us to this water yesterday." While they were eating lunch, a wayfarer came into view. The watchmen seized him and wrestled him to the ground. "Camels?" He said, "I have good news for you, cheer up!" He explained to them that the camels were at a certain well, with an escort of careless shepherds without concerns for their security. "Huge numbers of camels of pure Arabian stock." At this

الدبش ما يدرون وين مكانه. عدوا بالما هذا والجو مو هو بعيدٍ عنهم والجو ما ينهاط، العرب عليه قطين، عليه عربان ما تنتقايس. امّا لقوا اباعرٍ بالخلا، الجو عليه عربٍ واجد، ما يقدرون يكهمونه، وهم قوم ما هم كثير.

٩،٨ قال: يالربع من يجيب لنا علم البل. ويزعجون السبور وينكسون عليهم يقولون والله ما جبنا لكم علم، عربان ما ينتقرّبون. ومن نهج يبي يجيب علم ما يهوم الجو. وهم يقومون يتشاورون، ما هم بعيدٍ عن الما: الا وش به، الا وش به. ما يدرون الطرش وين هو قايد. قال: اغدينا ننكف، بليا هالغزو. يقوله امير الغزو. يوم قرّب الصبح قال: ياطويل العمر كان ترخص لي انا ابنهج أجيب لك الخبر، كان تتنانن ليا طلعة النجمه انا اجيب لك علم البل. يقوله شايع لامير الفضول. قالوا: خلوه يذلف وان جا جا وان ما جا عساوه ما يْثَنّي. قالوا خوياوه، عيال البطحي: لا، ان نهج خوينا والله ما تشدّون الا هو جاي الخبر منه حي والا ميت، والله ما تثورون من هذا الا هو جاي. قالوا: زاد ما يخالف خلوه ينهج. قالوا العيال، هل الزوامل: شف يالامير، لا ينهج خوينا وتنهزمون باكر وتخلّونه، والله لو تقعدون يومين أو تِذبَحون بهالمناخ فلا يركب راعي ذلول الا هو جاي. قال: بس انهج. قال لباد لخوياوه، اهل الجمل: اجلدوا بهذا واحزموا عليهم لا يمد احد، القوم هذي لا تنهج لا يمين ولا يسار، احزموا عليّه، وانا ترُو وعدكم طلعة النجمه الصبح، أوَبّت لكم عاد المحل، وان طلعت نجمة الصبح ما جيتكم تيّسروا. قالوا: عندنا لك، ما يتيَسّرون ابد ابد.

١٠،٨ وهو يركب ذلوله وهو يزعجه على الجو. يوم اقبل على الجو هات الذلول ونوّخه بْصَف الجو، وهو يعقله وهو يحبك موثبٍ على الجو، ينْكِفت على الجو. العرب نزيل

news, they lost no time in departing hurriedly. They sped to the basin, only to be halted in their tracks at the sound of merriment on the occasion of circumcision ceremonies and wedding parties. Loud voices and ringing shouts. They didn't have the faintest idea of the herds' whereabouts. They were looking down from the basin's rim, not far from those people down there at the well. It would be impossible for them to sally forth and confront the large crowds encamped below. They had to find a way to come upon camels somewhere in the desert. A small party of raiders was no match for such numbers.

The raid leader said, "Listen, men, who volunteers to find out about the camels?" The scouts returned empty-handed; they had nothing to report. "Really, we have no news. We cannot face such dense crowds. It is futile trying to walk down there and ask people without raising suspicion." Uncertain what to do, they deliberated for a while. The well was within reach, but how, how? They had not the faintest notion of where the herds were pasturing. The emir said, "Perhaps we have no choice but to turn back and forego the idea of capturing booty." Before dawn, Shāyiʿ spoke to the emir: "May your life be long, with your permission I will go and look for information. If you wait for me until the morning star twinkles, I might discover the camels' location." The other men said, "Let him go to hell! If he comes, he comes; if he does not show up, may he never return." His comrades, the sons of al-Baṭḥī, intervened: "No! If our companion undertakes this mission, you should not set out from here unless we know for certain whether he is still alive or dead. By God, you may not march from here unless he has come back." They shrugged and said, "Either way, we don't care. Let him go on his way." The brothers, the ones with the pack camels, said, "Look here, Emir! You cannot let our comrade go on his mission tomorrow morning and then leave him in the lurch. By God, even if you were to stay for two days or we were attacked and suffered casualties at this place, no one should ride out as long as he hasn't come back." "Just go!" the emir said. Labbād said to his companions, the brothers with the male camels, "You stay here and prevent them from leaving. They shouldn't go left or right. Just stay put. I promise to be back when the morning star appears. By then you'll see me coming. In case the star appears and I haven't shown up, feel free to act as you see fit." They said, "We are here for you. We won't let them do as they see fit. Never, never!" 8.9

He mounted his camel and steered it toward the basin. On his approach, he kneeled the camel at the terrain's edge, hobbled it, and ran down toward the 8.10

وفساقا، وعندهم لهم طِهر وليا الغنى والرقص. من تواله هكالبيت المطرّف وهو يزقط برواقه، يلبد بالرواق يبي اغديه يتسمّع لهم. يا هل البيت اللي لبد به شايع اثاريهم توّهم معرسين وناهجين بس يتفرّجون ونِكّس هو وايا زوجته. يوم راعي يا مير هذا الرجل، رجال البيت يوم جا وقام ينشّد الحشاش، وين الدبش؟ قال: الدبش بالمكان الفلاني وامان وضمان. راعي البيت عروسٍ توّه معرّس. ليا هذي راعية البيت يوم جت باثِرِه. ويثور الحشاش وينهج يتشطر يم منامه عند طرف البيت وينام. وهو يجي راعي البيت يبي ينام ويركّد السيف والهدوم على القش، فسّر هدومه وعلق السيف وهو يزرق بالمنام قدامَه. يوم جت عنده بالفراش قامت تْعامْلُه، يتعاملون يتغارشون بالفراش، وهي تقوم تستدني السيف قالت: الدبش متى قاد ياولد؟ قال: قبل امس. قالت: وين عزب؟ قال: بالمطب الفلاني. قالت: والله انك ما تعدى هالمكان اللي انت به الا كان تنطين الله وامان الله على البل المغاتير اللي معه القعود الاوضح اللي بخشمه الماوه، تراي مستعطيتك عليهن. قال: من انت؟ قالت: انا شايع الامسح. هي مسمية روحه شايع، تسمع بعلوم شايع. تمثيل هاللون بينهم ما دريوا بشايع ولا هولسوا ان شايع وزنهم يوحيهم. قال شايع بقلبه فالي وانا قبلته. قالت: انا شايع الامسح وتراي مستعطيك على نياقي. قال: عليك الله وامان الله ان نياقك بوجهي ما يحسّهن ما يمسّهن ولا يجيهن ما يضرّهن البل المغاتير اللي معه القعود الاوضح اللي بخشمه الماوه. وهي تركّد السيف وهي تدخل يمه يضحكون ويلعبون. يقول وتحكي هي ورجله هاللون مسمّية روحه شايع، ما دريت ان شايع لابدٍ بالرواق.

lower ground as fast as his legs would carry him. The people in the camp were having a good time. All around, the air was filled with raucous laughter. They made merry in processions celebrating a circumcision, amusing themselves with song and dance. He crouched down to hide under the flap at the back side of one of the outlying tents in the hope of hearing something of interest. It so happened that the couple living in that tent had just gotten married. They had gone out to gaze at the partying and returned to their tent. Before entering, the owner of the tent asked a worker whose job it was to cut and collect grass: "Where are the herds?" The worker told him the location and added that the animals there pastured in complete safety. The newly married husband was followed at a little distance by his bride. Therefore, the grass cutter quickly took his leave and withdrew to where he lay down for the night, not far from the tent. The husband entered, hung up his sword, loosened his clothes, and laid them on a pile of gear. Right away, he went to lie down for the night. She joined him in bed and began teasing him. They made a lot of noise, romping and frolicking on the bed. At some point in their fun, she jumped to her feet, grabbed his sword, and addressed him in a menacing tone: "Tell me, boy, when were the herds led to pasture?" "The day before yesterday." "Where are they grazing, away from the well?" He mentioned the name of the place, and she carried on: "By God, no way I'll let you move from this spot unless you promise me, solemnly in the name of God, to grant me the white camels and the white male that has a copper ring in its nostrils. My demand is for you to make those a special gift to me." "Well, first tell me who you are." She said, "I am Shāyiʿ al-Amsaḥ." She pretended to be Shāyiʿ because she had heard the stories of his exploits. They were playing an innocent game. They had no personal knowledge of Shāyiʿ. They could not possibly suspect that Shāyiʿ was right next to them and overheard what they said.[154] Shāyiʿ said to himself, "This is my omen. I have to accept it." Again, she said, "I am Shāyiʿ al-Amsaḥ, and my request is for these camels." He replied, "I promise to God that your camels are in my safekeeping. No one will lay a hand on them or even touch them. No harm will come their way, those white camels and the white male with the copper ring in its nose." At that she restored the sword to its place and turned to him in bed, laughing and playing. It was her manner of speaking, calling herself Shāyiʿ. She wasn't aware that Shāyiʿ was crouching there, hidden under the flap.

١١،٨ شايع سمع هالكلام وايقن ان الدبش يم المحل اللي هي تقول. وهو يسل روحه وينسبت على الذلول ويركبه وهو يجيك مع شنق الما، عليه لُه بشيتٍ اشهب. يامار هذولا الحواشيش جايين يغنّون ويعارضهم، حواشيش الخيل ينهجون مع الطرش ويحشّون للخيل بمجادل ويجيبون للخيل حشيش بالليل، ويا مير جايين، وهو يعانقهم: يالله حيّهم. كنُّه يعرفهم. قالوا: الله يحييك. ياعيال؟ قالوا: نعم. قال: يابعد حي انطونن لي حشيشٍ، عندي فرسٍ مفلٍي ولا آجد له عشا. قالوا: مبروكه انشا الله، وش تبي؟ قال: ابي حشيش. وكلٍّ يْغَرِز له شوي حشيش واقرطوه له. عيّنتوا الدبش؟ قالوا: بالفيضة الفلانيّه صدره وورده لله الحمد أمان وضمان. قال: الله يبشركم بالخير. وخذ الحشيش ودّه ذلوله وكبّه عنده. وعانق الاخرين: ابي لي حشيش لفلو عندي ابيه يبقم. قالوا: مبروكةٍ انشا الله، تبي حشيش؟ واقرطوا له له غمر حشيش. وخلهم يما فاتوا، قال: وين الدبش؟ قالوا: والله الدبش المغدرة (اللي امس صادره) والصادرة (اللي صدرت اليوم) والواردة (اللي تبي ترد باكر) هي هذي بفياض الهبيرة كله مجتمعه. وهو ياخذ الحشيش وهو ينهج على عينهم وهو ينحر هكالغار وهو يجي وهو يِلْغِف الحشيش بالغار، يخفيه. وهو يركب الوضحا وهو يزعَجَه.

١٢،٨ يوم جا يا مير الناس كل شادٍّ رسن ذلوله ويثني رجله على غرابته يبون يِنكْفُون، ويا جت تبي تنوض ضربه البطحي يا باركه، الارض. البطحي متحاشكين الغزو. من ركب ذلوله قْرِفوه ليا راكب راسه. يا قاهرينهم. قالوا: لعن ابوكم حنا زعجنا هالخبل، خبلٍ هذا لباد، وين لباد، نبي نرجي لباد! خبلٍ ذْلان تلقاوه يِجِل عند الحريم. يا مار خوياوه الثنين واحد مع ايمن القوم وواحد مع ايسرهم يوم يضربون الخيال يا طافحٍ مثل الجاعد: والله ما يمد الذلول الا يجي خوينا، ليه تقولون لخوينا

Shāyiʿ had heard enough. He knew the location of the animals. He slipped away, slid onto the back of his camel, and trotted past the well, dressed in a dust-colored cloak. On his way, he encountered a convoy of grass cutters singing merry songs as they rode, and he accosted them. It was their job to cut grass as fodder for horses. They moved apace with the herds and with sickles mowed grass to feed to the horses in the evening. Turning to them, he called, as if he knew them, "God's greetings, fellows! May you live long, could you spare some grass for me?[155] My mare has given birth and I couldn't find anything for her to eat." "A blessed birth, God willing, congratulations! What is it you want?" Each of them scooped up a handful of grass and flung it to him. "Did you see the herds?" They named a broad valley. "There they come and go at will, peace and security all around." "May God bring you glad tidings!" He took the grass and fed it to his camel. In similar manner, he spoke to the next group he met on his way. "I need some grass to feed to a foal that was born just now." "May she be blessed, if God wills. Do you want grass?" They tossed him an armful of grass. He waited until they had passed by, and asked, "Where are the herds?" "Well, the camels watered at the well yesterday and today, and the ones that are going to be watered today: all of those have collected in the valleys of al-Hibīrah." While they looked on, he picked up the grass and walked toward a cave. He stowed the grass in the cave, hiding it from view. From there, he rode straight back to his comrades, going at a lively trot. 8.11

As he came in, the raiders were tugging at the reins of their camels, one foot already placed on the saddle knob, ready to ride back home. Whenever one of them was about to let his camel rise, the Baṭḥī brothers gave him a blow and pulled the animal down to settle on its breast again. The Baṭḥī brothers kept the raiders in check. If someone mounted, they scolded him; and if he remained stubborn, they halted his mount. They became angry with the brothers: "God curse your father. The one we sent is an idiot. Stupid, this Labbād! Where is Labbād? Should we pin our hopes on someone like Labbād? Didn't you see how he used to hawk camel dung and offer it to women?" They protested to no avail. His two comrades, the brothers, one on the right and one on the left of the troop, were so strong that if they hit a horse rider, he'd fly through the air, as if he were as light as a skin spread on the saddle. "By God, you're not allowed to ride off until our comrade is here. Why then did you tell our companion, 'Go, we'll wait for you'? Why didn't you tell him, 'We will not wait for you'?" They kept them in check. And then, there he was. He cried, "I have found out 8.12

انهج ونتناك؟ ليه ما قلتوا ما نتناك؟ واحجموا عليهم طال عمرك. يوم راعوا والى هو هذا يوم لوّذ عليهم، قال: انا معاين وابي العيانه يالامير، امسح وجهك بالفود، ابشر بالبل اللي ما عنده الا الحلاب والصرار. قال: عيانتك من عينتك، عفية والله، حنا من طروشَه والله يحوشَه، وين البل؟ يا مار الموقع اللي به الدبش ما هو بعيدٍ عن خْوياوه. قال: البل قريب، لكن والله ما اعلمكم به الا تنطون على النياق المغاتير اللي معهن القعود الاوضح اللي بُه قلادة الماو اللي هاللون وصايفُه، عليه عطوى، البل هي وجمله. قالوا: ابد، عليك الله وامان الله يالو ما يجينا من الفود الا هن انهن ما يلحقهن شيّ. قال: من كفيلي؟ قال: اللي انت تبي. قال: كفيلي خوياي البطحي. قال: توكّلوا على الله، اركبوا.

وهم يركبون وهو يصلقهم عليَه. صار هالحين هو العقيد وهو يَمْزَعَه وهو يجيك ١٣،٨
الجيش تقل سور باثره. وهم يجونَه الصبح، ابدا مع الاصباحه. يوم خَذَوا خَدْم الفِرِسِن دِرهام واطَّلْبُوا للغاره وهو يَجْذِي حدى الزوامل وهو ياخذ قراميشه وهو يركب راعيَه معُه، حدى عيال البطحي. ويوم اقبلوا عليَه، قبل تقض الغاره وهو ياقف الاخر، وهو يحط قراميشه على جنبَه الآخر، وهم يترادفونه الثلاثه. وهي تروّح بهم. قال: إطّلب يالامير ترانا وصلناهم. وهو يِطّلِب وهي تِقِض الغاره وتَدْرَح به عن هالجموع كله. وغيروا على الدبش ويتِقّونه. والى ما جا هكالبل بمبركه وهم يطبّقون العيال بوسطه يا هذولي النياق المغاتير اللي معهن الجمل الاوضح، هي هذي عيّنةٍ بيّنه، وهم يطرحون راعيه ويبرّزونه بهذاااك. قال للراعي: روّح بهن لمعازيبك. حَرْجَمَوا على الطرش الباقي كله وهم ياخذونه وهم يصدّرون به، زخّوا البل وصدّروا به. انطلق راعيٍ من هل البل، ركب ذلوله وانحاش يم الجو. يوم راحوا، طال عمرك، يوم عبروا بالهزيمة، وهو يطري عليه انهم يبون يتذابحون

the location of the camels and I expect my reward, Emir! Upon my word of honor! It's a sure thing: the catch is yours! Rejoice! The herds are unguarded, except by shepherd boys who milk them and put wooden clamps on their udders to prevent calves from suckling them." The emir said, "Any animal that you fancy is yours. Bravo, well done, by God! We march and may God send the spoils our way. Where are the camels?" It was not a long ride. "The camels are not far from where we are. I'll tell you on condition that you let me have the white camels and their white stud camel with a copper collar." He gave a detailed description of them. "These camels and the stud were promised as a present." The raid leader said, "By all means, God is my witness that even if these camels are the only ones we capture, no one else will touch them." "Who is my guarantor?" "Your choice." "I take my comrades, the brothers al-Baṭḥī as my guarantors." "Done deal," he said. "Go, ride!"

They rode off. As their guide and leader, he steered them at a tearing pace 8.13
toward the target. In his trail, the raiders came surging like a wall of riders. They reached their destination at daybreak. As they were about to storm the herd and broke into a fast trot, one of the pack camels collapsed. The rider, one of the Baṭḥī brothers, took his gear and clambered onto the hind part of Shāyiʿ's mount. Just before the final onslaught, when they had come very close, the other pack camel stumbled. His gear was loaded on the other flank of Shāyiʿ's camel and he took his seat behind his brother. The three of them on one camel.[156] Thus, they sped off. "Launch the attack, Emir!" he called. "We are there!" The signal for the attack was given, and they rushed in like a whirlwind; the three took a different way from the other raiders. They rounded up the collected animals. Plunging into the herd at its resting place, they came upon the white she-camels and their white stud. These were the ones he was looking for, no doubt about it. They separated them from the rest of the animals and took the shepherd, telling him, "Take them home to your masters!" They rounded up the dispersed animals of the rest of the herd and made off, driving them hard. One of the shepherds had escaped on his mount and made it back to the basin. As the raiders commenced their homeward journey, it occurred to Shāyiʿ that the owners of the camels would likely start wrangling among themselves. They'd consider that the herds' location had been disclosed by the owner of the only camels that returned safe and sound. They'd accuse him of being the culprit who caused the loss. Next thing, decent men would start killing one another. He said to himself that he would not allow such a thing to

العرب، اهل الما، يبون يقولون اللي بلس علينا راعي هالبل، هاللي اباعره سالمه، هو اللي بلس علينا، على اباعرنا، وتبي تسير الكرام على الكرام، مير والله ما انا مخليهم يتذابحون على ظليمه. قال لخوياوه: يالفضلي كان لي قسم معك القاوه عند خوياي، ياخوياي تَرُو حقّي وداعة لِلّه ثم لكم، وانا والله ابنكس، انا ابي يم هالعرب وحقي تراوه بشواربكم ياخوياي، العرب كود يتذابحون على البل هاللي نْهَجت، ياكود يتذابحون، وانا ابحقن دماهم، بينهم، ابحقن دماهم. قالوا: ازهله.

١٤،٨ وانكس على العرب ونوخه بمناخه. يوم جاهم يا مير غادين صِفّتين، الهوشه، المكاون بينَهم، ناس تبي تذبح ناس. يقولون انتم اللي بَلَستوا علينا ياهل النياق والا وشّو له يِعْقِل نياقكم عليكم. وهم يقولون ما ندري عن شين. يا مير تبي تذابح الناس. ناسٍ تبي تذبح المره وناسٍ تبي تفكّه. قال لهم رجله: المرة هذي هاللون وهاللون، وهالكاينة وكاد عنده خبر منه. وهم يبون يذبحونه يقولون انك انتي اللي خبّرتي شايع، بينك وبينه علم. وانحر شايع هكالبيت قال: يامره عطينن ما وملحه. وهي تنطيه ما وملحه واقرض الملحة واشرب الما. قال: علّمي العرب لا يتذابحون يجون اعلمهم باللي عدّى على دبشهم. فرحوا وهم يجونه يتراكضون. قال: يارجال أنتم اصبروا نعلّمكم بالصايب، أما هالمرة اللي انتم متبلّين تبون تذبحونه والله انه ما تعلم بي الا كان هي تعلم متى يومه اللي هي تاتموت به. انا جيت لي حواشيش وعلّمونن بالبل وحطّيت الحشيش اللي انا خذيت منهم بهالمكان، وجيت الحواشيش الاخرين وحطيت من حشيشهم لذلولي بهذاك وجيت وقعدت برواق بيت هالرجل ابى آخذ من عِدْلُه والا من سلاحه، وهي تكلمت لرجله وتكلم له وتعرّضوا وجهي وهم ما دريوا بي. حطوا هالبل بوجهي وجبته بسبب حطّتهم لَه بوجهي. هذي اباعركم.

happen for no good reason. He told his fellow raiders: "Men of al-Fuḍūl, as for my share of the spoils, leave it with my brothers. My booty remains in your safekeeping.[157] I entrust myself to God and you. I must turn back. Twist my rights into your mustaches! Don't forget, your honor is at stake! Those folks are going to trade blame as they quarrel about their lost camels. They'll have furious altercations. They may start killing one another. I feel obliged to prevent unwarranted bloodshed. No blood should be spilled!" "Good luck achieving your mission and vision!" they said.

He turned back to where the tribe was, dismounted, and left his camel 8.14
behind. He continued on foot and at once saw the camp's men facing one another in two groups and scuffling. They scrimmaged and fought tooth and nail. They might have been about to kill one another. One party said, "You people with the camels have betrayed us. What else explains that they were held separately from the others and sent back to you?" The other party replied, "We don't know anything about this." Violence was about to flare up. Some asked for the woman to be killed; others disagreed and pleaded her innocence. Her husband said all sort of things about his wife, asserting: "This creature knows more about this business." They made ready to kill her on the suspicion that she was the one who informed Shāyiʿ. "The two of you must have been in touch!" Shāyiʿ went to a tent and said to the woman there, "Give me salt and water!" She did, and he took a bite from the food and drank the water.[158] Then he said, "Go and tell those people to stop fighting. Let them come, and I will explain how their camels were plundered." Surprised and exultant, they came at a gallop. "Listen, men," he said, "if you will bear with me, I'll tell the true story of what happened. This woman is unjustly accused and put under threat of death. By God, she doesn't know anything about this, as surely as she doesn't know when she will die. I ran into some grass cutters who told me the whereabouts of the herds. I stored the fodder in that place. I met another group of grass cutters, and I fed the grass they gave me to my camel in such and such a place. I came here and hid myself under the flap of this man's tent with the intention of taking some of his stores or arms. Inside the tent, she and her husband were having a conversation and my name came up. They had no inkling that I was right there. In their exchange, I was given responsibility for these particular camels of theirs. Hearing that, I took it as a matter of honor. For that reason, I kept my word and saw to it that their camels were returned to them."

١٥،٨ العرب نشدوا الحواشيش والحواشيش قالوا اي بالله جانا رجال هذا لونه وهذا لونه وطلب منا حشيش وعطيناوه. وراحوا للغار ولقوا الحشيش على قولته لهم. يا مير يوم وكدَت. قالوا: انت عاد وشّو له تنكس يمّنا يا صار انت قوماني؟ وش اوزاك عليه؟ يا صار انت اللي بلانا وش جابك لنا، وين تبي جايّنا وانت آخذٍ اباعرنا؟ قال: والله اني ما نكست من خوياي الا مشحّةٍ بكم ذلّيت واحدٍ يظلم واحد وتذابحون على سبب هالسالفة هذي، ايقنت انكم تقولون يا منه نكست البل، جت اباعره انكم كود تثورون عليه مثل هالثوره تقولون ما جا اباعرنا الا انت ياللي نكِسَت اباعرك وذليت والله عليكم انكم تذابحون بهالامر هذا، والبل هذي هاللي فكه فالٍ تفوّلوه هَلَه وتفوّلناوه. قالوا: احلف ان ما جابك الا هالمقصد. قال: ولله ما جابن الا هالمقصد، الا مشحّةٍ بكم لا عن واحدٍ يذبح واحد. قالوا: عز الله انك راعي جماله وهالحين بامان الله وعِدّك والله راجعٍ علينا كل طرشنا يوم فكّيتنا من بعضنا.

١٦،٨ ويسلم عليهم واركب ذلوله والحق خوياوه ويجيهم على الخاصره، عند التيم، قريب من هلُه. يا مطلّعين له خمسطعش ذلول عزلُه. قال: يالفضلي ابي ابشّر اهلنا، ابي قدامكم اغنّي. قال: انهج. يوم اقبل على الجو وهو يغنّي، من طلعة الشمس وهو يصوع الغنا، غنا الكْسِبه. يقول يامير مرته تفلي مرة الفضلي، تفلي راسه على فخوذه. يقول وهي تِنِزّ مثل نزّة عنود الصيد، وهي ترمز ليا مير واقفة يا راس ذيك يِدِنّ بالقاع، قالت: هلا بهالحس، شايع يابطن ابوي. قالت: وش تقولين؟ قالت: اقول ذيبٍ عوى. قالت: لا، تقولين لك حاجة اخرى. قالت: اقول ذيبٍ عوى بسم الله الرحمن الرحيم انحاشي عنه، آمنّا بالله واتكلنا عليه. وهي تثور وهي تخليَه.

١٧،٨ وهم يعارضونُه الشيبان، شيبان البطحي. قالوا: آه. قال: والله فود وسلامه. قالوا: ما عيّنت عيال لنا على لهم زوامل؟ قال: اي والله عيّنتهم، سرّا وغرّا،

They checked with the grass cutters, who confirmed that indeed they had met such a man who asked for grass and that they had given him some. They went to the cave and found a pile of grass, as he had said. The facts matched. Still, they didn't understand. "What made you risk coming to us, being an enemy? What made it such a pressing matter for you to act as you did? Aren't you the cause of our calamity? Nevertheless, you ventured into the lion's den. How dare you come visiting after looting our camels?" "Well," he said, "the only reason I came back after rejoining my companions is because I care about you. I feared that innocent people would fall victim to injustice and that you'd start killing one another because of this affair. I felt certain that if their camels were returned, others would take out their indignation and anger on them. If they were the only ones to get their animals back, violence might ensue and claim lives, I feared. It was fated that these camels should be handed back. It was providential for them, and we understood it as an omen too." "Take an oath that you came for this sole reason!" "I swear, honest to God," he said. "There is no other reason. I acted simply from concern lest blood would be spilled because of this matter." "Mighty God," they said, "you truly did us a great favor. Now go in God's safekeeping. As we see it, you forestalled a bloodbath and you've cleared the air among us. That is as good as a full restoration of our camels." 8.15

He took his leave, rode away, and rejoined his companions at al-Khāṣirah, al-Tayyim, not far from his own people's whereabouts. They had set aside fifteen camels as his share of the spoils. "Listen, Shaykh of al-Fuḍūl," he said, "it is time for me to bring glad tidings to my people. Let me ride ahead and intone my victory songs." Starting from daybreak, he continued to sing at the top of his voice all the way there. He erupted into joyful song, celebrating his haul of plunder. As he drew near, his wife was delousing the wife of the shaykh. She was ridding her of lice while balancing her head on her thighs. Suddenly she shot up like a gazelle doe. She jumped to her feet, letting the other woman's head bang on the ground. "Hear that wonderful sound? Oh, Shāyiʿ, oh my father's belly!" "Is it true what I hear you say?" the other lady said. "I hear the howling of a wolf," she answered. "No, I am positive that I heard you say something quite different!" "I said, a wolf howled in the name of God the Merciful and Compassionate. Stay away from him! In God we believe and in Him we put our trust." At that, she rushed off and let the other alone. 8.16

The graybeards came, the Baṭḥī graybeards, to take their measure. "So?" they asked. "By God, plunder and safety." "Didn't you see our boys, those 8.17

هالحين يجونكم معهم لهم اباعر. قالوا: ولا من غباشه ولا من دَخَل ولا من هوشه؟ قال: لا. قالوا: فود ما هو مبارك. الشيبان يبون المْعارَك. يوم جا العصر يا هي هذي البل يوم طْلَعت مثل خشوم الضلعان، البل والجيش والغزو والغنا والكْسِبه. وهم يقومون يسولفون ببيت الامير، اجتمعوا على الامير وقاموا يسولفون. عدينا عليّه هاك وقال لباد هاك ومشى بنا لباد هاك ولباد عمل هاللون، عقلان الله ثم هالخبل لباد.

١٨،٨ وايتَي يالحريم وهن يعلّمن الامير، قالت الانثى: حرمة خويكم هذا يوم سمعت الحس رْمِزت قالت ياهلا بشايع. قال: وكاد؟ قالت: وكاد، هذا ما هو لباد، يمكن هو شايع. قال: انا اخو ابوي هذا شايع ابن رمال. انهج انهج ياولد خله يتفضّل. شب النار وهو يجي ويقعد مقعده عند الرماد أول. قال: ثر، ثر ياشايع ابن رمال، اقعد على المركى، الله يحييك، ليه تجحد روحك تخيبل؟ قال: ابصير عند اللي يَحْمْل الردِي والا الطيب كل يبيه، وانتم على كل حال ما عملتوا خامل، والله جحدت روحي يوم ما من فعل بين، يوم بان فعلي علّمتكم. قالوا: الا عملنا خامل ولا ورّيناك قدرك ولا عملنا لك حساب، والله ما ندري وش نترضاك بُه هالحين. واذبح هكالناقة، سوّه نزالة له عِدّه الله اليوم جايهم.

١٩،٨ يقول امير يوم صار الى قعد بالمجلس تقوم بنات الفضول يتهايقن عليه ويرقبن يراعنّه، هكاللي اول لباد ما يراعن له، هالحين قامن يراعن له. يقول وهن يقومن يراعن، قالت هكالوحده: شايع ولا شايع خير، شايب وعَوَر. يا هو يسمعه. وهو يتمثل:

riding on pack camels?" "Of course," he said. "I have seen them and they are doing fine. They are on their way and will arrive shortly with the camels allotted to them as their share." "Really? Wasn't there any rough and tumble? Any acts of surrender in exchange for safety? Close combat in battle?" "To be honest, no," he replied. "Such loot is ill-starred," they grumbled. The old men were spoiling for bloody battles. In late afternoon, the great mass of camels approached, looming like a mountain range. Herd camels, riding camels, raiders, merry song, plunder. The favorable outcome was celebrated in the tent of the shaykh with endless storytelling. A ceaseless stream of tales flowed through the congregation: we attacked; Labbād said this; Labbād took us there; Labbād did this and that. The happy ending first decreed by God, and next by that idiot, Labbād.

The women came and informed the emir. One said, "The wife of your companion startled when she heard his voice and said, 'Welcome, Shāyiʿ!'" "Are you serious?" he said. "No two ways about it. He is not really Labbād. In truth, he might be Shāyiʿ." "This can't be true![159] Here we have Shāyiʿ al-Rmāl! Run, boy, run. Let him come!" A fire was lit, and Shāyiʿ came and took his usual seat at the heap of ashes. "Up, up, O Shāyiʿ ibn Rmāl! Sit here and recline on this camel saddle. Welcome in the name of God! Why did you dissemble and pretend to be a dimwit?" "I want to consort with those who tolerate wretched people. Everyone likes to deal with nice persons who are doing well. Don't worry, you haven't done anything dishonorable. I hid my identity until I had something to show for myself. Now that I have proved my mettle, I am fine with being known for who I am." The others said, "Well, we did not act as it behooves us, since we haven't met you with the respect due to your rank. We did not take account of you as we should have done. By God, how can we give you satisfaction and make up for being so remiss?" They slaughtered a fat she-camel in his honor, as if he had only now arrived as their guest for the first time. 8.18

The story goes that girls of the Fuḍūl tribe came craning their necks to catch a glimpse and gape at him while he was being lionized in the assembly. As long as he was Labbād, they had not deigned to take notice of him. Attracted by his newly won fame, they came flocking just to take a peek at him. Scanning his features, one of them said, "Shāyiʿ but not *shāyiʿ khēr*; renowned but not looking good."[160] He was graying and one-eyed. He heard what they said and composed these verses:[161] 8.19

قـال ابن مـرداسٍ فتى الجود شايع   من الجد الاقصى ما غـياي قريب ٢٠،٨
وراك يالعـذرا تقولـين شـايب   شيبت وانا ما جا لي حل مشيب
انا لو اتـــــــلي الهون والردا   نسّفت قـرونٍ كنهـن رطيب
واعلمك يازين الوصايف بشيـبي   من كثر ما شفّـن بالديار لهيب
من كثر ما نصطي على شمّخ الذرا   في ساعـة فيها الذليـل مـريب
شيبت يالعـذرا من قـران فاطري   من مـرقـبٍ يـزمي وذاك يغـيب
شيبت من ربعٍ كفى الله شـرّهـم   يـذبّون تـالى النـاجيات ذبيب
بيوم به الهلباج ركضه مسلفـح   ركضـه من بين الركاب دبيب
يا عاب تالى الجيش حولت قفوهن   في سـاعــة يوم السهوم تصيب
غـلبنا رجـال ما هقـينا بغلبهـم   وانا بفعـل الطـيبـات نجيب
جدعت ابن روقٍ والركاب زوالف   بكفٍّ لها بالموزمـات نصيب
عسـاك ياكفٍّ جـدعـتي محمـد   عساه عن شـر الليـال تغيب
لعيون بنـاتٍ من حمـام لكنهـن   سـردٍ غـشى فـخوذهـن سبيب

بنات حمام الرماليات، لهن جد اسمه حمام ورا عميره، يشبههن على الخيل الشقر. حمام ابو سعد جد عميره.

انخـنا واناخوا وعقّـلنـا وعقّـلوا   والكل منـا يـدّعي بنصيب
وعلّقـنا هـدوم الغي من فوق ضمّر   وطـير المـنايـا فوقـنا رقـيب

These are the words of Ibn Mirdās, 8.20
Shāyiʿ of ancient nobility, not a parvenu.
Why, girlie, despise me for being old:
my hair grayed well before its time.
Had I chosen pettiness and disrepute,
I'd flaunt tresses dark as bunches of dates.
I tell you, graceful damsel, why I'm gray:
It's from scalding winds on desert treks.
My high-humped camels plunge into danger
when the faint of heart lose their bearings.
Sweetie! I'm gray as one cinched to saddles,
hardy mounts hurtling past landmarks galore;
Gray from crossing swords with ferocious foes,
smiting like devils in defense of fine camels.
Scornful of good-for-nothings who flee in war,
I amble at ease in the churning melee.
If our rear falters, I battle to thwart foes,
careless of arrows whistling by my ears.
We bested men we thought unbeatable,
splendid feats worked by none but me:
See, Ibn Rōg flung from his fleeing steed
by my fist, inured to bearing fighting's brunt.
My fist! I pray, send Muḥammad flying—
may you be spared blows of evil fate:[162]
Fight for splendid daughters of Ḥamām,
purebred mares waving luxuriant tails.

—The "daughters of Ḥamām" are the ladies of the Rmāl. One of their early ancestors, even before ʿAmīrah, was named Ḥamām. He likens them to gold sorrel horses. Ḥamām was the father of Saʿd and grandfather of ʿAmīrah.

Dismounting and hobbling our camels, we fought
pitched battles, clamoring for victory.
Daredevils wrapped in panache, we plunged
into frays watched by hungry birds of death.

يقول وهي تقمز وهي تحب راسه قالت: طلبتك تاليه، انك ما تقول بي شين. ٢١،٨
قال: مسموحه. واقضبوه وصار عندهم محشوم وقاموا يغزون ويغزي بهم وينهج بهم على كل ديره. وخِذ عند الفضول له وقت وهو عندهم. ويجيك منهم عاد، روح منهم. وصار عند سبيع وصار عند عتيبه، ما خلى احد ما جاوه، راعي فرجه، راعي فْرَج يمين ويسـار.

As he finished, she came rushing up and planted a kiss on his head. 8.21
"I humbly ask you to close the subject. Please do not mention me anymore!" "Granted!" he said. They showered him with attention; from then on, he was treated with utmost respect. They raided together and journeyed in all directions. He stayed a long time before moving on to the tribes of Sbēʿ and ʿUtaybah. He visited all the tribes: he loved traveling far and wide, covering long distances and crossing vast deserts, every which way.[163]

شايع عند عتيبه

شايع فرسُه مهتّلَه تقل بغله وحاطٍّ عليه خياش، هو نزل عند عتيبه واثاري الشريف جا غزايٍ عليهم. قالوا: العن الله آبو حيّكم، الشريف جا الصبح يبي يصبحنا، وش نعمل؟ ويا مار فيه شعيب بْلُه جال ان توهّلوه قبل يلحقهم فهم سلموا منُه. قالوا: من يقعد يوقّد على النيران كننا مقيمين، حنا نبي نسري، نِهجّ؟ قعدوا هكالخياله، اربع خياله، هذي الا هذي، الفلانايه، المنيّهايه (= المنيّهات). وهو يقعد هو لبّاد عندهم، شايع، اسمه لباد. يوم قعد وسرت العرب وهذولاك يحطّون على النيران كن هذي نيران العرب مِجِلدِه. قالوا: ياالباد، وش علمك مجلدٍ بهذا؟ قال: والله ابي عندكم، ابي اعاونكم واوقّد على هالنيران معكم. قالوا: يابن الحلال. قال: خلّونَن انا، انا اعاونكم وباكر يا مشينا خلون أوخذ، وش لكم بي عاد، انا ابى اعاونكم هالحين ولا انا فقيدةٍ انا وهالبغله. اجلد عندهم وكل ما هذا يمر على النيران ويا ماريوم جا تالى الليل قاموا ينعسون، وهو يمر على النيران ويوضّيهن ويوضّي هذيك ويوضي هذيك، يْحورِف عليهن، يحط من هالحطيب وهالجله عليهن. يقول ياما جا الصبح، يما اصبحوا. القوم محزّبين للصباح، صباح العرب. يوم جا الصبح وهي تركب القوم وهي تِطّلِب يبون يصبحون هالعرب اللي هم ناوين. واثاري فرسه يوم اوجست نضّة الخيل، فرسه هاللي هو مهتّل، يا مير يوم قْمِزَت، وهي تِرهم وهي تجي وهي تَخَبط بيده، وهي تنتل هكالروث وهي تخبط. قال: خيلكم ياعيال، خيلكم ياعيال. قالوا: وش علمك؟ قال: الرجال جوكم. قالوا: عيّن خير، عين خير، توّنا يا هالحين، تونا. قال: والله جتكم الخيل يا لعنو ابو حيّكم. قالوا: وش ادريك؟ قال: ادري، كيف وش ادرين، اركبوا اركبوا. ولا صدّقوه. ١،٩

Shāyiʿ among the ʿUtaybah Tribe

Shāyiʿ was riding an exhausted mare that looked like a mule. He had covered her with sackcloth. He was staying with the ʿUtaybah tribe when they received news of the approach of the sharif at the head of a raiding party. "God curse your tribe," they said, "the sharif is coming, and tomorrow morning he will launch his attack. What to do?" They knew where to find a narrow valley hemmed in by cliffs: if they were swallowed by the gorge before getting caught, they'd be safe. "Who volunteers to stay behind and light fires to make them think all of us are still encamped here? We'll ride by night and make a run for it!" Four of them stayed behind, those with the fastest horses. Shāyiʿ, who called himself Labbād, joined the volunteers. When the others had departed, they lit fires to make it look as if everyone was there. "Hey, Labbād," they said, "what makes you stay here with us?" "Well," he said, "I'd rather be with you. I might be of some help. Tomorrow when we leave, let me be the one who is made captive. I am none of your concern. I'd like to be of assistance. No one will miss me and my mule." He remained in their company. They kept fires burning. Late at night, when the others had dozed off, he made the rounds of the fires, adding fuel here and there. He unceasingly patrolled the fires until daybreak: he kept throwing on more wood or feeding the flames with camel dung. The enemy troops stood at the ready to launch their attack at dawn, the traditional Bedouin morning attack.[164] Their cavalry asked the Lord for victory and booty, and off they rode to the tribe they had marked for attack. Shāyiʿ's mare, on sensing their approach from the drumming thud of hooves, became jittery, belying her worn-out looks. She neighed, moved about, noisily stamping her forelegs' hooves, and let droppings fall while beating the ground with her hooves. "Jump in the saddle, boys," he called. "Into the saddle at once!" "What's the matter?" they asked. "The enemy is coming at you!" "Take it easy, take it easy. We still have time, plenty of time," they said. "Damn it!" he called. "The charge is coming, curse your tribe!" "What told you?" "What do you mean, 'What told you?' I know! Ride, ride!" They didn't believe him. 9.1

يوم راعوا يما سمعوا نزيز الخيل. العن ابو حيكم. وهم يركبون. وهو يجيك بس مع اتلاهم، وهو يقصر لَه الرسن، بس مع اتلاهم. يا مير منيّهاه هن، والعرب سروا العشا، سروا، زْبَنوا هجيجٍ للضلع، يبون لهم شعيبٍ بالضلع غديهم يزبنونه. وخوذوا، خوذوا، يوم راعَوا يا والله لاحقتهم خيل الاشراف، هالسلايل جنك وقامن يلحقنّهم، ومنحاشين ومنحاشين. يوم لحقنهم السبّق، هاللي يحسبونهن ما اركض منهن شين خيلهم الثلاثه، هم ثلاثه وهو الرابع، وهو بس يتليهم، يتليهم من قَفُو. ويوم لحقتهم الخيل: هنا مير هنا، هنا مير هنا. ما من هنا، لحقوهم. وهو يزل عن وجههم، هو، وهو يزل عن وجههم. يوم حديهن وهي تجذي، وهي تجذي عن الثلاثه، وهم يلحقونهم. يوم لحقوَه وهو يوزّن وزنه على الفرس، قال: اركب، اركب، اركب. وهو يلوّح بوروكه وهو يلحق. وهو يقضب الثنين هذولاك. وهم يلحقونهم، وهي تْهَكَع بالثاني. يوم هْكَعَت بالثاني وهو بعد عنده عنده يما لحقوه وهو يميّل عليه. قال: اركب، اركب، اركب مع قفا خويك، اركب. وهو يلوّح مع قفا خويه، وهن ينهجن، وهي تطلعهم. وهي تجلد وحده. ويوم جا الظهر، جا الظهر، وهم يلحقونَه. يوم لْحقَوَه وهي بعد ايييه، امش، امش، امش، يا والله قال راحَيْه. قال: يالله اركب، اركب مع تالي خوياك على ظهره. وهو يركب، يلبّقه له وهو يلوّح قفو خوياوه. قال: تجوّدوا بي بس. وهي تنهج عطية الله وهي تروّح. وهو يخليهم، يخلي الخيل. ويما لحقوا خوياهم. قالوا: والله هاللون هذي جتنا مير تولّموا. يا مير هم هاوينٍ مع الريح وصيروا قدام بالريح وهم يفكون روحهم. قالوا: لعن ابو حيكم هذي اللي نحسبه بغله، هذي والله لولا الله ثم لولاه اننا ماخوذين حنا وماخوذاتنا، هذي اللي الحقتنـا. ٢،٩

Next thing they knew, they heard the whinnying of horses. Indeed, curse your father's tribe! They rushed off while he covered their rear. He kept his mare on a tight rein, following behind the last of his companions. Their steeds were of the highest quality. Their fellow tribesmen had already left the evening before and traveled all night, hoping to make it in time to the refuge in the mountain gorge: a narrow valley opening in a rocky range where they hoped to find safety. They kept running, on and on. Every now and then they threw apprehensive backward glances. They noticed that the sharif's cavalry was closing in on them, his fabled purebreds. The pursuers were closing the gap while they fled as fast as they could. The racers, reckoned to be the fleetest horses in Arabia, caught up with the three of them. He, the fourth, cleaved to their rear, with the enemy cavalry in hot pursuit, calling, "Here, here, here, here!" They stood no chance: the others were upon them. Shāyiʿ turned to a companion whose horse was faltering. He brought his mare side by side with the other, while galloping, and told him to vault onto his mare and sit behind him. He managed to do so, and they rejoined the others. He caught up with the two others, with the enemy in relentless pursuit. Again the enemy cavalry surged, just when the horse of the second of his companions stumbled. And again he came to the rescue. He docked his horse next to the other, bent over toward him, and told him to sit behind his other comrade. And he vaulted onto her back. The mare pulled them out of their predicament. Only one other horse of their bunch was still going. Around noon, the sharif's men closed in on her too. "Go, go, go!" But she had run out of steam. And so he said, "Ride with us. Sit on her back behind your friends." He maneuvered her into the right position and the other rider swung onto her haunches, the last one in a row of companions. "Hold on to me; grip me tightly!" he said. She extricated them: she was a gift of God, a mare in a class of her own. She outran the cavalry, which continued to chase them in vain, and they rejoined their companions. They told them about their harrowing escape and warned them to be prepared. In a compact group, they raced at top speed through the canyon and emerged safely on the other side. They had made it through the ordeal. "God's curse on your tribe! We thought this horse was no better than a mule. But for God and this mare we would have fallen into their hands, we and our wretched animals. She whisked us to where we are in your company." 9.2

شايع عند ابن عريعر

شايع عنده له فرس اصيل وطيبه، معروفه، أخذه ابن عريعر. جاهم انت ياشايع غزّاي وصْدفت انه طبّ عليهم، وباليوم اللي طب بُه عليهم صار عليهم نذر من لهم عقيدٍ يبي يصبّحهم. قالوا ما حنا لقانٍ له حنا، لكن نبي نخلي أطيب العريعر واطيب خيلهم على المراح يشب النيران ويحيي الحس، والغزو هذي تِمّن اننا مِصبحين، وحنا نبي نعلّق عليَهن من العشا ونسري، ونبي ليلنا كله ومن باكر كله، ويوم يغير ياميرعلى المِرح، والفرس هذي تِطلِع راعيَه. وهو يهزع فرسه شايع وهو يحوّل عند اللي حوّل من العريعر. قال: يارجل، ياللحية الغانمه، اتبع هالعرب، لا تقعد عندي بحلقي انت وايا عودتك هاللي تحتك. قال: والله انا طِرقي واردى ما فيها امانه على رقبتي، وش تبي بي؟ يقوله شايع. امرَحوا، يوم جا تالي هالليل ايوم قامت فرس ابن عريعر تْشَبّب وترْهِم. ويفوع من منامه. قال: نم، ما دام هالعودة ترعى بهالفيضة لا تثور من منامك، مشكّرٍ له ومخلّيه ترعى، انت ياشايع. ويوم بهّق الصبح يا مير ارهمت بطرف الفيضة وجت. وهو يثور ويقضب رسنه يتاعي له، ويكرب بطانَه ويكرب محزمه، قال: اركب فرسك. وهم يركبون. يوم بزغت الشمس يا مير هذولي هن تقل يتمازعن لهن خام مع العج. قال: ادفع، ادفع، لحقونا الرجال. ويقوم يتلبّطه رجّال العريعر بالسوط، من قفو ومن قدام. ويوم انهم فَطْنوا يا مير القوم: جاي على ارقابكم ياعيال، ياهل الخيل جاي على رقابكم. عليكم الله وامان الله، جاي على ارقابكم. ١،١٠

Shāyiʿ at Ibn ʿRēʿir

The thoroughbred horse of Shāyiʿ, a fine and reputed mare, was impounded by Ibn ʿRēʿir.[165] On one of his raiding expeditions, Shāyiʿ had stopped off at Ibn ʿRēʿir's place. While there, they received warning that a raid commander was going to launch a surprise attack at dawn. They said, "He is too strong for us. Let's leave al-ʿRēʿir's most valiant rider and the best horse to stay behind at this resting place of our camels. If fires are lit and there is noise, the raiders will believe that we are waking up and bustling about in the morning. Meanwhile, we should load up after supper and ride all night and all the next day. The enemy will attack the camp, but the horse of the rider left behind will deliver him to safety." Shāyiʿ pulled his mare aside and dismounted beside the rider who was staying behind. The rider told him, "Hey, good man, follow the departing tribe. Don't stay here with me! It will add to my burden if I have to look after you and that knackered horse you're riding. It will be another headache for me." "Easy now," Shāyiʿ replied. "I am just a poor wayfarer. No one cares about me. What would they gain from me?" The two of them remained at the resting place. Toward the end of night, the horse of Ibn ʿRēʿir became restless and began to whinny. Alarmed, its rider started from his sleep. Shāyiʿ said, "No reason for concern; go back to bed. As long as I see my old horse browsing on the greenery in the vale, there is no need to be stirred from sleep." To keep the mare comfortable, he let her roam freely around the camp. At daybreak, his mare whinnied at the edge of the vale and came back to him. He jumped to his feet, grasped the reins, and called to her in the language of horses. He tightened her belly girth and his own belt. "Get on your mare!" he ordered the other man. When the sun rose, they sighted a great glitter hovering in the distance. It looked like white cotton cloth being shredded in clouds of dust.[166] "Push her, push on!" he cried. "The raiders are at our heels!" At that, Ibn ʿRēʿir's man lashed his mount behind and in front with his whip. Before they knew it, the enemy had closed in and they raced to escape them. The enemy cavalry made ready to strike at them and go for the kill. God be with you and protect you! They were within a whisker of death. 10.1

٢،١٠ قال: وش تْهَقى بفرسك؟ قال: ما والله وراه العود، خْلِصَت. يقوله رجال ابن عريعر. قال: ابد؟ قال: ابد. قال: وش رايك تبين اهزمك والا اخلّيك بحلقهم؟ قال: لا والله لا تخلينن. يقول وهو يَرْدَعَه بالرسن يا مير يوم اجتمعت هالعودة راسه وذيله جميع فوق راسه، وهو يعانقه، قال: اركب، اركب. وهو ينزعه وهو يحطُّه على حاركَه وهو يزعجَه، يرخي رسنه ويزعجه. يوم خذت له ما خذت وتروّس له راس نبا وهو يوقف، قال: حوّل راع انت تشوف أحد؟ راعى، قال: والله ما اشوف العود. قال: اركب. وهم يركبون وهم يمزعونه. ويخلّيه على مغارَه. يوم غابت الشمس ياهو يطلع على العرب. العرب البارحة واليوم كله سراة. قال: حوّل، حوّل انحر معزّبك. وهو يحول وينحر معزّبه وهذاك يحول ينحر معازيبه. قال: وين فرسك؟ قال: فرسي خليته الضحى. قال: من جابك؟ قال: جابن شايع. قال: وكاد؟ قال: وكاد. قال: وشلون؟ قال: ياطويل العمر هاللون اللي صار وهاللون اللي صار وعمل بي هاك، وفرسه كل البارح عاذرة وانا مربوطةٍ بحذاي، قافل، وهذيك ترعى، ولولا الله ثم هو والله ما تشوفن. قال: وش تهَقى هالخيل اللي اطلبنّكم متى يجنّنا؟ قال: كان هن على مركاضهن يجن على النومه. قال: انهج خله يجي.

٣،١٠ يوم جا، قال: وش تقول يابن رمال. قال: وشّوا من طْرفُه؟ قال: متى يجوننا؟ قال: كان خيلهم على مركاضهن يجنّك باكر الضحى. قال: يعني على مركاضهن اليوم كله والليلة اللي تجي، هاللي حنا به؟ قال: ابد، كان مركاضهن ما بطّل، على مركاضهن اللي انا اخبر، اليوم والليلة هذي كله، يجنّك باكر الضحى. قال: ما هنا فرس تركض يوم وليله! قال: نم زاد على كل جنوبك منهم. قال: نبي الفرس مْنَك. قال: والله ما انطيه. قال: بيع. قال: ما ابيعه. قال: بفرسين. قال: ابدا، انا خذيته بيدي، انا جذبت شايته من تحت راعيه ولا انطيه. قال: اطلب اللي تبي.

“How much energy is left in your mare?” he asked his comrade. “By God,” the man of Ibn ʿRēʿir said, “the old beast is at the end of its tether. She’s done for.” “Really?” “Yes, for sure.” “Tell me what you think. Would you like me to help you escape, or would you rather be left at their mercy?” “No, no, by God,” he said, “don’t leave me in the lurch!” At once Shāyiʿ reined in his mare so forcefully that his mare’s tail and head almost touched above her body as she curved her back.[167] He brought her side by side with the other horse and told his companion to ride with him. Shāyiʿ grasped him and pulled him onto his mare’s haunches, let the reins go free, and gave her the spurs. After she had run for some time, he let her ascend to the top of a promontory and halted. “Get off,” he said. “Take a look—do you see anyone?” “No, I see absolutely nothing moving.” And they tore off again; he let her go at full throttle. At sundown, they caught up with the tribe, which had been traveling all night and all that day. They dismounted, and each of them went to his hosts. They asked Shāyiʿ’s companion about the whereabouts of his horse and were astonished to hear that he had been given a ride by Shāyiʿ. He explained what happened and what Shāyiʿ had done. “Yesterday his mare was all day at ease in the vale, grazing, whereas my horse stood shackled at my side, at the ready.[168] But for God and him, you wouldn’t be seeing me now.” “In your estimate, when can we expect the pursuers to get here?” “If they keep running as hard as they were, they might arrive while we are sleeping.” “Go get him, and let him come to me.” 10.2

Shāyiʿ came and was asked, “What would you say, Ibn ʿRēʿir?” “About what?” “What time will they be here?” “If they keep running as they did, tomorrow in the morning.” “You mean, running all day and the coming night, this night?” “That’s right. That is, if they can keep it up. This is an estimate based on the pace I’ve seen from them. A full day and night; then they’ll arrive somewhat early in the morning.” Ibn ʿRēʿir said, “As for us, we do not know of any horses capable of running a full day and night.” “Sleep at ease and turn on your other side for more sleep. There’s plenty of time before they get here,” Shāyiʿ reassured him. “We want your mare,” he said. “By God, I won’t give her to you.” “We’ll buy it from you.” “It is not for sale.” “In exchange for two other mares.” “No way,” he said. “I captured it by pulling the saddle from under its previous owner, and I will not give her away.” “Ask any price you wish!” “Well then, I will sell it to you on condition that her first foal is given to me.” (“First foal,” *mathnawī*, means that if the mare foals after the buyer takes possession 10.3

قال: ابيعه عليك بس ابي بَه مثنوي. المثنوي مثل ما تقول إلى افلت الفرس عند هالرجال اللي شراه أول فِلُو لك انت يالبياع تاخذُه منُه، لِك. أمر الله انه قبل ما يحصّل شايع مثنوي فرسه مات محمد ابن عريعر وشاخ عقبه اخوه حماد وعيّى على شايع بالمثنوي، قال: رح وراك ما تطلبنا شين ولا عندنا لك شين. الامير اللي مات له وليد صغير اسمه عثمان. واحسب ياشايع للولد يا ما تم خمسطعش سنه، يوم تم خمطعش سنه، كبر، غدى جذع، وهو يجيه شايع ويقول به هالقصيدة ، يقول:

٤،١٠ انا برجوى الله ثم عثمان ابن محمد   يا غاب عامينٍ رجيته عام
ياحيف يالصفرا جواد ابن خنشر   ما وقّفت بين الصفّتين تسام
وانا سومي له على ذارع من القنا   كما سابحٍ غاص البحور وعام

٥،١٠ الولد ما يدري وشّي القصيده. قصيدة مرت ولا يدري وشي! يوم جا يم امه، قال: عطون عشاي. جابت امه عشاوه يا مير ايدامه ما. قال: ياحيفك يايمّه، ليه ايدام عشاي ما؟ قالت: هذا قدر الرجل اللي ما يقوم بواجبه. قال: وشّوا واجبي اللي انا مقصّرٍ بُه؟ قالت: جَلِي ما سمعت قصيدة ابن رمال هاللي يتحسّف على فرسه. وِخْذَت منه لا بيع ولا شرى وهو ضيفٍ لابوك ويتناك يا ما حسب لك وارشدت وعلّمك بالقصيده. يوم اصبح الولد قال: ياشايع، قال: نعم. قال: وشو غرضك اللي انت ناصينا على شانه؟ قال له شايع: انا بْلِزَمكم يالبناخي، انا بْلِزَمك وعيّى عمّك بمثاني خيلي. قال الصبي: وعدك من هانا يما يبرق البرق بالوسم وانشا الله ما يكون الا خير، وانت ما لك رخصةٍ تِمِدّ يا ما يقع الوسم. يقوله عثمان. هم بالقيظ. قال: ياما يقع الوسم؟ قال نعم. قال: سمع وطاعه. وافصخ رسن الذلول واعزب به مع الدبش. ويحسب للوسم شايع يما دخل. وهو ينط هكالمرقاب إلى مير يوم ناض البرق يامير يخيله شايع غرب، على حروة ديرته. يوم اصبح الصبح وهو يجلس بالقهوه. قال:

of her, the seller will receive the first foal.) God decreed that Muḥammad ibn ʿRēʿir should die before Shāyiʿ received the foal. His successor as shaykh of the tribe, his brother Ḥammād, refused to cede the first foal to Shāyiʿ. "Beat it," he said. "Don't make any demands on us. We have nothing for you." The emir who passed away had a young son named ʿUthmān. Shāyiʿ put him on notice when he had reached the age of fifteen—that is, when he had grown up and become a young man. Shāyiʿ came and recited these verses:

I hope for God, then ʿUthmān, Muḥammad's son: 10.4
if two years' wait is in vain, I will wait another year.
What a pity, Ibn Khanshar's white purebred,
never put up for sale between rows of tents.[169]
I defied death, thrusting long-shafted lances,
as a swimmer at sea thrusts and pulls his arms.

The boy was in the dark as to the verses' meaning. He heard them, but 10.5
he had no inkling. When he asked his mother for supper, she brought him food, but without condiments. "Too bad. Why no condiments, Mother?" "That is what men get who do not fulfill their duty." "In what respect did I fall short, Mother?" "How come you don't know? Didn't you hear Ibn Rmāl's verses, composed in sorrow at the loss of his mare? It was taken from him, not through selling and buying, while he was staying here as your father's guest. He kept those verses in abeyance until he reckoned that you had grown up." Next morning, the boy asked Shāyiʿ, "What is your purpose in sending us this message?" Shāyiʿ said, "You owe me something, dear brother; you are under an obligation toward me. Your uncle refused to give me the foal, as had been agreed with your father." "I promise you," said the boy, "by the time we see the first flashes of lightning in fall, God willing, all will be fine. But you must stay here and not leave before the autumnal rains." It was midsummer when ʿUthmān spoke these words. "That long?" "Yes," the boy said. "Fine, I'll do your bidding," Shāyiʿ said. He took the halter off his riding camel and sent it to pasture with the other camels. Shāyiʿ counted the days and regularly climbed an elevation to scan the horizon. One day, he saw a flicker of lightning in the distance toward the west, in the direction of his homeland. Next morning, as he was in the majlis, cup of coffee in hand, he intoned:

١٠،٦ سرى البرق ياعثمـان ياكاسب الثنا على دار اهلنـا ياصـدوق الوعايـد
يشدى جلود الخيل يا مس جـلده بقٍّ من البـرغوث طـرار النواجـد
والا ارتعـاش الفـرخ لميع بـرقـه تسـري له الاظعـان من غـير رايـد
ولت ما ولت من عقب ليلٍ وغدّرت وبالظن عـاف المـا زبار النفـايـد

١٠،٧ قال: ابشر. الولد هذا له شبرية معروفه، مفضّضة بذهب. يوم جا الليل نام عمه هو ومرته بالقطيفه، واقضب يالولد شبريته وخِلّ به القطيفه على روسهم على الفراش من تحتهم واثبتَه يما هفّت بالقاع، ثْبِتَه على عصابته وغدفته وعلى الوساده، وهو يخلّيه وينهج عنهم. يوم جا الصبح تنبّه عمّه وجا يبي يثور يا مير ما يقوى يثور. قال: هاللي قاضبٍ راسي يامره وشّوا؟ قالت: قديمي. قال: سِلّيها. يوم سلّته، قال: هذي قديمي عثمان، من جانا جاوه الله! دونك ياعبد دونك، انهج يمّه وانصه عطه الختم، دوك الختم عطه اياوه. قال: ياعم عثمان مرسلن عمي يمك يقول هذا الختم. قال: ارجَع بُه يمُّه، الختم لي وله، هذا عمي وختمُه ختمٍ لي، يفطن لحاجة لنا عنده. وهو يرجع يَمُّه، قال: يقول هاللون وهاللون. قال: دونك اوراق المعاش من الدوله، سلمهن اياوه. وهو يرجع. قال: ارجع بهن يمّه، المعاش لي وله ويفطن للحاجة اللي لنا عنده، وان ما جيتن بخبر والله لادرّج راسك. وانكس يمُّه قال: يقول هاك وهاك. قال: انهج يمّه قل يقول عمي ود ثم والله انه ما يخبر الحق لا لك ولا لابوك الا فرس شايع ابن رمال هي هذي براسه وبناته ست، هي سابعتهن. يوم علمه، قال: زين، سلم لي عليه ويا جيته قل يقول عثمان مجيرٍ جيرةٍ تافي من عظم راسي، حارمٍ عليّ شرب الفنجال مع الغانمين انهن ما ياطن الا على زل من الجفرة – اللي يم الحسا هناك – ليا ما ياطن دكاك النفود. يوم علمه ويجمع كبار العريعر، قال: يالربع وش الحيله؟ وش نْعمل؟ وابلشوا، من

Distant flashes, ʿUthmān, my good boy! 10.6
Lightning's promise over my tribe's land;
Ripples like shivers of pain over a horse's skin
at the bite of a nasty midge's ferocious jaws.
A chicken's tremor: thus, lightning's quiver
makes camel trains run, no need for scouts.
One night it came without bringing rain:
it seems water is repulsed seeing the sands.

"Trust me, expect good news soon!" the boy exclaimed. He clasped his well-known dagger, its grip inlaid with gold carvings. His uncle and his wife slept under a rug. He pierced the rug with his dagger where their heads were and fixed it into the bed coverings under them. While doing so, he made sure to stick the dagger through a fold of his uncle's headdress and turban, and plunge it through the pillow. He left him pinned down tightly and left.[170] Come morning, his uncle discovered that he was unable to move when he tried to get up. "Hey, woman, have a look! What is it that keeps my head tied down?" "A dagger." He asked her to pull out the dagger, and on seeing it, he recognized it as ʿUthmān's. "May God get at the person who got at us! Hey, you slave, here! Go to him and give him this signet ring. Here is my ring, take it! Give it to him!" He did as he was told. "My uncle ʿUthmān, my master sends me with this ring for you, saying you should take it." "Return it to him. The ring belongs to him and me. My uncle's ring is also my ring. Let him ponder what else he owes us." The slave brought the report. "Here!" he said. "The documents for the allowances paid to me by the state. Hand him those!"[171] Again, the slave received the same response: "The allowances are for me and for him. Let him think about what he really owes us. And this time, if you do not bring me the correct answer, by God, I'll send your head rolling." On being informed, it dawned on him what was wrong. "Go and give your master's assurance that in all honesty the only obligation toward you and your father he can think of would be the mare of Shāyiʿ ibn Rmāl: the mare and its six daughters. The mare itself makes seven." The slave was given the reply: "Good. Bring him my greetings and tell him: ʿUthmān has taken a dear oath on his own life that he will stop drinking a cup of coffee with his kinsmen and friends if these mares are not made to walk on carpets from al-Jafrah in al-Ḥasā Province all the way to the sands of the Nafūd Desert."[172] Perplexed by this demand, the uncle called together the 10.7

اين زل نفرش من الحسا للنفود. قال ستاد الخيل، الصانع اللي يحذاهن: لا تبحلون، عندي حلّه، حذا ومسامير وجّدهن لي ومطرقه ومبراة وزلّيه وحده والى انصلت الفرس حذاته أحَذاه على زله. أحط الزل على قد قينه بينه وبين حذاه واسمّره والى منّه انصلت لا تمشي، تاقف نْحذاه، لما نجي النفود. ونِتِمّ دينُه.

قال عثمان: يالعريعر ترونا غزو، لا يقعد احد. وهي تعلّق العريعر وهي تركب خيل وجيش. يوم جوا خبوب الرضم هاللي عند تربه، هذولي، والى هذي البل مثل المخايم، اباعر شمر، وهم يغيرون عليّه. قال: شوفوا، لا يثور ولا رميه، ايتوا من وراه وحيطوا به. جوا من وراه حاطوا به، جموع لا تحِصَى ولا تعَدّ. وهم يضفّونه. قال: يابن رمال. قال: نعم. قال: البل هذي هي من شمر؟ قال: نعم. قال: هي تعز عليك. قال: آه. قال: يا خذيناه هو يلحقك ملام؟ قال: يا خذيتوَه خوذوا معه ذلولي هاللي تحتي. قال: قل وصلت ديرتك. قال: الله الله، هذي ديرتي. قال: عطونا الخيل يارجاجيل. يا مير جابوهن، هي براسه وست بناته معَه. قال: هذي فْرِسَك، تعرفه؟ قال: اعرفه. قال: هذولي بناته ست، مْعَلّقٍ عليهن، ماموناتٍ محفوظات واستلمهن وان كان لك مبَقّى حقٍّ علّمنا به. قال: كمال وجمال. قال: تروه حارمٍ علينا الكسب ياما نجي اهلنا ياهالغزو. غزوتنا نبي بياض وجيهنا مْنَك. وينكس وابن رمال يجيب خيله لهلُه. ٨٫١٠

principal men of al-ʿRēʿir and explained his quandary: "What will do the trick in dealing with this condition?" They were at a loss for a stratagem. How could we possibly lay a carpeted road all the way from al-Ḥasā to the Nafūd? Their blacksmith, the craftsman who shod the horses, said, "Don't twist yourselves into knots! The solution is very simple. Find me horseshoes, nails, a hammer, a file, and a carpet. If the mare loses its horseshoes, we'll replace it with fabric from the carpet. I'll fashion a horseshoe by cutting a piece from the carpet of the right size up to the coronet and nail it to the hooves. If it falls off, we halt and make another one in the same manner, and so on, until we have reached the Nafūd. That's the way to fulfill his oath."

ʿUthmān said, "Men of al-ʿRēʿir, join me on a raiding expedition. No one is allowed to stay behind." They packed, and the cavalry and camel troops rode off. When they came to Khbūb al-Riḍm, near Trubah, it looked as if the sand hills were dotted with shreds of white fabric: the camels of Shammar.[173] They launched their attack. "Hear!" he said. "Be careful now! No shot should be fired. Round them up from behind." They collected a huge number of camels by encircling them and compressing them into a compact mass. "Ibn Rmāl, are these the camels of Shammar?" he asked. "Yes, indeed," Shāyiʿ replied. "Are they dear to you?" "Yes, of course." "Well, if we robbed them, would you be blamed for it?" "If you rob them, then also take the camel on which I am riding." "Have we arrived in your tribal land?" "Yes, for sure, this is my homeland." He ordered his men to bring the horses: the mare and her six daughters. "This is your mare. You remember her?" "Yes, I recognize her." "And these are her six daughters. They come with her. We took care of them and they are in good shape. Take them, they're yours. And if some of what we owe you is still missing, let us know." "Everything is perfect and beautiful," he said. Then ʿUthmān told his men, "We are not allowed to take any plunder until we reach home, raiders! We embarked on this raid for the sole purpose of whitening our faces and freeing ourselves of any blame." Thus, Ibn Rmāl returned home to his kinfolk with his horses. 10.8

ذلوله تجفل وتخليه

١،١١ شايع نَهَج مع الخلا غزّاي لحاله ببسيطا، دَوٍّ خالي. وهو يجي بْلُه مظمايه وهو يغدّي ويدلي يسوي غداوه ويقيّد ذلوله. ما قَيّدَه، ذرّعه ذراع، عقد الرسن بْيِدَه، يخبرَه ما تشرد ولا تنهج عَنُه. يا مير الذلول ما عمرَه راحيْه (= راحت) وميلاف ولا عمره راحيْه. يوم جا هكالروض وهو يحول بُه، روض هكالكتاد (= القتاد)، به رِعي، بهالحماد. واثاريه فرّ من تِحْتَه له طير وهي تستجفل وهي تقمز. يوم قْمِزَيْه يا مار منقطعٍ الخيط. يوم جا يبي يَقِضْبَه وهي تنحاش. آه، ويقضب الحَقَب وتدلّي ترثع وهو يرثع باثره، وتضربه هكالرضمة يا واقع. وهي تولّي وتغدي. يا مار بهالمهمهيّه، بهالحماد، لا امواه ولا هذي ولا هذيك. اركض باثرَه اركض، اركض، ويمشي مع ثره، امير يوم راحَيْه. وهو يقعد بس مع ثره يمشي، يمشي. يوم تليّش، مع ثره. يوم تليّش وخلص.

٢،١١ قال: انا مار اغدين ابحَفر لي قبر ما زالي شديد وما زالي حي والا انا رحت. وهو يجي وهو يحفر له قبر ويحفره يّما غوّطه وهو ينجضع بوسطه يا مار طولُه. ويمرح هكالليله. يا مار عنده له بوم بله شنق رَسِم، طول ليله ما ينام. يقول واثاريه دِيّش به بعض التدييشايه، نعس. يوم ديّش، يعني غط عينه النوم، وهو عطشان ومتليّش وسهى بالنوم، وهو يجي له منابي، قال: ياشايع، ياشايع، اقعد، اقعد، شف ذلولك بالسدرة الفلانيه، بالمحل الفلاني. ما هي بعيد محل السدره. وهو ينهض راسه يا مير ما عنده احد. هو يسمّي وهو يرجع ينام. قال: ياشايع، اقعد، اقعد،

His Riding Camel Panics, Stampedes, and Leaves Him Behind

11.1 On one of his raids Shāyiʿ, traveling unaccompanied, traversed al-Busayṭā, a vast, empty wilderness.[174] On one particularly lonely stretch of waterless desert, he halted at lunchtime, fettered his she-camel, and prepared some food. He did not shackle her legs but only wound the rope of the reins around her forelegs. He knew that she would not wander off and abscond. She did not stray. She was sweet-tempered, not wayward at all. While traveling that barren plain of hard ground, he stopped at a rare thicket of acacia trees with some grazing around. Suddenly a bird flew up from under the camel with a loud whirring sound. Startled, the camel panicked and stampeded. At her brusque movement, the thin rope snapped as he tried to grasp it. She ran away. He hung on to the saddle girth, but she kept going at a wild gallop, dragging him along. Then he hit a big stone and had to let go of the girth. He kept running after her for a good distance, but he stood no chance in such an utterly desolate, flat expanse of desert. There was no drop of water to be found, nothing at all. He ran and ran, following her tracks until he was exhausted and could go no farther.

11.2 He said to himself, "Perhaps I'd better start digging a grave while I still have the strength to do so, in preparation for death.[175] Otherwise I'll be dead before I start." He started digging a trench until it was of the required depth. Then he lay down in it and turned on his side. Yes, it was of the right width and length. He spent the night resting in the grave. There happened to be an owl somewhere close by. All night, he hardly got any sleep. He dozed off a few times, overcome by drowsiness, no more. His eyelids fell shut a couple of times. He was thirsty, worn out, drifting in and out of sleep. Then he heard a call. A voice called to him:[176] "Shāyiʿ, Shāyiʿ, sit up, sit up! Look, your camel is at that acacia in such and such a place." It was a place not far from where he was. He raised his head and looked around: no one to be seen. He invoked the name of God and went back to sleep. Again he heard: "Shāyiʿ, Shāyiʿ, sit up, sit up! Your camel is at that place, at the acacia tree, caught in the branches of the tree." This time he started

شف ذلولك بالمحل الفلاني، بالسدرة، قاضبته السدره. وهو يثور وهو ينهج قال والله انا ابشوف هذا انشا الله منابي خير، هالمنابي هذا.

٣،١١ يوم طلع على السدره يا مير هي هذي ملتوي الرسن على غصنٍ مْنَه ولاويتّه يما هي واصلٍ الرسن صريمة الرسن اللي بهذا وقاضبه ومجلده. ويجْيَه وفكّه ويطلِقَ الرسن ويركبه ويجيك عليه، هاللي يقول:

٤،١١
العنك يارجالٍ تخلّي ذلولك بارض الخلا طِلقٍ بغير قياد
اغرّني حبل الرفلا من فاطري ثلاث منون وحديهن باد
خمّيتها وانا مِشْفِ بقضبه يا وان خطاها عن خطاي بعاد
وحفرت لي قبرٍ على راس منهل طويل النبا طول الزمان يعاد
ما عندي الا البوم ينعى شبابه وحاطٍّ له بين الصفرتين مَعاد
واجلدت انا والبوم في راس ما نبا وابكي وتهل العيون بْداد
البوم يجاوبني يبي هِجِن فاطره بالليل يندب ما هناه رْقاد
وش فاقدٍ يابوم لذّات الصبا ولا بطّ ماطاك شوك كتاد
ولا فاقدٍ يابوم بيضا غريره ولا فاقدٍ يابوم لين وساد
ولا فاقدٍ يابوم خيلان زوبع عليهن الغوى والدروع تقاد
أوصيك يابوم الخلا قل لعزوتي اهرج لهم عطهم علوم وكاد
ان جيت اخوي وسايلك عن مصيبتي تقول له وسط الفيافي باد
وان مت يدفنّي على جال منهل حيثه معادٍ للنضا ترداد
يردم على قبري ثمانٍ من الحصا يموت الفتى وسمولهن جداد

to his feet and went on his way, saying, "By God, I must go and see for myself. God willing, the caller is a good spirit, whoever it is calling to me."

When he came to the acacia, he saw that the camel's reins had become entangled in one of the thorny branches, becoming more entwined in the tree with every turn until the halter itself had become caught in it. The animal was fixed in that position. He put the camel at ease, pried it loose, and freed the twisted reins.[177] Then he mounted and rode back to his people. He said: 11.3

"Curse you!" Why leave your camel alone, 11.4
free to roam, untethered, in wilderness?
Blindsided by my camel's rotten rope,
three twisted strands, one threadbare,
I held on, gripping frantic with despair,
my steps no match for her mighty stride.
I dug a grave at the well's outer rim,
familiar to wayfarers, much visited,
To the tune of an owl lamenting youth,
from dusk to dawn awaiting its return.[178]
As I lay dying, owl hooting from above,
I cried my eyes out with floods of tears.
Does an owl call a mount by screeching,
shrieking all night, bereft of slumber?
Silly owl, pining for lost halcyon days,
are you hurt, treading barefoot on thorns?
Perk up! You don't long for a fair maiden.
You don't pine for comfort of soft pillows;
You don't miss the view of Zōbaʿ cavalry,
resplendent in battle colors and shining arms.[179]
Lonely desert owl, I trust you to find my kin:
tell them what you saw of my predicament.
Tell my brother if he asks about my grim fate:
"He came to grief in empty desert wastes."
If I die, bury me at a well, plain to see
for wayfarers and riders of hardy camels;
Raise eight slabs of stone over the grave!
Forever young, they point: "There lies a dead man."

وان عشت لا بدّي على الدار عايد كما فرخ شامٍ في حلول هداد
وانا بوجه اللي فرض حبة النوى تجلى عني كربٍ عَلَيّ وكاد
وانا الذي أصبر على كل ما بدا وانا الذي لهزلى الرجال سناد
ما يدرك الطولات كود من سعى لها وردي العزايم عن عناها حاد
وانا لخالقي وجّهت وجهي ونيّتي وبيني وبين الغانمين امياد
وتذكّرت خلدا صيفة البدر خدّها شمال من الضلع الكبير قصاد
وهي بنت من يحجي ويذري ويلتقى يا جرّدوا مصقول كل غْماد
نقيّة عرضٍ كن صفّة جعودها اذيال شقرٍ عرّضت لطراد
وانا سترها الضافي وانا ذوي حيها واضرب على صعب الامور عناد
سقاك ياسدرة الخلا الناعميه عساه من وبل الثريا تعاد

If I survive, I must be homeward bound,
like a Syrian falcon taking wing in fall.
In Him who turns seeds to sprouts I trust
to lift my worries' oppressive weight.[180]
Come what may, I'll bear it patiently;
let the weak lean on me for support.
Proud achievements are won by exertion:
not shirkers who waver and procrastinate.
My face and spirit I turned to my Creator,
nowhere near to my noble-hearted fellows.
Khaldā is on my mind, her cheeks like the moon,
where she lives, north of the Mountain;[181]
Daughter of a hero who shields, repels, fights[182]
if grim swords are drawn from scabbards;
Beauty pure, garlands of tresses tumbling:
fanned-out tail of a chasing sorrel mare.
I am her ample mantle, one of her kin;
doggedly I tackle tasks most daunting.
Lonesome acacia, let the blessings of rains
sent by Pleiades' stars refresh your life!

يودع ذلوله عند السبيعيات ويوصيهن عليه

١،١٢ هـذي قصيدة شايع الامسح يوم هو يودع ذلوله مع بنات السبعه من عنزه. ودع ذلوله الوضحا وهي منقطعة عقب مغزى. هزع من خوياوه وتخفّى يما جا البنات ووصّاهن. يوم نهج منهن وخلاه عندهن وهن يتطالبن عند العارفة عارفة عنزه، الكل تقول الذلول عندي. قالت حديهن: اذكر الله ياعارفه، الذلول عندي، يا عاد انا بنت من يشق ويرقع. قالت الثانية: اذكر الله ياعارفه الذلول عندي، يا عاد انا بنت من يصيبه قبل تقع. يعني صاحب الشور. وخذته بنت صاحب الشور. وخلاه عندهم ليا ما جا الصيف وربعت وجاه ونهج به وغزى عليه. يقول:

٢،١٢ قـال الغفيـلي والذي مـس كوره　　على كور وجنا ويّ والله زْمـاله
اوصيكن يانجل العيون بفـاطري　　وصاةٍ لمن منكن كد جـاد خـاله
قـرّبن مـبركه بالليـل عنـدكن　　عن البرد ياالخفرات ضَفّن جلاله
وعـلّمـن راعى الذود بفـاطـري　　يا استنن الحشوان يداري جفـاله
عفّيتهـا بالوسـم تسعـين ليـله　　وخمسين وقت الصيف هذا كماله
أبي عـليها نقضة الجـزو غـزوه　　يا بنّـن الخفـرات غـاوي دَلاله
نـبي عـليهـا ذود قـنٍّ مقصّـر　　قـليـل الحساني قـاطعٍ بيعياله

He Entrusts His Camel to Girls of the Sbaʿah Tribe of ʿAnazah

This is a poem by Shāyiʿ al-Amsaḥ, composed when he left his riding camel with seven girls of the Sbaʿah tribe of the ʿAnazah confederation. The animal was in bad shape, emaciated by arduous raiding. He let his companions go their own way and went into hiding until the girls came by. He spoke to them and left his mount in their care. After he had gone, they could not agree who should have the privilege. Therefore, they submitted their dispute to ʿAnazah experts in tribal law. Each vied for the honor of being the one responsible for his camel. One said, "Fear God, Judge, aren't you aware that I am the daughter of the man who gets others in a bind and extricates himself?"[183] The second said, "Fear God, Judge, the camel should be with me. Am I not the daughter of the man who hits the mark before disaster strikes?"[184] (That is, a man of wise counsel.) The daughter of the wise man won and was allowed to tend to the camel. Restored to strength from grazing on pastures of spring, the she-camel was reunited with Shāyiʿ in summer and they resumed their raiding practice. On that occasion, he said: 12.1

Hand on her saddle, al-Ghfēlī burst into song:[185] 12.2
Sweet-tempered lady camel, you're marvelous!
Large-eyed beauties, I entrust my mount to you,
girls endowed with maternal uncles' excellence.[186]
Couch her close by where you sleep at night;
cover her, dear maiden, against biting cold!
Instruct your shepherd boy to treat her well,
lest she panic if skittery calves dart about!
Ninety days on pasture lush from autumnal rain,
fifty more of spring grazing restored her shape.
Herbage wilts in heat; it is time for raiding,
for damsels to deck her out with ribbons,
For us to capture rich misers' camel herds:
grouches who scrimp on food for children,

بخيل على الجيران والضيف يا لفى　　يمناوه بالمدّات ما اعطت شماله
ويا قيّلوا ربعي نصيت راس مرقب　　عيني ورا ربعي وعيني قباله
والى قضوا طرباتهم من مقيلهم　　مسيت عليه ما ارتخى من حباله
ياطول ما وردتها تسبر العدو　　لو العطش والجوع موزي بحاله
ياما وردنا عقلة جاهليه　　طيرت حمام فرّخ بعرض جاله
واستجفلت بي وذارتن ثم عاودت　　مثل العنود اللي بغم له غزاله
لا تجفلين هداهد يافاطري　　حمام طار من قاعة البير لجاله

الى طار الحمام من البير يجفّله.

يوم اني درهشت له وعاوده　　على مثل حابوط الرحا من ثفاله
وحولت وخضيت القراح لفاطري　　يما عْطَنت بالما وفاخت جْفاله
يا بركت بيمركب فرجلت به　　وايّا مقيل للقطا ياظلاله

فرجلت يعني تفج فخوذه يا بركت يهوي الرجال من تحته من ضمره، قافل من المغازي والمماشي.

وان درهمت مع سهلة فرزة الحصا　　عوى الذيب من فرقاه وفرقا خَياله

عجز يلحقه الذيب.

ياكن يد الوضحا يا نزرته　　يد صانع يرجى العشا بالعماله
على كورها بالقيض لو حسّن الظما　　أخير عندي من برايد ظلاله

Who skimp on outlay for neighbors and guests:
a right hand no more generous than the left.[187]
Watchman, when my comrades recline in shade,
I climb heights to keep an eye left and right;[188]
They enjoy pleasant lazing in midday heat;
my evenings are in saddle, reins grasped tight.
Often I took her when I scouted out my foes,
battling weariness, throat parched, belly empty.
Many a time our stops at old desert water holes
startled doves from nests in stone-laid casings:[189]
Alarmed at her panic, I spoke words of calm,
as a gazelle doe soothes a bleating fawn.
Don't stampede! Be quiet, hardy mount of mine!
Just a dove, caught by well's bottom and wall!

—Camels panic at the sudden rush and whirl of a startled dove flying up from a well.

If I let her drink, she calmly lowers her lips,
slurps from a skin like leather under a quern.
I dismounted, scooped water from a hole:
at ease she kneeled, sated, fright gone.
If couched for rest, her forelegs folded,
sandgrouse may hide in the shade beneath.

—"Her forelegs folded" means that her axillae are widely spaced. In couched position, the camel has enough room under her body to let a man slide through underneath because the animal is so lean. The mount is sinewy from riding on long-distance raiding expeditions.

At a fast trot on plains with scattered rocks,
she outpaces wolves howling from vexation.[190]

—Impossible for wolves to keep up with her speed.

Scold her and the white mount's legs pump
like gesticulating workers anxiously awaiting wages.[191]
In the saddle, scalded by midsummer's glare,
I'm happier than in dense gardens' deepest shade.[192]

ياما حظينا فوقها من غنيمه   وياما قْطَعت بي من زيازي سهاله
علمتها للارداف وهي لِقِيّه   يوم ان ردي الخال عيّى واوى له

يوم ان ردي الخال ياوي لذلوله ولا يعرضه المخاطر.

عن جارنا والضيف ما كِفّ فضلنا   وبيوتنا بالقحط كل عنى له
ونمِدّ من مد الكريم لجارنا   ونعطيه من عطوى رفيع الجلاله

Untold are the riches I've amassed on her back
by crossing vast plains of desolate desert wastes.
Three years old, she'd be mounted by two men,
not soft riders, fastidious curs of lousy lineage.

—Wretches whose maternal uncles are no good show unwarranted compassion; they refrain from exposing their mounts to hardship.

Our wont is to coddle neighbors, pamper guests;
in spells of drought, our tents are everyone's refuge.
We are prodigal with gifts of the Beneficent,
the Almighty's favors shared with neighbors.[193]

عميره ولد شايع يِطلِع ابوه من حبس ابن عريعر

غزى شايع واخذ اباعر وخيل من المفلى لابن عريعر. واطلبُه ابن عريعر وامسكُه، قال: أدّ الخيل والبل. قال: والله الخيل والبل صكّوا بهن شمر واقفوا بهن ولا لي بهن حيله. واربطه، اجدعه بالحبس. وقعد بالحبس ثمان سنين. يوم كبر ولده عميره جاك ناحرٍ ابن عريعر. يوم جا وزنُهم وهو ينوخ الذلول ويضوي عليهم. يا مير موصوف له محل ابوه وانه بالحديد، بالرفه تحت الذرا. ويضوي عليه يوم نامت الخلق واهِمزُه. وهو يقعد وهو يحب راسه امير دموعه يوم تطارزن على وجهه. قال: هو انت عميره؟ قال: ما غيره. قال: انت على زماله؟ قال: اي بالله. قال: وش وَقْعه؟ قال: على غرضك. قال: ياولدي انا ما اقاضي، اللي يقاضي بي وْلِدُه، له ولد جذيع ما هو كبير ما يْعَدى بحضن ابوه بالنهار وبالليل ينام مع امه الى صارت ما هيب ليلتّه والليله ما هيب ليلتّه، حريمه يناومهن والليله ما هيب ليلة ام الولد، ينام معَه الجذيع، ان ادركتُه لنا الليله فانا تقاضيت وجليت صدا كبدي. ١٫١٣

وداور عَلْيَه ويلقاه نيمة ما عندَه احد، ودالِشٍ الوغد من الفراش وهي قَفْوُه ملَقّيِة وجهَه غاد وفاتخه، نيمه. وهو يْعَدي عليَه ويحط يدُه من تحت راس الوليد ويسلّه ويشلعه ويجيبه يم ابوه. قال: يابعد حيي وميتي، الدَوّ، الدو، وش وقع الذلول؟ قال: نعمك ونعمين. قال: الدو ولا هو انا اللي اوصيك بالمسرى، وانا ما ٢٫١٣

ʿAmīrah, Shāyiʿ's Son, Frees His Father from Ibn ʿRēʿir's Jail

On one of his raids, Shāyiʿ lifted Ibn ʿRēʿir's horses and camels from their pasture. Ibn ʿRēʿir went in pursuit, caught him, and demanded the return of his animals. "It can't be done," Shāyiʿ said. Shammar tribesmen had already made off with the horses and camels in one compact mass of animals. No way could they be made to reverse course. He was fettered and thrown in jail. Eight years he festered in his dungeon. When his son ʿAmīrah had grown up, he headed for Ibn ʿRēʿir. Close to the camp, he kneeled his mount and quietly glided toward them under cover of darkness. He had obtained a description of the place where his father was being held: he had information that he was shackled in iron under the overhang of the tent wall in the men's sitting room.[194] He slunk toward him and lightly touched him. Shāyiʿ sat up and kissed his head, his eyes filled with tears. "Is it you, ʿAmīrah?" He asked if he had come riding a camel and in what condition it was.[195] "Perfect for your purpose," he said. "My boy," Shāyiʿ said, "freeing me is no revenge. To get even, we must take his little son."[196] He had a little boy, Jdhēʿ, whom he always held in his lap during the day and who slept at his mother's place if it was not her turn to spend the night with Ibn ʿRēʿir. And it so happened that this night Ibn ʿRēʿir was with one of his other wives. He would sleep with his wives in a fixed order: each of them had been assigned a particular night to host him in her tent. This night Jdhēʿ was staying with his mother. "If you get hold of him tonight, I'll have obtained satisfaction, my revenge. You'll have sponged away the coat of dull grime on my liver." 13.1

ʿAmīrah found her sound asleep, alone. He lifted the child from the cover by slipping his hand under him. She slept next to the boy with her face turned to the other side, immersed in a deep sleep. He stepped forward, put his hand under the head, snatched the child, stole away, and carried him off toward his father. "You're dearer to me than my life and death. Off to the desert! To the desert! How fit is the camel?" "Excellent, more than excellent." "Off to the desert with you! Didn't I tell you to travel by night? I am not going with you. I'll stay here. Tomorrow morning, I want to enjoy watching the spectacle of 13.2

انا رايحٍ معك، ابشوف باكر جنونه على الورع حتى انّه ينقع الما على كبدي، وانت انحش. وهو يجيب الذلول وهو يخطّيه لَه خطوتين يبيّن جرّته على الرمل وهو يركبه وهو يسحب.

٣،١٣ يوم جا الصبح وجا ابن عريعر يعَمَل القهوه وهو يصَوِّت، قال: وين الولد؟ قالوا: الولد عندك. ايه، هات الولد رد الولد، ما لقوا الولد، والى سالفة اللي يقول: ياثوب من شقّك. ويفزع ابن عريعر وتفزع قومه معه يدوّرون الولد، يركضون يمين ويسار، المره والرجل والصغير والكبير والراعي والمعزّب. وشايع مبسوط عليهم يضحك. يوم تلَيّشوا من الدورِه وتليّمَوا. قال شايع: عرفت هالحين يابن عريعر غلا العيال؟ تخبر يوم انت اول تقول لي وش علمك تْحاتي وبالتالي سِكَتّ وقلت لك صْبَيّ وزلّت عجاريفه! سِكَتّ يوم اني ايقنت ان ولدي يجي ويْعَمل بك هالنيّه، عاد تَوّي انشرح خاطري. قال: انت صاق انت؟ قال: شف مبرك ذلوله بالمحل الفلاني، انهج وراع له.

٤،١٣ وينهجون يا مير هذا اثر الذلول واثر الليد (= الوليد)، خْطَيّواتُه عند مبرك الذلول. وارسل على عميره يسوم ولده انت يابن عريعر. قال: يجن خمسين بكره وسْلَعْهن خيل والخيل ما ياطن الا على زل من الحسا الى جبه وابوي معهن. قالوا: ما هي خلفةٍ البل والخيل، بس المشكل الزل من اين لنا زل نفرشه من الحسا الى جبه. يوم بلشوا، قال شايع: صوتوا للصانع. وهم يصوتون للصانع. قال له شايع: إحذ الخيل زل علشان تْتَمّم كلام ولدي عميره.

٥،١٣ عاد يقول شايع:

١ اخـذت ثلاث سنين في حبس خير　　والرابعـه جاني صدوق الفعـايـل
غــلامٍ ما بعــد خــط شــاربــه　　ولا جال في قلبه من الخوف جايـل

him beside himself with grief because of his little child. That will sprinkle clean water on my liver. And you: flee now!" ʿAmīrah brought the riding camel and made sure to have it pace up and down a few times and make its tracks in the sand conspicuous. Then he mounted and slipped away.

Next morning, Ibn ʿRēʿir was preparing coffee and called for the boy. On 13.3
being told that the boy was supposed to be with him, he gave orders to bring him at once, wherever he might be. But he was nowhere to be found. Now the story went: "O shirt, who has torn you up?"[197] Ibn ʿRēʿir raised the alarm and the entire camp joined the search. Everyone started running left and right—women, men, young and old, workers and their masters. Shāyiʿ was exhilarated. He openly laughed as he watched the commotion. When they gathered, panting from fatigue, Shāyiʿ said, "Do you understand now, Ibn ʿRēʿir, how dear one holds his children? Do you remember when you first said to me, 'What's the matter? Something troubling you?' After that, I kept my thoughts to myself and only said, 'A boy weaned from his childish pranks.'[198] I remained silent, feeling confident that my son would come and pay you back. I must say, my mood has much improved watching this scene." "You're not speaking in jest?" "If you don't believe me, go to where he couched his mount," and he pointed to the place.

They hurried over, and what they saw removed the last shred of doubt: the 13.4
tracks of the riding camel and the imprints of the little boy's tiny feet. He sent a messenger to ʿAmīrah to bargain for his son's return. Shāyiʿ's son imposed his conditions: "Fifty young female camels with a complement of horses.[199] The horses should come treading on carpets all the way from al-Ḥasā to Jubbah to accompany my father." They had no trouble with the horses and camels. The problem was the carpets: where do we find enough carpets to lay a road of carpets from al-Ḥasā to Jubbah? Puzzled, they groped for a solution. Shāyiʿ said, "Call a craftsman!" He told the craftsman, "Shoe the horses with pieces of carpet. That answers the conditions laid down by my son ʿAmīrah!"

Shāyiʿ then composed this poem: 13.5

Three years I was jailed by a worthy; *1*
  year four, a lionhearted savior came:[200]
Stout fellow, too young for mustache;
  no trace of fear stole into his heart.

دنّق علـيّ مظـنون عيـني واحبّـني   ودموع عينه فوق صدري شلايـل
وانا الحديـد بسـاق رجلي مغـلّق   والرجل كلّت من شبوك الحبايـل
تعـيش ياشبلٍ صطى ليـلة الدجى   على ولد شيخٍ عـامـلٍ بي هوايـل
صطى وجاب الورع من عند والده   ومن عند زين اللون شقرا جدايـل
حديته على دربٍ صعيبٍ ولا هفى   وجاب الذي ضَجّت عليه القبايـل
صطى وزَمّ الورع ومـرّن واحبّـني   وجلى عْني مِرٍّ على الكبد غـايـل
وشـاله على قطّاعـة الريـد وجنا   مـا يلحقنـه نـاتـلات الجـدايـل
اقفى على وضحا كما الهيق وصفها   تشـدي لهيقٍ مع شفـا الريع زايـل
طلب ثقيل الروز وضحٍ فطايـر   وضحٍ رِبَن بديار زوبع جلايـل
وطلب جوادينٍ من الخيل غيرهن   يعرفونهن من مكرمات الاصايـل
وعيّوا بهن زوبع على واضح النقا   وصكّوا قفاهن مقحمين الدبايـل
ومن عقب ما انا حافي الرجل عندهم   جوني بعـد ذلك يبون الجمـايـل
يعيش ابن شايع تقاصى بمطلبه   من الخيل وأيضا من خيار السلايـل
ومن عقب ما ني ضهيـدٍ عنـدهـم   اليوم تصلى كبودهـم بالملايـل
أخذ ثار ابوه وثار عمـه وعـزوتـه   وثارا وطمّـن راس من كان عـايـل
عسى غـلامٍ ما فعـل فِعِـل والده   تسفى عليه مسهسهات الرمايـل
يعيش ابن مرداس من مرقب العلى   رفـاع المباني من كبـار الحمايـل
وقرمٍ نِفَل بالفود من زايد السطر   ابوه وجـدّه مخضّبين السلايـل

Apple of my eye! You kneeled, kissed,
  wept, teardrops dripping on my breast.
You found me, ankles shackled in iron,
  feet numb from being tied with rope.
Hail, lion cub! You leapt from the dark
  to snatch the son of a shaykh, my scourge.
He pounced and grabbed his father's dearest;
  darling of a pearly, auburn-haired beauty.
I sent him the hard way; he didn't falter:
  his catch shook an entire tribe to the core.
He struck, lifted the kid, kissed me quickly,
  wiping out my liver's bitter crust of spite,
Swept him up on a strong desert crosser,
  too swift even for spirited thoroughbreds.
His getaway camel, ostrich white,
  zips over crests of distant sandy slopes.
The heavyweight claimed back his camels:
  mighty white herds on Zōbaʿ's land;
Claimed two steeds, golden purebreds:
  his noble racers, famous far and wide.
Loath to cede, Zōbaʿ declared open war,
  ready to risk life for proud possessions.[201]
Barefoot, I met from them callous unconcern;
  now they're all sweet talk and blandishments.
Hail to Shāyiʿ's son, harsh terms he imposed:
  horses and camels bred from champion strains.
Suffocating in cruel bondage, I rejoice,
  seeing red-hot torment bake their entrails.
He took glorious revenge for father and tribe:
  avenged, we stand tall, lower evildoers' heads.
If young men fail to match fathers' feats,
  let them be buried under windblown sands.
Long live Ibn Mirdās, nobility's crown,
  denizen of mighty tribes' lofty dwellings:
Extreme in exuberance, extravagant in loot,
  he outdid his ancestors, doughty warriors all.

قطيفان ابن رمال يفِكّ عميره ولد شايع من العريعر

عميره ولد شايع غزّاي معه له ركب. يوم انكف والى جيشهم مِنْتَلّ من طول الفْرَج. ويصادفه سلف ابن عريعر ويتقامعون هم واياهم. والى بنت ابن عريعر معهم على ظلّه تتلي السلف ويزبن عليّه عميره، لوّح على ظهر قعودَه وزبن عليه. قالت: سلمت وخاب طالبك. والى مير ولدٍ مزيون وشباب، على اوّله وعليه قْرون. ونزل عميره ضيف عند العريعر. عشقته بنت ابن عريعر وطلبته يجي عنده وتَعَذّرَه بس هي غْصِبْتُه، تبيه، ماتت عليه، غصبته على هالدرب. وكان هكالليله عليهم غِدر، مطر. وهو يثور يبي يلوّذ عليه مع قفو البيت وعلى ما برق البرق يامار يشوف الذيب فاتح افمه عاديٍ على الغنم، قال: ١،١٤

توافقت انا والذيب بليلة الدجا والكل منا يـدّعي بنصيب ٢،١٤
صارت خزيزة الذيب عيثا سمينه ينسف على فوق اليدين غصيب

غصيب شحم ولحم.

وانا من الخفرات بيضا غريره تنسف قرونٍ كنهن رطيب

يوم جا الصبح وثار من عندَه يا ريحة العنبر اللي عليّه صابغٍ بشيابُه، ريحٍ فاضح، ٣،١٤
عنبرٍ ما يوجد الا عند الشيوخ. وخاف ينفضح عند ابن عريعر، قاموا خوياوه

ʿAmīrah, Shāyiʿ's Son, Is Liberated from Ibn ʿRēʿir's Jail by Gṭēfān ibn Rmāl

The camels of ʿAmīrah, Shāyiʿ's son, were worn out from long desert journeys in search of plunder. On the way back, they encountered the armed vanguard of Ibn ʿRēʿir's camel train and skirmishes broke out. The daughter of Ibn ʿRēʿir rode in the camel train carrying the tribe's chattels and families, seated in her camel-borne palanquin. Seeking safety, ʿAmīrah vaulted onto the sturdy beast and beseeched her to grant him a personal pledge of protection.[202] She took him under her wing. "You're safe. Your pursuers failed!" she assured him. She saw that he was a handsome lad, an energetic young man in the flower of youth, wearing his hair in long greased tresses. She had given him asylum, and as a result ʿAmīrah stayed as a guest with Ibn ʿRēʿir. The daughter of Ibn ʿRēʿir had fallen in love with him, and she invited him to visit her tent, but he excused himself. She did not take no for an answer; she put him under such pressure that he had to oblige. She wanted him. She was head over heels in love with him. Dying of love. He was left no choice, and they spent the night together. It was foul weather, cold and rainy. He quickly made for her tent. As he took shelter at the wall of her tent in the midst of a thunderstorm flashing with lightning, he saw a wolf running with jaws in a grin, his glistening canines attacking a flock of sheep. Then he said: 14.1

Wolflike I prowl under cover of night, 14.2
each of us claiming his God-given prey.
Fatty ewe became wolf's delicious treat,
layers of juicy meat wobbling over feet;

—*Ghaṣīb* means "meat with fat."

Mine a unique white, silky-skinned beauty:
she shakes black tresses cascading down.[203]

Come morning, in a hurry to leave her tent, he carried her aroma of ambergris on his clothes. The scent gave him away. A perfume as costly as ambergris 14.3

قالوا: توّك ذبحتنا لعن ابوك. حطّوا عليه من عبس البل، البول، وعرّقوه كنه وجعان. قالوا: تغلمط ونِم كنك مريض لا تجلس عند العريعر يشمّون ريحتك تفضحنا. انتبهت البنت قالت: يايبه ترى ابن رمال ما صيده وجعان بس انه فشلان يجلس مع الرجال وهو ما عليه هِدْمٍ يلاحن (= زين) مير دونك هالعباة كبّعَه ايّاوه. قامت ارسلت لُه عباتّه جديده قالت لابوَه: عطو ابن رمال هالعباة تراوه مستحي لا يجلس معك وهو ما عليه هدومٍ تواجه. يوم جوا عيال العريعر شافوا عباة بنت عمهم عليه قاموا يتخازرون ويتقارصون بالعيون، نووا به النيه.

٤،١٤ يا مير قطيفان ابن رمال عندهم، وهو يدري بنيّتهم، انهم يعني نوَوا يذبحون عميره عيال العريعر. يوم ناموا العرب اشار قطيفان على عميره انه يهجّ عنهم، قال: اسرَوا، انحاشوا ترى هالعيال ناوينك. قدامهم لهم قاع وسيع. قال: آلى وصلتوا القاع الفلاني هاتوا ما وراهن واقرطوا خطوات المشعاب هنااااك، شَنَق، قرطَة الولد النشيط، واقرطوا خطواة الدلو، القلص، مع اثر الجيش. وهم يتقوّدونهن على هوينهم وبخفيه لما طلعوا من البيوت. يوم جوا القاع وهم يجيبون ما وراهن ويقومون لك يقرّطون من قشّهم يمين ويسار.

٥،١٤ العريعر يوم قعدوا الصبح والى ابن رمال وخوياوه ما هم عندهم. قال: خيلكم يالعريعر، اطلبوهم. قال قطيفان: يابن عريعر انا اشير عليك انك لا ترمّي بخيل العريعر، هذولي عندهم لهم شجرةٍ يرعن اباعرهم مْنَه وعظامهن صمّ ما هن على ما بخاطرك يعني ان الخيل تبي تلحقهن، والله انهن الى منّ الراكب شْعَبَه بالمحجان

was only found with shaykhs.[204] He grew scared that Ibn ʿRēʿir would find out about his escapade. His comrades said, "Well done. Now you've sealed our doom. God curse your father!" They poured camel urine over him and rubbed it in as if he had fallen ill. They told him to drape garments over his head and cover up, close his eyes, and show himself withdrawn as if he were seriously unwell.[205] They warned him to stay away from Ibn ʿRēʿir's majlis because the bouquet he carried would compromise him and expose him to the wrath of her kin. The girl understood their quandary. She said, "Father, he is not really ailing, but Ibn Rmāl is ashamed to sit in a majlis full of worthies while dressed in these wretched clothes. I'll give him one of my cloaks to put on." She sent him a brand-new set of clothes, telling her father, "Give this cloak to Ibn Rmāl. It is embarrassing for him to sit with you in such an improper outfit." When the clan's young adults joined them in the majlis, amazed to see him dressed in the girl's cloak, they exchanged malicious glances and meaningful winks. They had something in store for him.

It so happened that Gṭēfān ibn Rmāl had been staying with them for a while. 14.4
He knew that the young men of Ibn ʿRēʿir were plotting to kill ʿAmīrah. After everyone had gone to sleep, Gṭēfān urged ʿAmīrah to flee: "Go now, escape while it is dark! Those fellows are lusting after your blood." Away from the camp stretched a vast flat plain. "As soon as you have reached that plain, prod your mounts to run at their fastest pace! While galloping, you must throw your riding stick as far away as you can, with a strong youngster's energetic swing of the arm, whoosh, to the side. Throw whatever other utensils you carry—a bucket for drawing water, waterskins—so that they leave a trail of scattered gear in the wake of your camel troop!" Accordingly, they stealthily led out their camels and rode off with utmost quiet until they had left the camp behind. As soon as they came to the hard bottom of the vast plain, they urged their mounts to give it their all and began to throw their gear left and right in haphazard manner.[206]

At their morning gathering, the clansmen of al-ʿRēʿir found that Ibn Rmāl 14.5
and his companions were absent. "On your horses, sons of al-ʿRēʿir, catch them!" Gṭēfān said, "Ibn ʿRēʿir, if I were you I wouldn't exhaust your cavalry by going in vain pursuit. They feed their camels from certain bushes that grow in their land and their frames are as hard as stone. These riders are not what you think. Forget about your horsemen catching up with them! By God, if the rider hits his mount with a riding stick, the beast raises its tail and runs at a hot pace.

وقْمِصَت بذيله واحتمى ركضه انه من نشطه تفدّع بروحه وتجدّع قشه ومعاليقَه يمين ويسار من حمو ركضه. ما طاعوه واطلبوهم. يوم جوا القاع والى قشهم نثر. قال: جاي، جاي يالعريعر، صاقٍّ قطيفان، اللي هذا ركضهن ما حناب يمّهـن.

With the violent jerks of its movements, the mount throws off the rider's luggage and skins tied to its saddle, leaving the objects scattered left and right on the ground. That's because these camels run at such a blistering pace." Without heeding his advice, they raced off in hot pursuit. On reaching the plain, they found the scene as they had been told: the ground was littered with cast off utensils left and right. "Forget it. Back to where we came from!" he ordered his men. "Gṭēfān has spoken the truth.[207] We are no match for this kind of pace."

متفرقات

يقول شايع يتذكر الطيب: ١،١٥

ثلاث معـاني مـا يفعـلهن خَـيِّر   وانا احمد الله منهن هدومي نظايف
أولهـن من يسبي على بنت عمـه   وهو سترها الضـافي لو كان عـايف
والثـانيـه من يهِـــدّ وينْثِـني   يا حَـلّ ضَرْب مْصَقِّلات الرَهـايف
والثـالثـه من يعـطي ويطـري   لو جا من المِعـطَى عـلوم عنـايف
وانا مقدم الهيجا وانا ستر لابتي   وانا عقـيد عيـال غوشٍ ظـرايف
وانا دليـلتهـم يا خيّـــل الدجى   يا كَن عن ورد الدجى كل خـايف
وانا ثقيـل الرَوز وان كـاد كودهم   وبالسيف افـرّق للقـلوب الولايف
وانا ابن مـرداس فـتى الجود شـايع   قطّـاع بظهور الركاب التنـايف
يامـا حظينـا فوقهـن من غنيمـه   يا حـرّفوا سـرد المهـار العسـايف
اسوق النضـا بالقيض من يمّة العدا   ولا انْكِس الا عوص الانْضـا نحـايف
يامـا قـطعـنا ديـرة فوق ضُمَّـر   واسْري بهم واضْوي بحمر القطايف

Miscellaneous Verse

Shāyiʿ composed these verses on desirable character traits: 15.1

Three behaviors do not befit a gentleman;
thank God, they do not stain my clothes.
First, preying on daughters of one's kin:
her honor's shield you are, like it or not.
Second, soaring to pounce, and then recoiling
aghast when sharp blades hew and slay.
Third, vaunting one's charitable deeds,
though beneficiaries show ingratitude.
On battle's front line I cover my fellows:
a raiders' captain, I lead gallant youth;
Darkness closing in, I'm a desert pilot,
resolute when the gutless waver.
If perils mount, my resolve steels
my sword to sever hearts bound by love.
Ibn Mirdās, Shāyiʿ, without fear or reproach,
on camelback cleaves through the wilds.
Riding on and on, he harvests untold riches
from racing horses' numbing battle whirl.
In blistering heat I spur rugged mounts to foes,
homeward bound tramping woefully wasted,
Skeletal from vast distance crossed at night
to lift camel herds from well-appointed tents.

يقول يوم عيروه قالوا شايب على فاطر: ٢،١٥

انا ابن مرداس فتى الجود شايع   ازبّن المضيوم ريف القرايب
هو ليه ياربعي تسِبّون فاطري   تقولون له فاطر وراعيك عايب
ياما الحقت فاطري من قشّ بكره   وياما الحقت من عين شبٍّ وشايب
وياما سرت بي فاطري عقب عشوه   دليلٍ الى شدّوا لعوص النجايب
وياما ورّدت بي عقلة هجعة الملا   يوم ان خليف الليل عند الحبايب
وانا كما داب المرقب يا غط نابه   عيّى على القرّاي ولَفّ العصايب
ياما على كوره ندوج الدويّه   وياما على كوره ندور الجلايب
وياما دوّجنا بالفي فوق كوره   وياما سرت بي مع فروع الجذايب
وياما سحبنا هجمة من مفاليَه   وياما حظينا من شخيل الجلايب
وياما ثنيته خلف الرديّات باللقى   يا ثار حِسّ معجّلات الضرايب
عساك يابكاي من غير نايبه   عساك تِبكى من كثير النوايب
الا من يبكي لذة شبا به   ما الوم من يبكي ليالى العجايب
وانا ابكي على زوبع ليا ابعدَن بهم   سنين المحل فيها عجاج وهبايب
وابكي على خيلان زوبع الى اوجهت   على طرش العدو ياخذونه نهايب
وابكي على شمر ولا احدٍ يلومني   كرام النفوس مولّعين الحرايب
وابكي على غلبا ولا دست عايبه   هل المكارم مخَلّصين النشايب

One day people ridiculed him, saying, "How odd, such an old guy on camel-back!" In response, he said: 15.2

I am Ibn Mirdās! Shāyiʿ, virtuous knight,
who shelters victims, generously serves his kin.
Why, my fellows, heap ridicule on my camel,
snickering: "Frail gray perched on an old bag!"
Many a time my old beast outran lithe lasses;
caught and overtook riders young and gray.
Through many a night she sped with me,
noble trotters' desert pilot on course.[208]
In dark she sniffs out remote water holes,
while weaklings cavort in women's quarters.
If I sink my fangs into flesh, like a rock viper,
Qur'an readings and bandages are no remedy.[209]
Often we rode wearily across lonesome plains,
tireless and tenacious in search of plunder,
Or wended our way through shady patches,
plotting a route in valleys' upper reaches:
Beyond belief the countless camel herds;
unfathomable the sheer size of our hauls.
My delight is in shielding fear-stricken stragglers in retreat;
I revel in earsplitting roars, crackling shots.[210]
If the faint of heart wail at scratches,
what tears they'd shed at true disaster!
Crying for one's halcyon days is different:
who does not pine for sweet nights of yore?
I grieve seeing the Zōbaʿ tribe chased off
by years of drought and storms of dust.
I grieve for splendid horsemen of Zōbāʿ
raiding enemy herds to seize spoil galore.
Grieving for Shammar brings no disgrace:
noble souls, eager to light flames of war.
Let's weep for warriors of the Victorious Plume;
great heroes, they solve tangled knots.[211]

ويقول يتذكر ربعه: ٣،١٥

قال ابن مـرداس فـتى الجود شـايع   سيـلٍ تحـدّر من هَفوف شفـيف
أحب الوغى واتعب على الطيب والوفا   وعـرضي عن درب المعيـب نظـيف
واعـشي الجـيران واكـرم ضـيوفي   وقت المجـاعـه والزمـان كسيف
ياما غـزيت وجبت عـيرات النضا   ومن قفوي عجلات الركاب زفيف
وانا سبرهـن يا اقْفَن وانا عقـيدهـن   وانا الدليـله وباللقـــا ظـريف
وادل الوعد واضوي على عزبة العدا   واضوي الى كَنّ الذليـل مخـيف
كم منهلٍ شـربت مخبث غـريفـه   لو مـاه من كثر العجـاج غـريف
وكم شيخ قوم بالملاقا جـدعتـه   لو هو في يوم الكتـــال عنـيف
وانا من اهـل الضـلع الطويـل البين   اللي على كل الجبـــال منـيف
حيـد سكن به قبلنـا حـاتم الصخا   من خـلقـتـه للغـانمـين شـريف
سقـاوه من نَوّ الثـريا مخـــايـل   وسيـله على كل الديار مطـيف
تقـافا مزون الوسـم تخضـر جوانبه   وتلقى زمـاليق السـليـح تغـيف
دار بهـا ربّو ربوعي بالصخـــا   عفّوا جوانـبهـا بكل رهـيف
ونطـرّد الاجنـاب مـا ياصـلونهـا   عسى يسقّـيها من المزون خـريف
وبايمـانـنا زرق العـتل عـدلة القنـا   ومن فوقهـن ريش النعـام يغـيف
من مات ما حاش الثنا وادرك العـلا   ممشاوه من جوف العبـاد ضعـيف
وانا ابن مـرداس فـتى الجود شـايع   ما صـرت يوم للمهـزلـين ولـيف

Saluting kinsfolk, he said: 15.3

Ibn Mirdās, generous Shāyiʿ, unleashed verses
like torrents released by rain-laden clouds.
I love din of battle, faithful to my struggle
to keep honor unstained by ignoble deeds.
I feed my neighbors and pamper guests,
though beset by hunger and starvation.
I love raiding, loot of lean-bellied camels,
a tight-knit band speeding along in my wake.
On the march, I am scout and commander,
skilled desert pilot, adroit if battle is joined.
At night I stalk enemies, find the rendezvous,
when weaklings cower and hunker down.[212]
Often I scooped up foul dregs from holes,
water roiled with dust and windblown sand.[213]
A dueling knight, I unsaddled many a shaykh,
no matter how fearsome in battle he loomed.
I hail from the Mountain, visible from afar;
tall and proud, it dominates the surrounding land:
Granite rock dwelling of Ḥātim al-Ṭāʾī
of generous disposition, hospitality's paragon.
May rains of the Pleiades shower his land,
unleash torrents to drench the plains;[214]
May a cumulus sail in to lay carpets of green,
and a softish breeze stir succulent stalks of *silīḥ*.
My homeland sprouts a munificent breed:[215]
victorious, sword in hand, they keep it safe;
Rival tribes are chased away—they don't get close.
Clouds of fall, sprinkle our blessed realm!
Tilting long-shafted lances, we gallop forth,
tufts of ostrich feather aflutter at the blade.
To die in obscurity, short of eternity's rock,
is to cut a poor figure among God's folk.
I am Ibn Mirdās, famed as generous Shāyiʿ,
not one to suffer weaklings, not a single day.

ويقول في جماعته: ٤٫١٥

يقول ابن مرداس فتى الجود شايع   أنا بطـل لا شـك ربعي هـلايـم
لى جبت لهم بالليل علم يسرهم   الصبح راحوا للعـدا بالنـمايـم
انا من اتلى جيل كسابة الثنا   وجيل الثنا ما باقي الا الذمايـم
وانا باول جيل منّانة العطا   مشاورة النسوان عنـد اللزايـم
انا من قوم هـــات لا هـاك   لا جاضعتهم رادعات الوشايـم
وانا مثل داب الرجم لى ناش نوشه   ما ينفعه قاري وكثر الحزايـم

These verses are addressed to his kinsmen: **15.4**

Thus spoke Ibn Mirdās, generous Shāyiʿ: *1*
I'm a hero; for kin I have rotten slackers.
If I do them a good turn in the evening,
come morn, they malign me to my foe.
I'm the last of a long line of honorable men;
the rest of my kinsmen are odious rogues:
First in a generation that boasts of its giving,
that are reminded of duty by women;[216]
Folks apt to say "Give!" not "Take!" *5*
—May tattooed beauties refuse their bed!
If my head whips forward, rock viper-like,
Qur'an verse and cloth don't cure its bite.[217]

Notes

1 For Ibn Gidrān (CA Ibn Qudrān), see Introduction. The Asaʿidah have largely led an existence separate from other sections of ʿUtaybah, a confederation based in the area between Riyadh and Mecca in central Najd. It is believed that the Asāʿidah first settled in al-Zilfī, and moved from there to Bagʿā in the fifteenth century (al-ʿUṣaymī, *Shuʿarā' ʿUtaybah*, 1:19).

2 This is the first of Shāyiʿs many marvelous feats. The one-eyed hero has eyesight far stronger than that of ordinary beings, a physical trait that bespeaks his shrewdness and farsighted leadership. See Introduction, n. 2.

3 Though matchlocks and early flintlocks were used in the seventeenth century, and a reference to these weapons occurs in a Nabaṭī poem addressed to Barakāt al-Sharīf al-Mushaʿshaʿī (d. 1615 or 1610), it seems unlikely that in the seventeenth century hunters in remote areas such as these would have routinely used firearms. See Kurpershoek, *Love, Death, Fame*, xvii; lii n27; 119; 271n373.

4 "Hear": *yā-khāl*, the poet addresses his maternal uncle, whose identity is not given or known.

5 The same image occurs in §15.2, v. 7 and §15.4, v. 7.

6 "Rock hole": *jibuw, jibiyyah*, pl. *jibāwah, jibūwah, jibā*, "water hole in rocks (*ṣifā*) with a narrow mouth of considerable depth" (*ǵaltah* is a smaller water hole in the rocks) (Hess Archive).

7 The sayings of this and the previous verse make the point that for ventures to be crowned with success certain preconditions must be fulfilled.

8 The verse is almost identical to Ibn Ẓāhir's line: "Do not purvey the vile gossip of the depraved; / honest men decline a drink of melted fat" (*wla yingil al-mingāl rajlin bi-jayyid / wla yishrab ad-dahn al-mdhāb rjāl* (Kurpershoek, *Love, Death, Fame*, 55); i.e., they do not practice dishonesty and dissimulation, a virtue expressed by Abū Qays ibn al-Aslat: "Prudence and firmness are better than / dissimulation, weakness and wavering" (*al-ḥazmu wa-l-quwwatū khayrun mina l / -idhāni wa-l-fakkati wa-l-hāʿī*) (al-Mufaḍḍal, *Dīwān al-Mufaḍḍaliyyāt*, 1:568; 2:226).

9 A common note struck in the poetry of the period, e.g., "We aim to manipulate the world's grindstone, yet attempts at guiding her must come to naught" (Kurpershoek, *Love, Death, Fame*, 31).

10 The poet cautions that circumspection in and of itself may not protect one from the fickleness of Fate: the benefits you enjoy today may go to someone else tomorrow. Almost the same words are found in a poem with the same rhyme and meter by Rumayzān (mentioned in Kurpershoek, *Arabian Satire*, xliv, xlv, 146n98): *w-kam gāʿidin bi-ẓ-ẓill w-inzāḥ ẓillih / w-kam gāʿidin bi-sh-shams jāh ẓlāl* ("Often shade forsakes those in its shelter / to favor those who were roasted by the sun") (Sowayan, *al-Shiʿr al-Nabaṭī*, 425); and Ibn Ẓāhir: *fa-kam mistiẓillin zāl ʿanh ẓlālih / w-kan jālisin fī sh-shams jāh ẓlāl* ("Don't forget: your spot in the shade may yet fade; / comfort one who bakes in scorching heat") (Kurpershoek, *Love, Death, Fame*, 55).

11 The motif of a girl suspected of going to a tryst while in fact on the lookout at night for distant flashes of lightning, the conventional heralds of rains and fertility, also occurs in the story of Bahīj, the chief of the Sinbis, a branch of ʿBēd (ʿUbayd) of Ṭayy and ʿIgdah, a village in Jabal Ajā, a tribe that was ousted from the area by Shammar (Sowayan, *Ayyām al-ʿarab*, 245).

12 A simile borrowed from poetical usage, as in this image of snowflakes fluttering down: "At dusk, a cover of white like shredded shirts" (Kurpershoek, *Bedouin Poets of the Nafud Desert*, §52.3, v. 10).

13 "Foothills": *lughf*, pl. *lghūf*, a synonym for *sāhid*, pl. *syāhid*, "steep side of a sand hill; the foot of a sand hill" (Hess Archive).

14 The identity of those who appealed for help is not mentioned. Certain quarters of al-Jawf were partially inhabited by families of the Rmāl, the tribe of Ibn Gidrān and Shāyiʿ, who had migrated there from Jubbah (Madawi Al Rasheed, *Politics in an Arabian Oasis*, 151). Starting in 1838, the campaign of ʿAbdallah ibn Rashīd and his brother ʿUbayd ended in 1842 with the incorporation of al-Jawf into the Rashīdī domains (al-Suwaydāʾ, *Manṭiqat Ḥāʾil ʿabra al-taʾrīkh*, 364–68).

15 Formulaic numbers such as pitched battles being fought for seven nights and the drawn-out peregrination that follows give a Hilālī touch to the tale.

16 "Barriers": *mitārīs*, sg. *matras*, "wall made of stone, a mass of rock, used as a rampart or used as cover by hunters when shooting at game" (Euting, *Tagebuch einer Reise in Inner-Arabien*, 2:71).

17 The reference is to the northern Bedouin settled in Mghērā and other communities in al-Jawf before being put to flight by Ibn Gidrān and his Shammar troops.

18 At the time, there was no country called Jordan. The narrators sometimes use the names of modern states in the area in order to give the listeners a rough indication of the geography of tribal movements. Shammar tribal movements were generally in a northern direction, hence the names Jordan, Syria, and Iraq feature whenever the dramatis personae cross the borders of the current state of Saudi Arabia.

19 When Hind, the sister of the poet Imru' al-Qays, sought refuge with 'Uwayr ibn Shajnah following the death of their father, Ḥujr, 'Uwayr's fellow tribesmen used the same words and argument: "Let's usurp [lit., 'eat'] their possessions since they are already done for anyway [lit., 'eaten']." But 'Uwayr rejected their advice and conducted her and her retinue to safety, and was praised for doing so in verses by Imru' al-Qays (al-Iṣfahānī, *al-Aghānī*, 9:89). The betrayal of strangers and refugees under one's protection is one of the gravest infractions of the desert code of honor.

20 Lit., "to cut their horns."

21 A mare is led alongside the camel on which its owner rides in order to keep her from becoming fatigued and save her energy for battle, as was already the custom in pre-Islamic Arabia (Imru' al-Qays, *Dīwān*, 174).

22 Another image borrowed from poetry but more usually employed to compare a camel train carrying the howdahs of the women as they sway back and forth to the crowns of palm trees in a breeze, and not the armed vanguard as here.

23 In the desert, a fettered or chained prisoner was held in a hole in the ground. Tent poles were laid across it and "corn-sacks and other heavy articles heaped upon them, so as to leave only a small opening over the prisoner's face through which he may breathe" (Burckhardt, *Notes on the Bedouin and Wahabys*, 163).

24 The coded oral message, sent from captivity in the presence of one's enemy masters, has a long pedigree in Arabian storytelling. One pre-Islamic example is the message sent by Nāshib ibn Bishāmah al-ʿAnbarī of Banū Tamīm, held prisoner by the Lahāzim tribe, warning his fellow tribesmen about an imminent raid by the Lahāzim. See, e.g., *al-ʿIqd al-Farīd* under the heading "Ayyām Bakr ʿalā Tamīm, Yawm al-Waqīṭ."

25 "Desert well": *ʿiglah*, "a well by a channel or in a valley, which caves in after heavy rains and has to be restored" (Musil, *The Manners and Customs of the Rwala Bedouins*, 676); "well deeper than a *thamīlah* (water hole hidden under the ground) and less deep than a *rakiyyah* (well without stone casing) from which water may be hoisted with the help of a rope the same length as a rope used to hobble a camel, *ʿuqāl*)" (al-Suwaydāʾ, *Min shuʿarāʾ al-Jabal*, 2:214).

26 See Introduction, p. x.

27 "Three days for escape": *al-mharribāt* (CA *haraba*, "to flee, escape"). Three days are given to someone who has contracted a blood guilt (known as a *dwumī*) and his close kin to make their escape and put themselves under the protection of another tribe, where such a person is known as a *jalawī*, "an exile from a tribe who has sought asylum with another tribe" (Hess Archive, 7867).

28 "Style of the Banū Hilāl": *mithl ṭawy al-Hlālāt*; the comparison is with the construction of a well's stone casing, *ṭawy*.

29 The poem that follows in §1.15 resembles a poem with the same rhyme that is recited in the Najdī Banū Hilāl cycle of narrative and verse. It is ascribed to the tribal leader Ḥasan ibn Sirḥān in response to a challenge by the Hilālī hero Abū Zayd. Verses 4–7 of this poem open with the formula "That night we halted at" (*ʿashiyyah ʿashshēnā*), which also occurs nine times in the Banū Hilāl poem (Sowayan, *Ayyām al-ʿarab*, 1031–32).

30 "They surged": On the use of the Hilālī word for "to set out" (*tigallalaw*, "to pack up and carry loads," CA *istaqalla*, "to lift; transport") and its occurrence in this position of the verse, see Kurpershoek, *Love, Death, Fame*, liv n43.

31 Implicit is the notion that even ranking maidens of the tribe, who would normally keep inside the tent, are hard at work because of the exceptional circumstances of migration.

32 Lit., "she draws the hem of her cloak over the ground."

33 In the Banū Hilāl poem (see n. 29), al-Aṭwā is mentioned as a well marking one of the stages. The transmitter of that poem comments that it is fifty fathoms deep and situated far inside the Nafūd sands.

34 Anbaṭ is situated in the area of Wadi al-Khirr; written as Qaṣr Ambaṭ by Musil, who also reports the presence of extensive surfaces covered with salt (*Northern Neǧd*, 13, 170).

35 As expressed in §1.15, v. 8, the ancestors are, as it were, fighting side by side with their offspring. The fighters' battle cries encourage them to give it their utmost. In the genealogical scheme (see Introduction), Ibn Gidrān is the great-grandson of ʿAmīrah, the first ancestor of the Rmāl tribe.

36 Cf. Imru' al-Qays: *wa-dhā shuṭabin ghāmiḍan kalmuhū*, "a sword leaving wounds too deep to measure" (*Dīwān*, 86). Praise for the enemy in war songs is common practice in boastful poetry, based on the notion that defeating valiant adversaries lends greater luster to one's victory. Because tribal warfare and rivalry are deeply personal, expressions of respect for the enemy reflect the importance attached to the maintenance of a measure of stability in a society of perpetual tribal competition.

37 In Hilālī-style poetry, the male camel carrying the tribe's leading maiden in her howdah is conventionally described as fast and indefatigable, in spite of the weight on its back, e.g., "A mighty bull, [. . . .] when it hears the caravan leader's chant, the camel keeps pace with the pack in front" (Kurpershoek, *Love, Death, Fame*, 85).

38 In the various genealogical schemes for Shammar, the name Zōbaʿ is especially associated with the tribal division of Sinjārah. The Rmāl used to head the Ghfēlah section and in addition were considered paramount shaykhs of the Sinjārah division (Von Oppenheim, *Die Beduinen*, 1:156–58).

39 Herdsmen are usually from the tribe's lower ranks or servants, not skilled in fighting. Without the presence of armed guards, *janab*, they are defenseless against enemy

raiders. The verse boasts that their tribe's redoubtable reputation deters attackers. Therefore, even its humble herdsmen feel at ease and speak derisively of other tribes.

40 "Fat-Laden Platters": the sobriquet is meant as an encomium to the shaykh's boundless hospitality and slaughtering of fat animals for his guests.

41 Gidrān and Mṣabbiḥ are the sons of Khanshar, who was one of the nine sons of ʿAmīrah, the first ancestor of the Rmāl. In this genealogical scheme, Shāyiʿ ibn Mirdās is a grandson of Mṣabbiḥ. Jārid, the great-great-grandson of Shāyiʿ, is held to be the origin of one of the branches of the Rmāl at this time.

42 "Energetic": *yrakbin*, "to ride out frequently and with great vigor," derived from *rićib*, "to ride" (communication from Saad Sowayan).

43 "Lowlands of Iraq": *sīb al-ʿIrāq*; here, *sīb* means "flowing line seen at the horizon"; i.e., the confluence of the Euphrates and Tigris rivers, known as the Shaṭṭ al-ʿArab, as it appears from afar to camel riders coming from the higher desert ground to the river's southwest.

44 The return at the twinkling of the morning star is a common motif; cf. §8.9.

45 As described in *The Iliad*: "The sharp stone hit him in the forehead and smashed both brows in on each other, nor could the bone hold the rock, but his eyes fell out in the dust before him there at his feet" (Homer, *The Iliad*, trans. Lattimore, 371).

46 At this point, an ordinary Bedouin yarn transfigures into a narrative that more properly belongs to the magical world of fantastic storytelling in the style of *The Thousand and One Nights*, of which it is the sole example in this corpus (see Introduction).

47 Ḥātim al-Ṭāʾī is similarly solicitous about the mother of only one child: "O Māwiyah, I captured many a mother's only child, only to let him live and free to go" (al-Iṣfahānī, *al-Aghānī*, 17:385).

48 With similar wording, a woman called Gwayyilah, the wife of a lower-class Bedouin who decided to join a raiding party in spite of his lack of experience and a suitable mount, beseeches the raid leader, Bkhīt al-ʿAṭāwī, to take him in his care (Kurpershoek, *The Story of a Desert Knight*, 232–39). Like Gwayyilah, the mother of ʿĀmir ibn Khafājī entrusted her son to the Hilālī heroes Dhiyāb ibn Ghānim and Abū Zayd by presenting to them two large mutton chops (Sowayan, *al-Ṣaḥrāʾ al-ʿarabiyyah*, 300).

49 In Arabian storytelling, an old woman, *ʿajūz*, living alone by herself somewhat separate from her kin group's dwellings, often plays such a role as an initial informant and guiding contact for the story's protagonist.

50 In Najdī oral tradition about Banū Hilāl, the *ṣlubī*, in the role of evil messenger, appears on the scene to bring the Hilālī hero, Abū Zayd, the tragic news. In the majlis, the same piece of theater is enacted as the one that made the fiancée of Shāyiʿ abandon hope of ever seeing her beloved again. Abū Zayd had to be convinced of the death of ʿAlyā in

order to make him start on the Hilālī westward migration away from Najd. The motif remains the same, though in each example the narrative takes different turns.

51 Shāyiʿ's model, Ḥātim al-Ṭāʾī, is no stranger to this epic strain and its fondness for bloody detail. He boasts of the many generous gentlemen who through his thrusts "thunderously tumbled into the dust, peritoneum ripped open, entrails laid bare." The graphic detail of violent death is reminiscent of Aias driving his spear into an enemy who "dropping in the dust, clawed the ground in his fingers" (Homer, *The Iliad*, trans. Lattimore, 327).

52 For a similar scene, but inverted, with the shaykh lighting a fire in the morning and asking about the whereabouts of his missing daughter or son, see §7.10 and §13.3.

53 "Real man": *rajlī aṣ-ṣiǵǵ* (for *ṣidǵ*, CA *ṣidq*).

54 The motif of a bride and her promised husband being treacherously separated in favor of another contender for her hand is a familiar one in Arabian storytelling, though not with such gruesome detail as here. See Introduction, n. 41.

55 "Extinction": *hāfīn*; *hafā*, "to perish; to fall down" (CA *hafā*).

56 From the context, it appears that the old man was not Ibn Gidrān's father but rather an uncle or other elder relative.

57 Artful speech spoken by a person in the throes of death is a time-honored motif in Arabian lore, as it is in Italian opera. For example, advice to posterity given by dying poets or the poem composed by a poet known as Muṭawwaʿ Ushayqir, one of the lyrical "martyrs of love," that literally ended in his last gasp (Sowayan, *al-Shiʿr al-Nabaṭī*, 383–92; Kurpershoek, *Love, Death, Fame*, xvii).

58 Legend does not show Shāyiʿ as pious in a religious sense but rather as inspired by the traditional codes and customs of the Bedouin. The narrator's comment clearly stems from §2.12, v. 5, which itself may represent a later addition meant to bring the lore in line with the stern religiosity introduced by the later rise of Wahhabi doctrines, as may have happened to other early pieces of verse. Also, the narrator may have taken the opportunity to advertise his own views on the subject.

59 Early ancestors, legendary or real, are by definition powerful because they are the ones who presumably established the lineage or tribe in the first place, while further down the generations, decline is an ever-present danger. In §2.12, vv. 2–8, we see a loose collection of gnomic wisdom commonly found in this type of poetry.

60 See n. 58.

61 Pugnacious advice of the "eat or be eaten" kind is typical for Najdī poetry of the era, e.g., Ḥmēdān al-Shwēʿir: "If the enemy strikes and you fail to repay in kind, your foe does not get stung and feels no fear" (Kurpershoek, *Arabian Satire*, 51).

62 "Black-haired": *sūdān al-rūs*, one of the nicknames of Shammar tribesmen, "a reference to the pride and power exhibited by them when, unlike the other Arabian tribes, they refused to comply with the Wahhabi practice of cutting their long hair and shaving their heads" (Sowayan, *The Arabian Oral Historical Narrative*, 9).

63 According to the tribe's genealogists, the earlier ʿAmīrah was Shāyiʿ's great-great-grandfather.

64 Hunting with cheetahs is a trope in Hilālī poetry (cf. Kurpershoek, *Love, Death, Fame*, xviii–xx), although it has a much longer history in Arabic poetry (cf. Montgomery, *Fate the Hunter*, §24). Here it is used by the narrator to imbue his story with a Hilālī atmosphere.

65 "Revenge": *abā th-thuwāriyyāt*, "hereby I take revenge for (so-and-so)," as Imruʾ al-Qays shouted, "*Yā-li-thārāt al-Malik! Yā-li-thārāt al-Humām*" ("I avenge al-Malik! I avenge al-Humām") (al-Iṣfahānī, *al-Aghānī*, 9:90; CA *thaʾr*, "revenge, vengeance, blood revenge"). In other narratives, ʿAmīrah resurfaces to free his father from bondage in an enemy camp; see §13.1.

66 Jubbah, a little oasis town at the edge of the sands, was traditionally known for the high-quality wooden saddles manufactured by its craftsmen.

67 The camel's tall neck is compared to the two stout poles planted in the ground at the sides of a well in order to support the roller on which the rope runs. The simile is apposite given the common comparison of a running camel's legs to the rapid movement of a pulley wheel suspended over a well as the bucket falls down in the shaft.

68 Shāyiʿ's son ʿAmīrah had other ideas about women at the caravan's rear; see §14.1.

69 The transmitter explains that the verse refers to a purebred camel mount, but the wording is typical for descriptions of horses. The nervous impatience of the horse might be taken in a general figurative sense as a call to action.

70 The generosity of a shaykh or ruler brings prosperity to the receivers, as do the rains of late fall and early winter, this verse's "buckets" (*dlā*, sg. *dalw*; i.e., the constellation of the Pleiades, so called because it catches "water in a large bailing bucket and then pours it over the scorched land," Musil, *Rwala*, 226). Rain results in *ribīʿ*, a springtime of lush grazing for livestock, and lavish spenders are compared to "grassy plains" (Kurpershoek, *Arabian Satire*, §22.36).

71 Ibn Gidrān's complimentary nickname; see §2.1.

72 In poetry, deep winter in the northern Arabian desert represents the pinnacle of deprivation and hardship. It is too early in the season for new growth of herbage, while camels and Bedouin may suffer from cold and lack of food. If she-camels have not enough milk to feed their young, the owner may decide to slaughter an otherwise healthy she-camel in order to live up to the expectations of guests and his fellows. "Yearning": *mirzimāt*,

lit., "groaning she-camels"; i.e., they long for their young and yearn to suckle them, but in this case, they are lacking in milk. An axe is used to slaughter a camel by cleaving the animal's breast.

73 The members of the Āl Miflih family are the descendants of Miflih ibn ʿAwwād ibn Fālih al-Asʿadī. Al-Msattit, so called because he had six fingers, belonged to the Jʿafar branch of the ʿAbdah of Shammar. He concluded a pact with Ibn Jʿēthīr of the Asāʿidah to divide the area of Bagʿā between them. The Asāʿidah arrived in Bagʿā in exile (*jalwah*) following an internecine struggle in their tribal area in the Hijaz. According to local tradition, their arrival in Bagʿā dates from about 1520. See also n. 1.

74 Possibly the reference is to Saʿd ibn Ḥtērīsh, the leader of the Asāʿidah in their exile to Bagʿā.

75 Qaṣr Mārid is a pre-Islamic fortress in the ancient settlement of Dūmat al-Jandal in the region of al-Jawf. For the Bedouin it served as a symbol of unassailable strength and might.

76 Ibn Ḥatrūsh, see n. 74; other sources refer to the diminutive Ḥtērīsh.

77 The Asāʿidah of Bagʿā trace their descent to the Rūgah division of the ʿUtaybah confederation in central Najd.

78 Ajā is the principal chain of granite mountains, and the area around it is known as Shammar Mountain.

79 See Introduction.

80 The defiant wording clearly borrows from the common Hilālī stock. "Surmise": *yiḥrī*; i.e., the *ḥarāwī*, "whereabouts, place where one expects someone or something to be" (in this case, the enemy).

81 Again, common moral guidance given in oral Bedouin poetry of the time, e.g., one of many verses on the importance of friendship by al-Māyidī ibn Ẓāhir: "Be smart, overlook a friend's shortcomings: your kin may turn a deaf ear to your appeals" (Kurpershoek, *Love, Death, Fame*, 55).

82 The conventional Robin Hood ethic prominently featured in Bedouin poetry from pre-Islamic days on; see Introduction.

83 The reference is to the poet Muḥammad al-Sudayrī, a scion of a family that intermarried with the Sauds, and Ibn Ṭwālah, the chiefs of the Aslam division of Shammar.

84 See Introduction, Note on the Text.

85 Ḥmēdī al-Jarbā is known as the father of Muṭlaq, whose son Miṣlaṭ was killed in the decisive battle of Shammar against the Wahhabi troops in 1791, as a result of which the Jarbā shaykhs and their Shammar tribes emigrated to Mesopotamia. Muṭlaq himself was killed in 1798. No further information on Ḥmēdī is available.

86 "Sha'thā and Na'āmah": names for female riding camels of the highest quality that are given or impounded as blood money, taxes, or in other ways claimed by a higher authority or powerful leader (al-Suwaydā', *Manṭiqat Ḥā'il 'abra al-ta'rīkh*, 301).

87 The 'Ajarrash family belongs to the Thābit of the Sinjārah division of Shammar. Shwēsh al-'Ajarrash distinguished himself under the leadership of Ṣfūg al-Jarbā in battle against 'Anazah, earning him the title of "Knight of Shammar" (*fāris Shammar*) and "Falcon of Shalwā" (*ṭēr Shalwā*); see n. 88. Ṣfūg ibn Fāris al-Jarbā was killed by the Ottoman Turks in 1847.

88 "Brothers of Shalwā" (*ikhwāt Shalwā*): explained as the three sons of 'Ajarrash—Shwēsh, 'Adāmah, and Hīshān—who were brought up in Iraq by their grandmother because their father and mother died when they were still infants. They were taken under the protection of the leading Shammar shaykh, 'Abd al-Karīm al-Jarbā. Under the shaykh's banner, the brothers distinguished themselves in fighting the Ottoman Turks, shouting their battle cry: "I am the falcon of Shalwā (*anā ṭēr Shalwā*)," after the name of their grandmother who went around begging food for the infants, "my little birds" (*ṭwērātī*). This nineteenth-century phrase became an epithet for persons of an exceptionally brave, loyal, and generous disposition.

89 "Hobbled": *'gāl* (CA *'iqāl*) is a short rope used for hobbling a camel. In this context, the word was also used to denote a tax imposed by rulers on camel breeders, usually one of the finest camels (*sha'thā w-na'āmah*, see n. 86) from each sizable herd.

90 The same scene occurs in an episode about the al-Jarbā shaykhs in Iraq (Sowayan, *Ayyām al-'arab*, 46).

91 Ibn Ḥmēd (Ḥumayd) is the family name of the chiefs of the Bargā division of the 'Utaybah confederation in central Arabia.

92 Possibly the reference is to the "great epidemic that killed many in al-'Uyaynah, including the chief" in 1725–26 (Al Juhany, *Najd before the Salafi Movement*, 61; Kurpershoek, *Arabian Satire*, 163). It is not known for certain who Muḥammad al-Sharīf is, but one may conclude from his depredations that the historical memory evoked in this episode predates the establishment of Saudi rule in al-Dar'iyyah and after that in Riyadh, and the extension of Egyptian-Turkish control over the Hijaz (see Introduction). The seventeenth century was a time when "the Hijaz was completely independent under its Sharifs, who seem to have regarded themselves as the natural overlords of their desert hinterland, into which they were in the habit of making incursions either for punitive purposes, or for the replenishment of their treasuries. The first such raid, of which we are told by Ibn Bishr, took place in 1578, when Sharif Hasan abu-Nami [Abu Numayy] reached Riyadh with an army of 50.000 [sic] men, and spent a considerable time there, plundering and killing" (Philby, *Sa'udi Arabia*, 12). This corresponds to the motives

ascribed to the sharif in this story and the dating of the Shāyiʿ al-Amsaḥ legend's origins to the seventeenth century (see Introduction and the passage about Muḥammad ibn Aḥmad ibn Muḥammad al-Ḥārith ibn Abi Numayy, "Raids of the Sharifs against the Mountain," *Ghazawāt al-Ashrāf li-l-Jabal*, in al-Suwaydā', *Manṭiqat Ḥā'il*, 296–305).

93 Another anachronism: the poet Ibrāhīm ibn Juʿaythin from Tuwaym in Sudayr Province lived from 1844 to 1943.

94 Another example of legend being put in a time frame that corresponds to the better-remembered parts of the area's oral culture, i.e., early-nineteenth-century or late-eighteenth-century personalities and events, in this case the dynasty of the Ibn ʿAlī family prior to the Ibn Rashīd rule that represented the highwater mark of Bedouin culture. See Kurpershoek, *Bedouin Poets of the Nafūd Desert*, xxv.

95 The important settlement of Mōgag was the base of the Ghfēlah branch of the Sinjārah of Shammar. See Introduction.

96 Some lineages of Shammar maintain that they are genealogically related to the Great Sharifs of Mecca. See Introduction.

97 Ninety is a formulaic number often used in Hilālī-style narrative and verse, with the general meaning of "a large number."

98 Al-Ṣāyiḥ is a genealogical designation sometimes used for "the three divisions of Shammar that descend from Ṭayy—that is to say, al-Aslam, al-Khriṣah, and Sinjārah," which "are closer to each other that any of them to ʿAbdah" (Sowayan, *The Arabian Oral Historical Narrative*, 7). For Zōbaʿ, see n. 38; here and §5.5, v. 14, where it is used as a synonym for al-Ṣāyiḥ.

99 "The collective *ʿizwah* (war cry) of Shammar is *al-Ṭanāyā* (from *ṭanā*, 'to swell with anger') because its warriors swelled with anger when attacked" (Sowayan, *The Arabian Oral Historical Narrative*, 9).

100 They did not do so because of their putative descent from an ancestor who was one of the Sharifs of Mecca. See Introduction, pp. xi and xii.

101 "Damn it in the name of the Merciful": *ḥatt ar-rḥamān*; similarly, *ḥatt khayyāl ar-rḥamān Sinʿūsī*, "*Ḥatt*! I am the rider of His Grace! I am Sinʿūsī!" (Sowayan, *The Arabian Oral Historical Narrative*, 169).

102 The story is reminiscent of Gharrāf, the slave of Saṭṭām ibn Shaʿlān, who "surpassed all the other slaves in generosity and bravery and was no less esteemed by the Rwala than if he were a chief himself." Attacked by the Fidʿān tribe when he came to the rescue of his master's herds, he was pinned under the body of his slain horse. The Fidʿān "slashed him with their sabers" until "nearly all the fingers on his hands and the toes of his feet had been cut off" (Musil, *Rwala*, 602).

103 Ninety; see n. 97.

104 "Ḍayāghim" and "Sanā'īs" are collective war cries of the 'Abdah division of Shammar (Sowayan, *The Arabian Oral Historical Narrative*, 9–10); they feature in the saying "before you, Bahīj was driven out by al-Sanā'īs," from a verse by the military leader of the Ibn Rashīd dynasty, 'Ubayd ('Bēd) ibn Rashīd, in which he menaces an opponent (al-Suwaydā', *al-Amthāl al-sha'biyyah al-sā'irah fī manṭiqat Ḥā'il*, 324). For Bahīj, see n. 11.

105 "Muḥammad's boys": *'yāl al-Mḥammad*, a branch of the 'Abdah division of Shammar to which belong the Jirbān, the section of the al-Jarbā shaykhs of the Shammar Bedouin.

106 Praise for pain inflicted by the foe is part of the contention that the sharif shares blood ties with his Shammar opponents. That the sharif echoes this locally touted claim is sufficient proof that the poem is a Shammar composition.

107 Āl Thābit is a branch of the Sinjārah division of Shammar to which belong the 'Ajarrash family.

108 The second hemistich is a repetition of the line in §5.5, v. 6.

109 Shalwā is the moniker bestowed on the 'Ajarrash of Shammar. See n. 88.

110 See Introduction and n. 100 on a presumed kinship with the Sharifs of Mecca.

111 For this tale's many parallels with the legend of Ḥātim al-Ṭā'ī, the pre-Islamic poet who became the celebrated embodiment of boundless generosity for ever after, see Introduction.

112 Al-Kalbān: the descendants of Musallam, one of the nine sons of 'Amīrah, are nicknamed al-Klāb (Sowayan, *Ayyām al-'arab*, 230).

113 Al-'Awājī is the name of the family of shaykhs of the Wild Slēmān tribe of 'Anazah, the most redoubtable and much-feared Bedouin adversaries of Shammar (Von Oppenheim, *Von den Beduinen*, 2:347). Unlike, for instance, the prominent Rwalah tribe of 'Anazah, the Wild Slēmān dominate a contiguous area to the west of Shammar. Si'dūn al-'Awājī ordered his sons 'Gāb and Ḥjāb to usurp the settlement and well of Bēḍā Nithīl from Miṣlaṭ al-Ṭimyāṭ, the shaykh of the Tūmān division of Shammar. Subsequently, 'Gāb and Ḥjāb were killed by Shammar around 1830 in the course of a long-running vendetta that became the subject of an epos that is considered the highwater mark of the Shammar-'Anazah rivalry (Sowayan, *The Arabian Oral Historical Narrative*). Therefore, the narrator's reference to the 'Awājī as the culprits is related to more recent tribal memories: there is no news of such inroads by the Wild Slēmān in earlier centuries.

114 Cf. the poet al-Hirbīd checking with the lady of the tent whether perchance she had stored away some tobacco for her own usage without her husband's knowledge in Kurpershoek, *Bedouin Poets of the Nafūd Desert*, §42.6.

115 For the miraculous vision of Shāyi', see n. 2.

116 Probably the presence of an artisan, always considered lower class, has been chosen for this detail on the assumption that a well-bred Bedouin would not commit such a

flagrant breach of etiquette. The detail also shows that lower-class craftsmen always live in fear of losing their possessions, whereas the Bedouin are supposed to bear losses with studied nonchalance.

117 See n. 100; this verse explicitly lays claim to kinship with the prestigious Hāshimī house of the Great Sharifs of Mecca.

118 Similarly, Ḥātim al-Ṭā'ī boasts that all he will leave behind are a coat of mail, a horse (*sābiḥ*, as in this verse), and a spear (*Dīwān*, 41). Not meant to be taken entirely literally, the phrase became a figure of speech denoting an attitude of austere bravery. Anne Blunt characterized 'Ubayd ('Bēd) ibn Rashīd, "the principal hero of Shammar traditions," as someone who "left no property but a sword, a mare, and a young wife, having given everything away during his lifetime" (*Pilgrimage*, 194).

119 As a child, Ḥātim al-Ṭā'ī refused to take any food unless he had someone to share it with; otherwise, he would cast it away (al-Iṣfahānī, *al-Aghānī*, 17:366–67).

120 See Introduction.

121 See n. 216. To broadcast one's munificence for ulterior motives is to stain the purity of deed and reputation.

122 The second hemistich is identical to the one of §15.4, v. 5. "Nuptial bed": *jāḍa'athum*, lit., "they (the women) are lying belly to belly with them (the men)"; i.e., to sleep with, have sexual intercourse. It is a synonym of CA *tabaṭṭana*, as in "[as if] I have not lain belly to belly [*wa-lam atabaṭṭan*] with buxom girls wearing anklets" (Imru' al-Qays, *Dīwān*, 143).

123 They unleashed deceit against a smarter schemer. See Introduction.

124 Enlisting as a free servant (*fidāwī*) is a ruse often resorted to by men who do so for reasons other than making a living. Musil gives the example of a man who found employ with the Sirḥān tribe in order to track down someone marked for blood revenge (Musil, *Rwala*, 500). The noble herdsman on a secret mission is also a narrative motif, e.g., in the tragic love story of Mḥēsin al-Rebshānī of the Rwalah tribe. The father of the girl he loved refused to give him permission to marry her, and in his desperation, he sent a poem imploring Khalaf al-D'ējā, a chief and gallant knight of the Sharārāt tribe, to come to his aid. As his battle cry, *nakhwah*, was invoked, the hero took it as a matter of honor. Incognito, al-D'ējā enlisted as a herdsman with the father and quickly rose in his esteem, not least because of his feats as a marksman and hunter of ibex. Al-D'ējā was recognized for who he was by the Rwalah shaykh Fayṣal ibn Sha'lān (d. 1864, murdered in blood revenge) on a visit. The embarrassed father agreed to let al-D'ējā marry his daughter on Mḥēsin's behalf, but it was too late: on their arrival, they found he had already died, joining the cohorts of Arabian martyrs of love (Sowayan, *al-Ṣaḥrā' al-'arabiyyah*, 434–37, and *Ayyām al-'arab*, 1075–80).

125 *Ghaḍā* (*Haloxylon persicum*): a "large shrub or small tree" that "is important for camel grazing and a source of excellent firewood," and *irṭā* (*Calligonum comosum*), similarly, a shrub of sandy terrain, "furnishing camel grazing and excellent firewood" (Mandaville, *Bedouin Ethnobotany*, 249, 256). These popular species from the sand dunes "are very desirable because they burn slowly and produce plenty of hot charcoal with few if any sparks, and nontoxic smoke" (Watts and al-Nafie, *Vegetation and Biogeography of the Sand Seas of Saudi Arabia*, 63). Huber notes that *ghaḍā* is more common to the north of al-ʿLēm, a rocky landmark on the way from al-Jawf to Jubbah through the Nafūd, and *irṭā* is more common to its south (*Journal d'un voyage en Arabie*, 337).

126 "Improvised seat": *ḥwāyah* (CA *ḥawiyyah*, pl. *hawāyā*, "a garment stuffed with dry herbage wound around the hump of a camel by way of decoration" (Imru' al-Qays, *Dīwān*, 133); "a contraption that is prepared for a woman to ride on" (Lane, *An Arabic-English Lexicon*, 679).

127 One visualizes the narrator's gesture. It is a reminder of the recorded story's performance context.

128 A girl and a youth who elope to some distant tribe and put themselves under the protection of a powerful chief "can then marry and live as man and wife in the same tent but are always threatened with the revenge of the *eben al-ʿamm* [*ibn al-ʿamm*]. An elopement is punished in the same way as murder, and the thirst for revenge must be satisfied" (Musil, *Rwala*, 138). In this case, al-Bijādī might have pleaded that Shāyiʿ had broken the bargain he offered—letting his stud cover his she-camel in exchange for the hand of his daughter—but such equivalence would find no support under tribal law.

129 In other poems, this description of the camel's rearing highlights the great care taken to produce the strongest and fastest riding camel possible (e.g., Kurpershoek, *Arabian Romantic*, 55–57).

130 Similarly, Imru' al-Qays measures the jumps made by his riding camel in fathoms (*Dīwān*, 159). The Banū Hilāl of the legend trained their horses to jump over a wide trench so as to best the horses of Khalīfat al-Zanātī at their own game. This Hilālī motif has been grafted lock, stock, and barrel onto the legend that sprouted around the nineteenth-century poet-hero Rākān ibn Ḥithlēn of the ʿIjmān tribe, and his training of Ottoman horses in Serbia to do the same (Sowayan, *al-Ṣaḥrāʾ al-ʿarabiyyah*, 301).

131 "I am of no use": *lā agāḍī lak anā, yibih*, lit., "I, my person does not settle accounts for you, gives you no satisfaction by way of revenge, Father," as Imru' al-Qays was told by an old woman of Banū Kinānah, *lasnā lak bi-tha'r* "we will not do for you by way of blood revenge" (al-Iṣfahānī, *al-Aghānī*, 9:90). See Introduction.

132 "Kept inside": lit., "hidden." An aristocratic daughter was exempt from menial tasks outside the tent and allowed to stay inside, "hidden," much like a gem or an object of high value, awaiting a qualified suitor.

133 "To the horses": *bi-l-maʿārig*, sg. *maʿrigah*, "a soft, light horse saddle" (Musil, *Rwala*, 385).

134 This was the normal procedure for a chase at night; cf. Ibn Sbayyil's verse: "Behind them the torch of a shaykh in hot pursuit" (Kurpershoek, *Arabian Romantic*, 87, 135, 218n242). The technique is explained by Hess, *Von den Beduinen*, 102.

135 "Reins held": *mass ḥablah*, lit., "he gripped her rope"; i.e., she is a trained female riding camel, *dhilūl*; the opposite is *lam yamsash al-ḥabl*, "no steering ropes are attached to it"; i.e., a male stud camel exclusively used for breeding (al-Iṣfahānī, *al-Aghānī*, 11:19).

136 A similar simile is found in Kurpershoek, *Bedouin Poets of the Nafūd Desert*, §1.2.

137 Jabr ibn Sayyār (d. 1708; see Kurpershoek, *Arabian Satire*, 158) uses the same simile: "Saddlebags aflutter, she runs, swaying her head, like the hands of a peasant sowing seeds" (*ṭaffāḥat al-khirjēn yūmī bi-rāshā, shirwā yidin awmā bhā badhdhārha*) (Sowayan, *al-Shiʿr al-Nabaṭī*, 437).

138 *Mēs* is a kind of hard wood used for the manufacture of camel saddles and rollers of pulley wheels suspended over wells (CA *mays*, hackberry, genus *Celtis*). In this verse, the noise produced by friction on the hard wood of both the saddle and the roller is indicated.

139 The verse echoes al-Mutanabbī's famous "Horses, the night, desert wastes know me, smiting and thrusting, pen and paper"(*fa-l-khaylu wa-l-laylu wa-l-baydāʾu taʿrifunī, wa-l-ḍarbu wa-l-ṭaʿnu wa-l-qirṭāsu wa-l-qalamū*) (*Dīwān*, 3:369); and Khalaf al-Idhn, a nineteenth-century knight and poet of the Rwalah tribe: "My sword testifies for me, and my lance; all of Mesopotamia is witness to my feats" (*wa-s-sef yishhad lī wa-yishhad lī az-zān, wa-yishhad bi-fiʿlī min sikan bi-l-jazīrah*) (al-Sudayrī, *Abṭāl min al-Ṣaḥrāʾ*, 268).

140 See Introduction.

141 Similarly, §15.4, v. 3.

142 The Fuḍūl tribe has largely disappeared from the Arabian Peninsula. They were related to the Banū Lām, a tribe that in the tenth/sixteenth century migrated from the peninsula to an area beyond the Tigris River in Iraq. The Fuḍūl remained in the northeastern corner of Arabia. The tribe was weakened and scattered during decades of warfare against the first Wahhabi state.

143 Shāyiʿ acts in accordance with some of the most popular sayings: "If they do not treat you with regard and distinction, get up at once, leave without another word!" (Kurpershoek, *Arabian Romantic*, 85); "I'd rather have a slab of rock for a pillow than sleep on a soft carpet in a land of ignominy" (Kurpershoek, *Arabian Satire*, 111); or Labīd in his

Muʿallaqah poem: "I leave places not to my liking, unless one is forced by Fate" (*tarrāku amkinatin idhā lam arḍahā, aw yaʿtaliq baʿḍa al-nufūsi himāmuhā*) (al-Zawzanī, *Sharḥ al-muʿallaqat*, 109).

144 "Idiot": *khibil*, "of a troubled understanding" (Doughty, *Travels in Arabia Deserta*, 1:647).

145 If camels have a salt deficit, generally because they have not been grazing on saltbushes for an extended period, "they become weak and thin and have a tendency to eat bones and carrion" (Mandaville, *Bedouin Ethnobotany*, 87).

146 Shāyiʿ, himself incognito like a king who plays the beggar, recognizes a similar sleeper champion among the camels. Similar shrewdness and dissemblance are on display in the choice of such an unrecognized superior desert cruiser in stories of Abū Zwayyid. Cf. Kurpershoek, *Bedouin Poets of the Nafūd Desert*, and al-Māyidī ibn Ẓāhir (Kurpershoek, *Love, Death, Fame*, 153).

147 "All Bedouin women are equally fond of ear-rings, nose-rings, ankle-rings, and bracelets. [....] The male Bedouin care little about their own dress, but love to decorate their wives, and dress them in good clothes, which they think reflect honour upon themselves" (Burckhardt, *Notes*, 232).

148 "The poorest wife will have some box [....] in which are laid up [....] her poor inherited ornaments, the ear-rings and nose-ring of silver or even golden [....] But if her goodman be of substance [....] she has a locked coffer painted with vermilion from Medina. [....] Commonly the housewife's key of her box is seen as a glittering pendant, upon her veil backward" (Doughty, *Arabia Deserta*, 1:268).

149 Mange, a highly contagious malady, is greatly feared by the Bedouin, in part because the treatment demands nasty and difficult labor.

150 The "small water hole" is a *migr*, described by Musil as a "half natural, half artificial well, five to ten meters deep, dug in a rock, into which the rain water flows. The opening, which is usually narrow, can be covered with a stone of moderate size" (*Rwala*, 681). CA *al-mumqir min al-rakayā*, "well holding little water" (Ibn Manẓūr, *Lisān al-ʿarab*, 4243).

151 In this version of the story, Shāyiʿ had not used this camel on raids before. Yet the phrase points to a long-lasting companionship of man and mount on perilous journeys.

152 A note to the Arabic explains that *gaṣṣadhum* means: "He gave each of them a little share (*qist*) of his water."

153 No particular girl is meant. Ditties often end with such a flourish, as if the song or acts described are dedicated to a pretty girl.

154 The hero overhearing a conversation, unnoticed, in which he himself features is a recurrent motif. See Introduction, p. xix.

155 "May you live long": *yā baʿad ḥayy*, lit., "may you still be alive (after I and others have passed away)," a Shammar expression of endearment. The expression is foreshadowed

in a verse of Ḥātim al-Ṭāʾī: "If one day we are separated by death, may you, Wahm, be the one who goes last!"; *idhā mā atā yawmun yufarriqu baynanā, bi-mawtin fa-kun yā-Wahmu dhū yataʾakhkharū,* with the note that in the dialect of Ṭayy *dhū* has the meaning of the relative pronoun *alladhī*, "who" (*Dīwān*, 16).

156 The scene is a stock narrative motif: the unlikely hero and his apparently second-rate mount come to the rescue of other riders and carry them to safety at an unflagging blistering pace. See Introduction, p. ix.

157 A standing expression, lit., "entrusted to God and after Him to you" (*tarū ḥaggī wdāʿat li-llāh thumm lukum*); and the lower-class Bedouin's wife, Gwayyilah, to the desert knight Bkhīt al-ʿAṭāwī, "I have entrusted him first to God and then to you" (*tarāhā imānt allah thumm imānatk*) (Kurpershoek, *The Story of a Desert Knight*, 235).

158 According to ancient tradition, a visitor is under someone's protection, even if he stands accused with his host, once he has been given to eat and drink. This is usually the case when the visitor's identity is not known to the host at the moment of his arrival and is offered food. On meeting a hostile party, "their declaration, 'We have eaten salt in such or such a tent,' is a passport that ensures them a safe journey; or at all events, the testimony of their host would release them from the hands of any Arabs, whether of his own or some friendly tribe" (Burckhardt, *Notes*, 172).

159 Lit., "I am my father's brother."

160 Shāyiʿ means "leading a herd by singing; widespread, well known."

161 Another well-known narrative motif: female disappointment at the hero's unimpressive looks that do not correspond to the glowing stories about his feats, followed by the hero upbraiding them in verse for their immature view of things; cf. Introduction, p. ix.

162 As explained to me by ʿAbd al-Raḥmān al-Suwaydāʾ, the editor of an early collection of Shammar poetry, the reference is to Muḥammad al-Rōg, a paramount chief of the ʿUtaybah confederation.

163 Similarly, his contemporary al-Māyidī ibn Ẓāhir's "travels covered the entire country, no place excepted. He went everywhere by camel or on foot. It was almost as if he spent all his life on camelback" (Kurpershoek, *Love, Death, Fame*, 153).

164 "The Aenezes [members of the ʿAnazah tribal confederation] never attack by night; this they regard as *bōg*, or treachery; for during the confusion of a nocturnal assault, the women's apartments might be entered, and violence offered, which would infallibly occasion much resistance from the men of the attacked camp, and probably end in general massacre—a circumstance which the Arabs constantly endeavour to avoid" (Burckhardt, *Notes*, 141).

165 Ibn ʿUrayʿir (Ibn ʿRēʿir) is the popular name of the dynasty established in al-Aḥsāʾ in eastern Arabia bordering the Gulf by Barrāk ibn Ghurayr of the Āl Ḥumayd family of the

Banū Khālid tribe; see Introduction. Ibn 'Rē'ir is the name generally used in Bedouin lore, unspecified and without historical basis, about persons in the tales and verses. The names mentioned here are Muḥammad, his son 'Uthmān, and Muḥammad's brother Ḥammād. Their exact identity is unknown, but the name Muḥammad occurs in historical records as a possible contemporary of Shāyi'. After his conquest of al-Aḥsā' in 1669, Barrāk was succeeded by his brother Muḥammad ibn Ghurayr (d. 1691) (Philby, *Sa'udi Arabia*, 26–27).

166 The image is familiar from early Arabic poetry. Imru' al-Qays describes attacking cavalry, seen from a distance: "like wings of locusts, swarming the sky, is the glitter of iron-shod hooves" (*Dīwān*, 160). See n. 173.

167 A common image for a spirited horse forcefully and abruptly being reined in.

168 In preparation for battle, horses would be evacuated and would not be fed so as to maximize their fitness, much as athletes do not eat a short time before a race.

169 Khanshar is an early ancestor of Shāyi', one of the nine sons of 'Amīrah. He may be referring to himself by this sobriquet.

170 A note in the Arabic text points out that a similar scene occurs in stories about the Jarbā shaykhs of Shammar and the Aslam division of Shammar (Sowayan, *Ayyām al-'arab*, 42 and 664–65).

171 Presumably, the narrator refers to the Ottoman rulers, but in this context it has an anachronistic ring. The Ottoman state paid a *ṣurrah* (lit., "purse"), an amount of money, to Bedouin tribes for safe-conduct on the road of the pilgrimage caravan to Mecca. In the area of Shammar Mountain, important tribal shaykhs were rewarded for their loyalty by Ibn Rashīd. By the term used here, *ma'āsh*, "pension," the narrator seems to refer to the practice of the Saudi state used to pay important tribal shaykhs a yearly "gift" (*ikrāmiyyah*) or the regular pay received by shaykhs who act as tribal representatives vis-à-vis the local government authorities.

172 Coffee has taken the place of wine, but otherwise the oath taken by Imru' al-Qays on learning about the killing of his father is similar: "I will not touch wine and women until I have killed one hundred of the Banū Asad and cut the forelocks of a hundred others" (al-Iṣfahānī, *al-Aghānī*, 9:87).

173 For other examples of distant white or light-colored specks compared with pieces or shreds of cloth, see §1.6 and nn. 12 and 166.

174 Al-Busayṭā is "a vast stretch of desert between Syria and Iraq [. . . .], without any water or pasture, God's place most remote from human habitation. It was crossed by al-Mutanabbī on his flight from Egypt to Iraq." In verses, al-Mutanabbī describes how his servants were deluded by fata morgana shapes hovering in the desert's quivering hot air (al-Jāsir, *al-Mu'jam al-jughrāfī li-l-bilād al-'Arabiyyah al-Sa'ūdiyyah, Shamāl al-Mamlakah*, 1:206).

175 The desert dweller's concern for ensuring a proper grave in preparation for his own demise is a motif in its own right (e.g., Kurpershoek, *Love, Death, Fame,* 284n458). As explained by Lane, "a traveler, in such circumstances, has even to make his own grave: completely overcome by fatigue or privation, or sinking under a fatal disease, in the desert, when his companions, if he have any, cannot wait for his recovery or death [...] having made a trench in the sand, as his grave, lies down in it, wrapped in his grave-clothes, and covers himself, with the exception of his face, with the sand taken up in making the trench: thus he waits for death to relieve him; trusting the wind to complete his burial" (*Manners and Customs of the Modern Egyptians,* 516).

176 The intervention of supernatural forces and mysterious voices (here called *mnābī* and elsewhere also *hātif*) guiding the hero-poet has been a motif since the earliest days of Arabic poetry and storytelling, e.g., the *hātif* that warned Muhalhil that he had been mistaken to order the live burial of his daughter, according to a pre-Islamic custom (al-Iṣfahānī, *al-Aghānī,* 11:52).

177 Another ancient motif. The pre-Islamic poet-hero Aws ibn Ḥajar was thrown off by a sudden violent movement of his camel while riding alone at night. Injured in both legs, he was unable to get up and the camel ran away. In the morning, the camel was found by tribal girls who had gone out to gather truffles and herbage, its nose rope entangled in the branches of a tree. He himself was nursed back to strength, in particular by the youngest of the girls, the shaykh's daughter and the only one not to run away in fear, for which she was duly rewarded with his verses (al-Iṣfahānī, *al-Aghānī,* 11:72–73).

178 Since the early days of Arabic poetry and storytelling, the owl, known for its hair-raising screeches and hooting, has been a symbol of everything sinister and ill-fated.

179 Similarly, §1.15, v. 35.

180 Q An'ām 6:95: «God causes the seed grain and the date stone to split and sprout».

181 The Mountain is a common shorthand for the area of Jabal Shammar (Shammar Mountain), also called the Two Mountains; i.e., the granite mountain ranges of Ajā and Salmā in the general area of Ḥā'il.

182 Similarly, §4.2, v. 4. It is a verse in the style of Banū Hilāl.

183 Lit., "he whose tears can't be patched up (*yishigg*) but he finds a fix (*yarga'*, makes a patch) for himself." "It means that he is resourceful: he puts others in a fix they can't get out of, but he can extricate himself from any fix. He can stitch any torn-off part, but his torn-off part can't be stitched" (communication from Saad Sowayan). See also n. 197 on the saying "he caused a tear that cannot be repaired."

184 Lit., "he who hits the mark before it happens" (*min yiṣībah gabl taga'*); i.e., someone whose foresight and dexterity wards off misfortune, for example by giving shrewd and timely advice.

185 This opening closely resembles §7.13, v. 1.

186 It is a common conviction among the Bedouin that a child's character is to a large extent determined by genes inherited from the mother's father. This is regarded as an important factor when deciding on the selection of a marriage partner. Hence, in poetry, praise for a married woman is mostly phrased as praise for her father; cf. Kurpershoek, *Bedouin Poets of the Nafūd Desert*, xix, xxxvi.

187 As in poetry and tales of pre-Islamic robber barons, persons who stand accused of being misers are routinely presented as legitimate targets of Bedouin plundering expeditions; see Introduction. Thus framed, misers are by definition lacking in courage, which if true would also make them easy prey. Noble deeds are performed with the right hand, while the left hand is reserved for tasks like cleaning oneself after defecation.

188 Climbing an elevation and watching out for danger while others take a rest are marks of a desert chief's energy and sense of responsibility. It is an ancient trope in boastful poetry, e.g., Imru' al-Qays in his verse: "I raise the alarm when they have gone to sleep; I make them lift their sleepy heads" (*wa-anā al-munabbihu baʿda mā qad nawwamū, wa-anā l-muʿālī ṣafḥata l-nuwwāmī*) (*Dīwān*, 164). And Ḥātim al-Ṭāʾī: "Many a lookout pointing to the sky I climbed, watching over endless deserts on all sides" (*wa-marqabatin dūna l-samāʾi ʿalawtuhā, uqallibu ṭarfī fī faḍāʾi sabāsibī*) (*Dīwān*, 29).

189 A man and camel are depicted as an inseparable whole, as in a verse of another desert knight, Shlēwīḥ al-ʿAṭāwī. See Introduction, n. 4.

190 As on a desert journey of al-Ḥuṭayʾah: "On nightly desert stretches the wolf, at a sprightly pace, kept running with us in tandem" (*wa-l-dhiʾbu yaṭruqunā fī kulli manzilatin, ʿadwa l-qarīnayni fī athārinā khababā*) (*Dīwān*, 10).

191 Cf. §7.13, v. 6.

192 The face of a rider who thus exposes himself to the sun and inclement weather would bear the *wasm al-khalā*, lit., "the brand, imprint of the desert." Compare the heading "A Face Marked by the Sun" in Kurpershoek, *The Story of a Desert Knight*, 168.

193 It is customary for the Bedouin to regard hospitality extended to visitors and the needy as a duty and privilege granted to them by the Lord. Therefore, the guest is a guest of God: "Bedouins bless the host and yield their thanks unto Ullah" (Doughty, *Arabia Deserta*, 1:274).

194 As described by Burckhardt, if a robber is seized and made a prisoner (*ribīṭ*, lit., "fettered"), "a hole is formed in the ground of the tent, about two feet deep, and as long as a man: in this hole he is laid, his feet chained to the earth, his hands tied, and his twisted hair fastened to two stakes on both sides of his head" (*Notes*, 162–63).

195 A repetition of the question put to him by his abducted daughter in the camp of al-Bijādī (§7.8).

196 Again, almost a repetition of the scene and wording used in §7.8.

197 Once badly torn, a shirt cannot be mended, as in the saying "he caused a tear that cannot be repaired" (*shagg shaggin mā yirgaʿ*) (al-ʿUbūdī, *al-Amthāl al-ʿāmmiyyah fī Najd*, 689). Here the question is: who caused this disaster?

198 "Childish pranks": *ṣbayy w-zallat ʿajārīfih*, a saying: "a little boy, but the time of his spontaneous, charming behavior has ended"; i.e., "little boys grown up," also used in a more general sense, e.g., *ʿajārīf al-hawā*, "the daring follies of love" (Kurpershoek, *Arabian Romantic*, 29). CA *ʿajrafiyyah* "rude, obstreperous, unruly behavior," e.g., as said of the poet ʿAqīl ibn ʿUllafah in al-Iṣfahānī, *al-Aghānī*, 12:254.

199 "Complement": *slaʿ*, sg. *silʿah*, "a rare object of high value." As part of the blood price for a person killed, one riding camel, "a mare, a black slave, a coat of mail, and a gun [. . .] constitute what is called the *sola*," in addition to the *diyyah* (blood money) of fifty camels (Burckhardt, *Notes*, 153). "In the Bedouin parlance, it usually refers to a horse, camel mount or a rifle" (Sowayan, *The Arabian Oral Historical Narrative*, 275).

200 The time spent in captivity varies: the narrative mentions eight years (§13.1).

201 The reference is to Ibn ʿRēʿir, who claimed the animals Shammar had stolen from him and kept Shāyiʿ as his prisoner as long as his demands were not met. Ibn ʿRēʿir's gambit turned against him when instead he was confronted with more losses as ransom for his kidnapped son. The poem makes it look as if it was worth the eight years Shāyiʿ languished in his improvised dungeon. Revenge was the ultimate pleasure. "Heavyweight": *thigīl al-rōz*, a standing expression for someone with long experience, self-possessed, and calmly confident; the opposite of *khafīf al-rōz*, "a lightweight loose talker"; *rāz*, "to take someone's measure."

202 The scene is reminiscent of the pre-Islamic bard Imru' al-Qays vaulting onto the camel and entering the palanquin of ʿUnayzah, as described in his *Muʿallaqah* poem: "When I entered the litter, the litter of ʿUnzayzah, and she said, 'Woe, oh woe is me, you'll make me go on foot!' / As she spoke, the palanquin tilted, the two of us inside: 'You cripple my camel, Imru' al-Qays get out of here!'" (al-Zawzanī, *Sharḥ al-muʿallaqāt*, 12).

203 On the sexual connotations of the wolf and sheep motif, see Sowayan, *al-Ṣahrā' al-ʿarabiyyah*, 645; similarly, in a poem ascribed to the daughter of the poet al-Māyidī ibn Ẓāhir (Kurpershoek, *Love, Death, Fame*, 141, 277n403). See Introduction, p. xxv.

204 Sowayan, *al-Ṣaḥrā' al-ʿarabiyyah*, 281–82.

205 Sitting as if slumped down and head covered with a garment or coat often occurs within the context of mental depression; cf. Imru' al-Qays (*Dīwān*, 81); ʿUrwah ibn Ḥizām (al-Iṣfahānī, *al-Aghānī*, 24:154); Doughty (*Arabia Deserta*, 1:274).

206 See Introduction.

207 "Spoken the truth": *ṣāğğîn Gṭēfān*; the *dāl* assimilated to the *gāf* (for CA *qāf*, *ṣādiqun Quṭayfān*).

208 In emphatically boastful style, seven of the Arabic verses §15.2, vv. 3–10 open with the cry "and how many times" (*wa-yāmā*), as the early classical "how many" (*wa-kam*), or the repetition of "and we" as opening of four consecutive lines in the *Muʿallaqah* poem of ʿAmr ibn Kulthūm. It is followed by four lines (vv. 13–16) opening with the words "and I cry for" (*wa-abkī ʿalā*), while vv. 11–12 also open with forms of the verb "to cry for."

209 Similarly, §15.4, v. 6.

210 Though the first mention of firearms in this kind of poetry dates from the early seventeenth century (Sowayan, *al-Shiʿr al-Nabaṭī*, 379–82), it seems unlikely that matchlocks were regularly used in seventeenth-century Bedouin desert warfare.

211 "The plume," *ghalbā*, is a commonly used metonym. It refers to the ostrich feathers that lend panache to the blade fastened on a lance or spear.

212 The rendezvous (*al-waʿd*), lit., "the promise, agreed meeting place and time," is an important element of long-distance raiding. In this type of serious raiding, the attack on the enemy camel herds is made by horse riders, while the camel troops carrying the supplies of food and water await their return with the loot at an agreed meeting point. If for whatever reason the raiders miss the location, they might find themselves in a precarious position: without water, they cannot make it back to their base, and the nearest well might be too far away or in enemy hands. If they do not succeed in linking up with their fellows in charge of the supplies, they may have to abandon the horses to face certain death in the waterless wilderness. Cf. a similar description in the verse of Ibn Sbayyil (Kurpershoek, *Arabian Romantic*, §§22.7–9).

213 Having no choice but to drink from a well with foul water has been part of poetry's descriptions of arduous desert crossings since pre-Islamic days.

214 The rains of the Pleiades, a period in late fall (*thruwwī*, from al-Thurayyā, the Pleiades constellation), are the most important and "the decisive factor for the future grazing" (Musil, *Rwala*, 9).

215 "Munificent": *al-ṣakhā* (CA *sakhāʾ*, "liberality, munificence"), in the area of Shammar Mountain especially associated with Ḥātim al-Ṭāʾī. See Introduction.

216 On the sin of vaunting the good turns one did to a certain person, see §6.7, v. 10 and Introduction.

217 See §15.2, v. 6.

Glossary

ʿAbdah the principal division of the Shammar confederation. They may have migrated from Yemen about seven centuries ago. The ruling families in Ḥā'il during the nineteenth century, Āl ʿAlī and Ibn Rashīd, are both from the Jʿafar section of the ʿAbdah.

Abū Zayd al-Hilālī hero-poet who led the Banū Hilāl on their western migration (*taghrībah*) from Arabia to Tunis.

Āl Ḥumayd See Ibn ʿRēʿir (ʿUrayʿir).

ʿAmīrah Shāyiʿ al-Amsaḥ's son. He is named after the early ancestor of the Rmāl tribe.

ʿAnazah one of the oldest and largest Arabian tribal confederations, supposedly named after an eponymous ancestor, ʿAnnāz. Around the beginning of the eighteenth century, they moved from their base around Khaybar in the Hijaz north toward Syria and Iraq. Genealogically, they are reckoned among the northern Arabs, Rabīʿah, whereas their hereditary rivals, Shammar, trace their origins to the southern Arabs. Around 1800, a second northward migration of the tribes of ʿAnazah and Shammar occurred, this time caused by Wahhabi pressure.

ʿAntar ʿAntarah ibn Shaddād, one of the most famous pre-Islamic poets and composer of one of the seven *al-Muʿallaqāt* poems. He is also the hero of a cycle of storytelling in the Middle East.

al-Asāʿidah a branch of the ʿUtaybah tribe in the village of Bagʿā (CA Baqʿā).

Banū Hilāl Arabian tribes that in 1050 set out from Egypt to invade North Africa, the so-called "westward journey" (*taghrībat Banī Hilāl*) described by the historian Ibn Khaldūn (732–808/1332–1406), who was the first to give examples of *hilālī*-style "Bedouin" poetry that later became known as Nabaṭī poetry. In more recent times, the Banū Hilāl featured in a popular saga whose characters included Abū Zayd and other heroes known throughout the Arab world.

Banū Ṣakhr (also: al-Ṣukhūr) originally from the northern Hejaz, these nomads and seminomads are the dominant tribe in the hinterland of northern

Jordan. By causing trouble for pilgrim caravans, they leveraged their influence with the Ottoman Turks. At the outbreak of the First World War, the only tribe that still paid tribute to the Banū Ṣakhr was the Sharārāt. After the war, they supported Emir ʻAbdallah of Transjordan against raids of the Saudi Ikhwān in 1922 and 1924.

ʻGēl see ʻUqayl.

ghaḍā (*Haloxylon persicum*) a large shrub used for camel grazing and a source of firewood.

al-Ghūṭah an area to the west of the Ajā mountains; its principal settlement is Mōgag.

Ḥātim [al-Ṭāʼī] a symbol of prodigious hospitality, the pre-Islamic Bedouin poet Ḥātim al-Ṭāʼī is one of the most widely known ancient figures in Saudi Arabia today. He is especially associated with the region of Ḥāʼil, whose inhabitants claim him as one of their own. The tribe may have gone, but the mountain ranges are still called Jabal Ṭayyiʼ.

Ḥāyil (Ḥāʼil) the capital of northern Najd, the province of central Arabia, it is situated at an almost equal distance from Mecca, Damascus, and Riyadh, halfway between the Red Sea and the Gulf. It is the center of Jabal Shammar, formerly Jabal Ṭayyiʼ, an area of mixed nomadic and sedentary modes of life. Economically, it was primarily orientated toward the Mesopotamian riverine areas of Iraq, and caravans plied the old pilgrim road, *darb Zubaydah*, that skirted the southern edge of the Nafūd Desert. Historically, Ḥāʼil has been in close interaction, and often in competition, with the oases and trade hubs of al-Qaṣīm Province and its major towns of ʻUnayzah and Buraydah, a few hundred miles to the south.

howdah (*ʻutfah*, pl. *ʻiṭāf*) a camel-borne litter in which the tribe's women travel. It is a larger version of the *ghabīṭ*, a camel's saddle for women upon which the howdah is bound.

Ibn Mirdās the patronymic of Shāyiʻ al-Amsaḥ, the ancestor of the Shammar tribe of the Rmāl.

Ibn Rashīd the ruling house in Ḥāʼil and Jabal Shammar from 1834 to 1921. The name Ibn Rashīd is a shorthand designation for the house, its members, and the ruling emir.

Ibn ʻRēʻir (ʻUrayʻir) the popular name for the Āl Ḥumayd dynasty of the Banū Khālid tribe that ruled the eastern al-Aḥsāʼ Province from 1669 to 1793, continuing the traditions of the Jabrid dynasty, who ruled the same area in the fifteenth and sixteenth centuries. Their independence was ended by the Saudi rulers. A later episode of semi-independence ended in 1830, when the Ibn ʿRēʿir were defeated by Turkī ibn Saʿūd and surrendered on honorable terms.

Ibn Saud also Ibn Saʿūd or Ibn Sʿūd family, the principal rulers of Najd and the political leaders of the religious reform movement known as Wahhabism.

al-Jarbā the first known Bedouin shaykhs of Shammar, of the Khriṣah division. They led the Shammar tribes that in the late eighteenth century moved from Najd to Iraq after their defeat by the first Saudi state. With Ottoman permission, the Jarbā crossed the Euphrates, entered al-Jazīrah Province, and in 1802/03 reached Sinjār Mountain in the north of Iraq. ʿAjīl al-Yāwar (Turkish for "adjutant, aide-de-camp," 1882–1940, in this edition ʿAgīl al-Jāwar) represented Mosul in the first Iraqi parliament in 1924. His grandson Ghāzī al-Yāwar was the first president of Iraq after Saddam Hussein.

al-Jawf also known as al-Jōbah, a large agricultural area and a town, which includes the area of Sakākā, in a depressed plain bordering on its south the northwestern side of the Nafūd Desert and on its north opening to Wādī Sirḥān. Al-Jawf has been a trading town of Shammar, the Rwalah, and the Sharārāt.

Jubbah a village and small oasis at the southern edge of the Nafūd Desert, old enough to be mentioned in a verse by the *mukhaḍram* poet Namr ibn Tawlab al-ʿUklī. Poets present it as a place teeming with wildlife, in particular oryx. Early Arabic sources praise its excellent pastures and remoteness from human habitation. For European travelers coming from al-Jawf, the miniature oasis offered the first vista of green on their way to Ḥāʾil, fifty-five miles (ninety kilometers) south of Jubbah. The town was known for the manufacture of wooden camel saddles. Nineteenth-century Bedouin poetry and stories are equally effusive in descriptions of Jubbah and the sands of the Nafūd as a natural paradise for camels and Bedouin.

Maʿān a town in southern Jordan.

al-Muʿallaqāt "the suspended poems," a pre-Islamic collection of poems, which, in the early centuries of Islam, were among the most admired long poems of the qasida type. They are so called because the poems, written on cloth in letters of gold, were said to have been hung on the walls of the Meccan Kaaba, but other explanations are also given.

Najd generally understood as the central part of the Arabian Peninsula—the plateau area roughly situated to the east of the mountain ranges of the

Hijāz, south of the Nafūd Desert, west of the Dahnā' sands, and including Wādī al-Dawāsir in the south but not beyond it. This large region is subdivided into areas that differ greatly in character. Historically and environmentally, its society has been characterized by contrast between sedentary and Bedouin groups. Nabaṭī poetry is essentially a Najdī phenomenon with roots in classical Arabian culture, a pedigree shared by many of the sedentary and Bedouin tribes in Najd.

Nafūd Desert the Great Nafūd, or al-Nafūd, is the second-largest body of sand of the Arabian Peninsula, though it is less than a tenth the size of the Empty Quarter. These two sand bodies are connected by the sand belt of al-Dahnā', which runs more than 870 miles (1,400 kilometers) from the southeastern al-Nafūd to the northern edge of the Empty Quarter. The Nafūd sands, with their rich vegetation after rainfall and plentiful firewood, are considered a Bedouin paradise.

al-Rmāl the shaykhs of the Rmāl section and the chief of the Ghfēlah branch of the Sinjārah of Shammar. Based in the small oasis of Jubbah, the Rmāl are the nomads of the Nafūd sands par excellence.

Sakākā see al-Jawf.

Sa'ūd see Ibn Saud.

Shammar the tribal confederation after which the area around Ḥā'il is called Jabal Shammar (it is also called "the Two Mountains" after Ajā and Salmā). As early as the seventeenth century, Shammar families began wandering toward Mesopotamia, while the thrust of 'Anazah was toward Syria, as far as Aleppo. The area between the Euphrates and Tigris rivers is the northern heartland of Shammar. Genealogically, Shammar belongs to the southern Arabs, Qaḥṭān, of Ṭayy, while 'Anazah is north Arabian, 'Adnān.

Sharīf the family of the Great Sharifs of Mecca.

Shaṭṭ al-'Arab the confluence of the Euphrates and Tigris rivers before they exit into the Gulf.

si'dūniyyah a type of Bedouin striped cloak made in Sūg al-Shuyūkh, Iraq, that became fashionable in nineteenth-century Iraq. Some of the first to wear it were the shaykhs of the al-Muntafiq confederation, Āl Sa'dūn, hence its name.

silīḥ a name given to a number of annual crucifers of large, spreading stature with showy red or purple flowers (information taken from Mandaville, *Bedouin Ethnobotany*, 313).

Sinjārah one of the four divisions of Najdī Shammar. Its territory and wells stretch from al-Ghūṭah District in the west through the Nafūd sands to the wells of the water-rich area of al-Ḥuzūl in the east. Though Sinjārah were the most "Bedouin" of Shammar, many of them owned permanent water holes and palm groves. They were known as independent-minded raiders with a particularly rich tribal and Bedouin lore.

al-Sirḥān a tribal group, probably named after Wādī Sirḥān. They are neighbors of the Banū Ṣakhr in the southern reaches of Ḥawrān in southwestern Syria. In 1925, they lost most of their camel herds to attacks by the Saudi Ikhwān.

ṣlubī (pl. ṣalab) a member of the pariah tribe of handicraftsmen who used to accompany the Bedouin tribes on their migrations. Renowned as skilled hunters, they dressed in the hide of the game they killed and rode donkeys, not camels. They shod the Bedouin's horses, repaired their metalwork, and performed other manual jobs, but otherwise lived a life completely separate from them and did not intermarry with them. A *ṣlubī* is often chosen to play the role of messenger, spy, or carrier of information in a context of tribal sensitivities and tensions.

'Utaybah (pronounced 'Tēbah) a tribal confederation territorially based in the area between Riyadh and Mecca in central Najd.

Wādī al-Khirr a riverbed that terminates at the Euphrates and upcountry comes close to al-Ḥazl (also al-Ḥuzūl), the wells of the Sinjārah division of Shammar.

Wahhabi used in reference to the doctrines and practices preached by the Muḥammad ibn 'Abd al-Wahhāb, and later established as the foundational principles of the Kingdom of Saudi Arabia, it is perceived as a pejorative term in its native country. In Saudi Arabia, the movement is called Salafī: a return to the religious practices of the *salaf*, the early generations of Muslims. Its adherents call themselves "those who profess the unicity of God" (*al-muwaḥḥidūn*).

Bibliography

Alf laylah wa-laylah ("The Thousand and One Nights"). 2 vols. Edited by Muḥammad Qiṭṭah al-ʿAdwā. Cairo: Maṭbaʿat Būlāq, 1810–11.

ʿAqīl, Abū ʿAbd al-Raḥmān ibn, al-Ẓāhirī. *Dīwān al-shiʿr al-ʿāmmī bi-lahjat ahl Najd*. 5 vols. Riyadh: Dār al-ʿUlūm, 1982–86.

Ayoub, Abderrahman. *Sirat Beni Hilal: Actes de la permière Table Ronde Internationale sur la Geste des Béni Hilal, 26–29 June 1980, al-Hammamat, Tunisia*. Edited by Abderrahman Ayoub. Tunis: al-Dār al-Tunisiyya li-l-Nashr and al-Maʿhad al-Qawmī li-l-Athār wa-l-Funūn, 1989.

Bell, Richard. *The Qurʾān*. 2 vols. Edinburgh: T. and T. Clark, 1937. Reprint, 1960.

Blunt, Lady Anne. *A Pilgrimage to Nejd*. 2 vols. 1881. Reprint, London: Frank Cass, 1968.

Burckhardt, John Lewis. *Notes on the Bedouins and Wahabys*. London: H. Colburn and R. Bentley, 1830. Reprint, Cambridge: Cambridge University Press, 2010.

Doughty, Charles M. *Travels in Arabia Deserta*. 2 vols. London: Jonathan Cape, 1936. Reprint of the third edition, New York: Dover, 1979.

Euting, Julius. *Tagebuch einer Reise in Inner-Arabien*. 2 vols. Leiden, Netherlands: E. J. Brill, 1896–1914.

Gary, Jane, and Hasan El-Shamy. *Archetypes and Motifs in Folklore and Literature: A Handbook*. Armonk, NY: M. E. Sharpe, 2005.

Al-Ḥaqīl, ʿAbd al-Karīm ibn Ḥamad ibn Ibrāhīm. *Alfāẓ dārijah wa-madlūlātuhā fī al-Jazīrah al-ʿArabiyyah*. Riyadh: Maṭābiʿ al-Farazdaq, 1989.

———. *Kanz al-ansāb wa-mujammaʿ al-ādāb*. 11th ed. Riyadh: Maṭābiʿ al-Farazdaq, 1988.

Ḥassān ibn Thābit. *Sharḥ dīwān Ḥassān ibn Thābit al-Anṣārī*. Edited by ʿAbd al-Raḥmān al-Barquqī. Cairo: al-Maṭbaʿah al-Raḥmāniyyah, 1929.

Ḥātim al-Ṭāʾī. *Dīwān Ḥātim al-Ṭāʾī*. Beirut: Dār Bayrūt li-l-Ṭibāʿah wa-l-Nashr, 1982.

Hess, J. J. *Von den Beduinen des innern Arabiens*. Zurich: Max Niehaus Verlag, 1938.

Holes, Clive. "The Language of Nabaṭi Poetry." In *Encyclopaedia of Arabic Language and Linguistics On-Line Edition*, ed. R. De Jong and L. Edzard. Leiden, Netherlands: E. J. Brill, 2012.

Homer. *The Iliad of Homer*. Translated by Richmond Lattimore. Chicago: University of Chicago Press, 2011.

Huber, Charles. *Journal d'un voyage en Arabie (1883–4)*. Paris: Société Asiatique et la Société de Géographie, 1891.

Huber, Charles. "Voyage dans l'arabie central." *Bulletin de la Société Géographique* 7, no. 5 (1884): 304–63, 468–530; no. 6 (1885): 92–148.

Al-Ḥuṭay'ah. *Dīwān al-Ḥuṭay'ah bi-riwāyah wa-sharḥ ibn al-Sikkīt*. Edited by Mufīd Muḥammad Qamīḥah. Beirut: Dār al-Kutub al-'Ilmiyyah, 1993.

———. *Dīwān al-Ḥuṭay'ah bi-riwāyah wa-sharḥ ibn al-Sikkīt*. Edited by Nu'mān ibn Muḥammad Amīn Ṭāhā. Cairo: Maktabat al-Khānjī, 1987.

Ibn Khaldūn, 'Abd al-Raḥmān ibn Muḥammad. *Muqaddimat Ibn Khaldūn*. Edited by Darwīsh al-Juwaydī. Beirut: al-Maktabah al-'Aṣriyyah, 1999.

Ibn Khamīs, 'Abd Allāh ibn Muḥammad. *Al-Adab al-sha'bī fī l-jazīrah al-'arabiyyah*. 2nd ed. Riyadh: n.p., 1982.

Ibn Mandīl, Mandīl ibn Muḥammad, Āl al-Fuhayd. *Min ādābinā al-sha'biyyah fī l-jazīra al-'arabiyyah, qiṣaṣ wa-ash'ār*. 4 vols. Riyadh: n.p., 1981–84.

Ibn Manẓūr. *Lisān al-'arab*. Cairo: Dār al-Ma'ārif, n.d.

Imru' al-Qays. *Dīwān*. Beirut: Dār Bayrūt, 1986.

Ingham, Bruce. *Bedouins of Northern Arabia: Traditions of the Al Dhafir*. London: Kegan Paul, 1986.

Al-Iṣfahānī, Abū l-Faraj. *Kitāb al-Aghānī*. Cairo: Maṭba'at Dār al-Kutub al-Miṣriyyah, 1928.

Al-Jāsir, Ḥamad. *Al-Mu'jam al-jughrāfī li-l-bilād al-'Arabiyyah al-Sa'ūdiyyah, Shamāl al-Mamlakah*. Imārāt Ḥayil wa-l-Jawf wa-Tabūk wa-'Ar'ar wa-l-Qurayyāt. 3 vols. Cairo: Maṭba'at Nahḍat Miṣr, n.d.

Al Juhany, Uwaidah M. *Najd before the Salafi Movement: Social, Political and Religious Conditions during the Three Centuries preceding the Rise of the Saudi State*. Reading, UK: Ithaca Press, 2002.

Al-Juhaymān, 'Abd al-Karīm. *Al-Amthāl al-sha'biyyah fī qalb al-jazīrah al-'arabiyyah*. 10 vols. Riyadh: n.p., 1982.

Kurpershoek, P. Marcel. *Oral Poetry and Narratives from Central Arabia*. 5 vols. Leiden, Netherlands: E. J. Brill, 1994–2005.

— I. *The Poetry of ad-Dindan: A Bedouin Bard in Southern Najd*. Leiden, Netherlands: E. J. Brill, 1994.

— II. *The Story of a Desert Knight: The Legend of Shlewih al-'Atawi and Other 'Utaybah Heroes*. Leiden, Netherlands: E. J. Brill, 1995.

— III. *Bedouin Poets of the Dawasir Tribe: Between Nomadism and Settlement in Southern Najd*. Leiden, Netherlands: E. J. Brill, 1999.

— IV. *A Saudi Tribal History: Honour and Faith in the Traditions of the Dawasir*. Leiden, Netherlands: E. J. Brill, 2002.

— V. *Voices from the Desert: Glossary, Indices and List of Recordings.* Leiden, Netherlands: E. J. Brill, 2005.

Kurpershoek, Marcel, ed. and tr. *Arabian Satire: Poetry from 18th Century Najd. Ḥmēdān al-Shwēʿir.* New York: New York University Press, 2017.

———. *Arabian Romantic: Poems on Bedouin Life and Love. ʿAbdallāh ibn Sbayyil.* New York: New York University Press, 2018.

———. *Bedouin Poets of the Nafūd Desert.* New York: New York University Press, 2024.

———. *Love, Death, Fame: Poetry and Lore from the Emirati Oral Tradition; Al-Māyidī ibn Ẓāhir.* New York: New York University Press, 2022.

Lane, Edward William. *Manners and Customs of the Modern Egyptians.* 1836. Reprint, London: Everyman's Library, 1966.

———. *An Arabic-English Lexicon.* London: Williams and Norgate, 1863. Reprint, Beirut: Librairie du Liban, 1980.

Lerrick, Alison. "Taghribat Banī Hilāl Al-Diyāghim: Variation in the Oral Epic Poetry of Najd," vol. 1, Introduction, Overview, Description; vol. 2, Arabic Composite of Text. PhD diss., Princeton University, 1984.

Lyons, Malcolm C., tr. *Tales of the Marvellous and News of the Strange.* London: Penguin, 2014.

Mandaville, James. *Bedouin Ethnobotany.* Tucson: University of Arizona Press, 2011.

Metlitzki, Dorothee. "On the Meaning of 'Hatem' in Goethe's West-Östlicher Divan." *Journal of the American Oriental Society* 117, no. 1 (Jan.–Mar. 1997).

Montagne, Robert. "Notes sur la Vie Sociale en Politique de l'Arabie du Nord: Les Šammar du Neǧd." *Revue des Études Islamiques* 6 (1932): 61–79.

———. *Contes poétiques bedouins (recucillis chez les Shammar de Gezire).* Bulletin d'études Orientales 5. Damascus: Institut Français de Damas, 1935.

———. "Le Ghazou de Šayeʿ Alemsah (conte en dialect des Šemmar du Neǧd, sous-tribu des Rmāl)." In *Mélanges Maspéro.* Cairo: Imprimerie de l'institut Français d'archéologie orientale, 1935–40.

———. "Sālfet Šayeʿ Alemsah, Ǧedd Errmāl (texte en dialecte de Šammar du Neǧd)." In *Mélanges Gaudefroy-Demombynes.* Cairo: Imprimerie de l'institut Français d'archéologie orientale, 1935–45.

Montgomery, J. E. *Fate the Hunter: Early Arabic Hunting Poems.* New York: New York University Press, 2022.

Al-Mufaḍḍal, Abū ʿAbbās ibn Muḥammad aḍ-Ḍabbī. *Dīwān al-Mufaḍḍaliyyāt.* Edited by Charles James Lyall. Vol. 1, Arabic text (1921); vol. 2, Translation and notes. Oxford: Clarendon Press, 1918–21.

Musil, Alois. *The Manners and Customs of the Rwala Bedouins*. Oriental Explorations and Studies 6. New York: American Geographical Society, 1928.

Musil, Alois. *Northern Neǧd*. Oriental Explorations and Studies 5. New York: American Geographical Society, 1928.

Al-Mutanabbī, Abū l-Ṭayyib. *Dīwān Abī l-Ṭayyib al-Mutanabbī bi-sharḥ Abī l-Baqāʾ al-ʿUkbarī*. 4 vols. 2nd ed. Cairo: Maṭbaʿat Muṣṭafā al-Bābī al-Ḥalabī, 1956.

Palgrave, William Gifford. *Personal Narrative of a Year's Journey through Central and Eastern Arabia (1862–63)*. London: Macmillan, 1871.

Philby, H. St. J. B. *Saʿudi Arabia*. Beirut: Librairie du Liban, 1968.

Al Rasheed, Madawi. *Politics in an Arabian Oasis: The Rashidi Tribal Dynasty*. London: I. B. Tauris, 1991.

Reynolds, Dwight Fletcher. *Heroic Poets, Poetic Heroes: The Ethnography of Performance in an Arabic Oral Epic Tradition (Myth and Poetic)*. Ithaca, NY: Cornell University Press, 1995.

Sowayan, Saad Abdullah. *Nabaṭī Poetry: The Oral Poetry of Arabia*. Berkeley: University of California Press, 1985.

———. *The Arabian Oral Historical Narrative: An Ethnographic and Linguistic Analysis*. Wiesbaden, Germany: Otto Harrassowitz, 1992.

———. *Al-Shiʿr al-nabaṭī: dhāʾiqat al-shaʿb wa-sulṭat al-naṣṣ*. Beirut: Dār al-Sāqī, 2000.

———. *Fihrist al-shiʿr al-nabaṭī*. Riyadh: self-published, 2001.

———. "The Hilali Poetry in the *Muqaddima*: Its Links to Nabaṭi Poetry." *Oriente Moderno* 83, no. 2 (2003).

———. *Al-Ṣaḥrāʾ al-ʿarabiyyah, thaqāfatuhā wa-shiʿruhā ʿabra al-ʿuṣūr, qirāʾah anthrūbūlūjiyyah*. Beirut: Arab Network for Research and Publishing, 2010.

———. *Ayyām al-ʿarab al-awākhir: Asāṭīr wa-marwiyyāt shafahiyyah fī l-taʾrīkh wa-l-adab min shamāl al-jazīrah al-ʿarabiyyah maʿa shadharāt mukhtārah min qabīlat Āl Murrah wa-Subayʿ*. Beirut: Arab Network for Research and Publishing, 2010.

———. "A Poem and Its Narrative by Riḍa ibn Ṭarif al-Shammarī." *Zeitschrift für arabische Linguistik* 7 (1982): 48–73.

Sowayan, Saad Abdullah, ed. *Al-Thaqāfah al-taqlīdiyyah fī al-mamlakah al-ʿarabiyyah al-suʿūdiyyah*. Riyadh: The Circle for Publishing and Documentation, 1999.

Al-Sudayrī, Muḥammad ibn Aḥmad. *Abṭāl min al-Ṣaḥrāʾ*. Riyadh: al-Dār al-Waṭaniyyah al-Saʾūdiyyah li-l-Nashr, 1981.

Al-Suwaydāʾ, ʿAbd al-Raḥmān ibn Zayd. *Faṣīḥ al-ʿāmmī fī shamāl Najd*. 2 vols. Riyadh: Dār al-Suwaydāʾ, Maṭābiʿ al-Farazdaq, 1987.

———. *Min Shuʿarāʾ al-jabal al-ʿāmmiyyīn*. 3 vols. Riyadh: Dār al-Suwaydāʾ, 1988.

———. *Al-Amthāl al-shaʿbiyyah al-sāʾirah fī manṭiqat Ḥāʾil*. Riyadh: Dār al-Suwaydāʾ, 2007.

———. *Manṭiqat Ḥā'il ʿabra al-ta'rīkh*. Riyadh: Dār al-Suwaydā', 2009.

———. *Al-Nakhlah al-ʿarabiyyah adabiyyan wa-ʿilmiyyan wa-iqtisādiyyan*. Riyadh: Dār al-Suwaydā', 1993.

Thompson, Stith. *Motif-Index of Folk-Literature: A Classification of Narrative Elements in Folktales, Ballads, Myths, Fables, Mediaeval Romances, Exempla, Fabliaux, Jest-Books, and Local Legends*. Bloomington: Indiana University Press, 1966.

Al-Tibrīzī, Abū Zakariyā Yaḥyā ibn ʿAlī. *Kitāb sharḥ al-qaṣā'id al-ʿashr*. Edited by Charles J. Lyall. Calcutta: Asiatic Society of Bengal, 1894. Reprint, Farnborough, UK: Gregg Press, 1965. Commentary on ten ancient Arabic poems.

Al-ʿUbūdī, Muḥammad ibn Nāṣir. *Al-Amthāl al-ʿāmmiyyah fī Najd*. 5 vols. Riyadh: n.p., 1979.

———. *Muʿjam al-kalimāt al-dakhīlah fī lughatinā al-dārijah*, 2 vols. Riyadh: Maktabat al-Malik ʿAbd al-ʿAzīz al-ʿĀmmah, 2005.

———. *Muʿjam al-azwāj fī l-turāth*. Riyadh: Dār al-Thalūthiyyah, 2017.

———. *Muʿjam al-anwā' wa-l-fuṣūl*. Riyadh: n.p., 2011.

———. *Muʿjam al-uṣūl al-faṣīḥah li-l-alfāẓ al-dārijah*. 13 vols. Riyadh: n.p., 2008.

———. *Muʿjam al-ḥayawān ʿind al-ʿāmmah*. 2 vols. Riyadh: Maktabat al-Malik Fahd al-Waṭaniyyah, 2011.

———. *Muʿjam al-malābis fī l-ma'thūr al-shaʿbī fī l-manṭiqah al-wusṭā' min al-Mamlakah al-ʿArabiyyah al-Suʿūdiyyah*. Riyadh: Dār al-Thalūthiyyah, 2013.

———. *Muʿjam alfāẓ al-maraḍ wa-l-ṣiḥḥah*. Riyadh: Dār al-Thalūthiyyah, 2015.

———. *Muʿjam al-tijārah wa-l-māl wa-l-faqr wa-l-ghinā*. Riyadh: Dār al-Thalūthiyyah, 2012.

———. *Muʿjam wajh al-arḍ*. Riyadh: Dār al-Thalūthiyyah, 2014.

Al-ʿUṣaymī, Muḥammad ibn Dakhīl. *Shuʿarā' ʿUtaybah*. 2 vols. Dammam, Saudi Arabia: Maṭābiʿ al-Mudawkhal, 1995.

Wallin, Georg August. *Travels in Arabia*. Cambridge, NY: The Oleander Press, 1979.

Watts, David, and Abdulatif H. Al-Nafie. *Vegetation and Biogeography of the Sand Seas of Saudi Arabia*. London: Kegan Paul, 2003.

Al-Zawzanī, Abū ʿAbd Allāh al-Ḥusayn ibn Aḥmad ibn al-Ḥusayn. *Sharḥ al-muʿallaqāt al-sabʿ*. Beirut: Dār Bayrūt, 1982.

Index of Poems and Editions

This edition is based on a published collection of recorded oral narratives and poetry. The poems have been ordered by their numbered position in this book's text. Unless otherwise indicated, the meter of the poems is a variant of the classical Arabic *ṭawīl* meter called *hilālī* in connection with the poetry of this volume (see Introduction, n. 31 and §1.14).

The shorthand references at the beginning of each source listed below indicate where a particular poem can be found. These references are followed by page numbers and the relevant number of verses of the poem in that edition.

Editions:

SO *Ayyām al-ʿarab al-awākhir: asāṭīr wa-marwiyyāt shafahiyyah fī l-taʾrīkh wa-l-adab min shamāl al-jazīrah al-ʿarabiyyah maʿa shadharāt mukhtārah min qabīlat Āl Murrah wa-Subayʿ*. Edited by Dr. Saad Abdullah Sowayan. Beirut: Arab Network for Research and Publishing, 2010.

SU *Min shuʿarāʾ al-Jabal al-ʿāmiyyīn*. Edited by ʿAbd al-Raḥmān ibn Zayd al-Suwaydāʾ. 3 vols. Riyadh: Dār al-Suwaydāʾ, 1988.

يا خـال شفت الشوف قبل يشوفني   مـمشـــاة يومٍ للذلول اهـذالـــ

§1.2: SO 248–49, 16 vv.

سـرى البـرق يابوي يا موَدِّتي   برقٍ بعيد ومن شفا البعد اخايلـه

§1.5: SO 249, 3 vv.

زاعن من الزبيـــدي ظعونٍ تِقَـلّلت   صـبح ليـل تنصى المغـارف صبوره

§1.15: SO 254–55, 40 vv.; SU 157–64, 40 vv.

قال ابن قدران بيوت يولّفها كما الدنانير بين عَدٍّ ونقّاد

§2.11: SO 260, 8 vv. Meter: *rajaz*.

قال ابن مرداس بيوت يولفها كما سَدْي الخام بين مبرم وغزال

§2.12: SO 260–61, 11 vv. Meter: *rajaz*.

قال ابن قدرانٍ بنفسٍ رفيعه عين عنٍ للضعيف صخيف

§2.15: SO 262, 19 vv.; SU 179–82, 17 vv.

قال ابن مرداس فتى الجود شايع حداني زماني والحمول ثقال

§3.2: SO 262–63, 17 vv.; SU 186–89, 17 vv.

ألى ياخوي دورّ لعيني الدوا يم صنعا وهيضات سوقه

§4.2: SO 263, 6 vv.

قال الشريف من حليات الامثال برّقت بالدنيا وانا قبل فاكر

§5.5: SO 266–67, 37 vv.

يقول ابن مرداس فتى الجود شايع اشوم كما حِرّ المراقب شام

§6.6: SO 269, 21 vv.; SU 204–8, 19 vv.

يقول ابن مرداس فتى الجود شايع وايا بطل واكثر علومي قدايم

§7.6: SO 270, 14 vv.; SU 210–11, 7 vv.

قال الغفيلي والذي مَسّ حبلَه على بنت قودا من خيار الزمايل

§7.13: SO 274–75, 20 vv.; SU 200–3, 19 vv.

وردنا قُطِري من عقب عشوه   لا علامات ولا رجومٍ تسوّى

§8.7: SO 277–78, 2 vv.

قـال ابن مـرداسٍ فتى الجود شايع   من الجد الاقصى ما غـياي قريب

§8.20: SO 282, 15 vv.; SU 169–72, 14 vv.

انا برجوى الله ثم عثمان ابن محمد   يا غـاب عـامـينٍ رجيتـه عـام

§10.4: SO 285, 3 vv.

سرى البرق ياعثمـان ياكاسب الثنا   على دار اهلنـا ياصـدوق الوعايـد

§10.6: SO 285, 4 vv.

العـنك يارجــــلٍ تخـلّي ذلولك   بارض الخـــلا طِـلقٍ بغـير قيـاد

§11.4: SO 287–88, 24 vv.; SU 173–78, 22 vv.

قــال الغفيـلي والذي مـس كوره   على كـور وجـنا ويّ والله زْمـاله

§12.2: SO 288–89, 24 vv.; SU 212–16, 19 vv.

اخـذت ثلاث سنين في حبس خـير   والرابعـه جـاني صـدوق الفعـايـل

§13.5: SO 290, 20 vv.; SU 190–98, 20 vv.

توافقت انا والذيب بيليلة الدجا   والكـل منـا يـدّعي بنصيب

§14.2: SO 291, 3 vv.

ثلاث معـاني مـا يفعـلهـن خَـيّر   وانا احمد الله منهن هدومي نظايف

§15.1: SO 292, 11 vv.; SU 183–85, 11 vv.

انا ابن مـرداس فـتى الجود شـايع   ازبّـن المضـيوم ريف القـرايب

§15.2: SO 292, 16 vv.; SU 165–68, 16 vv.

قـال ابن مـرداس فـتى الجود شـايع   سيـلٍ تحـدّر من هَفوف شفـيف

§15.3: SO 292–93, 23 vv.

يقول ابن مرداس فتى الجود شايع   أنا بطـل لا شـك ربعي هـلايـم

§15.4: SO 293, 6 vv.

Index

جامعة نيويورك أبوظبي

NYU ABU DHABI

About the NYUAD Research Institute

The Library of Arabic Literature is a research center affiliated with NYU Abu Dhabi and is supported by a grant from the NYU Abu Dhabi Research Institute.

The NYU Abu Dhabi Research Institute is a world-class center of cutting-edge and innovative research, scholarship, and cultural activity. It supports centers that address questions of global significance and local relevance and allows leading faculty members from across the disciplines to carry out creative scholarship and high-level research on a range of complex issues with depth, scale, and longevity that otherwise would not be possible.

From genomics and climate science to the humanities and Arabic literature, Research Institute centers make significant contributions to scholarship, scientific understanding, and artistic creativity. Centers strengthen cross-disciplinary engagement and innovation among the faculty, build critical mass in infrastructure and research talent at NYU Abu Dhabi, and have helped make the university a magnet for outstanding faculty, scholars, students, and international collaborations.

About the Typefaces

The Arabic text is set in Sakkal Kitab Medium, a font from the Sakkal Kitab family of fonts designed by Mamoun Sakkal and Aida Sakkal. Sakkal Kitab is an Arabic Naskh text typeface family with elegant cursive tatweel/kashida and swashes in multiple lengths. It is ideal for setting long text passages in books and magazines. The family has five well coordinated weights.

The English text is set in Adobe Text, a new and versatile text typeface family designed by Robert Slimbach for Western (Latin, Greek, Cyrillic) typesetting. Its workhorse qualities make it perfect for a wide variety of applications, especially for longer passages of text where legibility and economy are important. Adobe Text bridges the gap between calligraphic Renaissance types of the fifteenth and sixteenth centuries and high-contrast Modern styles of the 18th century, taking many of its design cues from early post-Renaissance Baroque transitional types cut by designers such as Christoffel van Dijck, Nicolaus Kis, and William Caslon. While grounded in classical form, Adobe Text is also a statement of contemporary utilitarian design, well suited to a wide variety of print and on-screen applications.

Titles Published by the Library of Arabic Literature

For more details on individual titles, visit www.libraryofarabicliterature.org

Classical Arabic Literature: A Library of Arabic Literature Anthology
Selected and translated by Geert Jan van Gelder (2012)

A Treasury of Virtues: Sayings, Sermons, and Teachings of ʿAlī, by al-Qāḍī al-Quḍāʿī, with the **One Hundred Proverbs** attributed to al-Jāḥiẓ
Edited and translated by Tahera Qutbuddin (2013)

The Epistle on Legal Theory, by al-Shāfiʿī
Edited and translated by Joseph E. Lowry (2013)

Leg over Leg, by Aḥmad Fāris al-Shidyāq
Edited and translated by Humphrey Davies (**4 volumes**; 2013–14)

Virtues of the Imām Aḥmad ibn Ḥanbal, by Ibn al-Jawzī
Edited and translated by Michael Cooperson (**2 volumes**; 2013–15)

The Epistle of Forgiveness, by Abū l-ʿAlāʾ al-Maʿarrī
Edited and translated by Geert Jan van Gelder and Gregor Schoeler (**2 volumes**; 2013–14)

The Principles of Sufism, by ʿĀʾishah al-Bāʿūniyyah
Edited and translated by Th. Emil Homerin (2014)

The Expeditions: An Early Biography of Muḥammad, by Maʿmar ibn Rāshid
Edited and translated by Sean W. Anthony (2014)

Two Arabic Travel Books
Accounts of China and India, by Abū Zayd al-Sīrāfī
Edited and translated by Tim Mackintosh-Smith (2014)
Mission to the Volga, by Aḥmad ibn Faḍlān
Edited and translated by James Montgomery (2014)

Disagreements of the Jurists: A Manual of Islamic Legal Theory, by al-Qāḍī al-Nuʿmān
Edited and translated by Devin J. Stewart (2015)

Consorts of the Caliphs: Women and the Court of Baghdad, by Ibn al-Sāʿī
Edited by Shawkat M. Toorawa and translated by the Editors of the Library of Arabic Literature (2015)

What ʿĪsā ibn Hishām Told Us, by Muḥammad al-Muwayliḥī
Edited and translated by Roger Allen (2 volumes; 2015)

The Life and Times of Abū Tammām, by Abū Bakr Muḥammad ibn Yaḥyā al-Ṣūlī
Edited and translated by Beatrice Gruendler (2015)

The Sword of Ambition: Bureaucratic Rivalry in Medieval Egypt, by ʿUthmān ibn Ibrāhīm al-Nābulusī
Edited and translated by Luke Yarbrough (2016)

Brains Confounded by the Ode of Abū Shādūf Expounded, by Yūsuf al-Shirbīnī
Edited and translated by Humphrey Davies (2 volumes; 2016)

Light in the Heavens: Sayings of the Prophet Muḥammad, by al-Qāḍī al-Quḍāʿī
Edited and translated by Tahera Qutbuddin (2016)

Risible Rhymes, by Muḥammad ibn Maḥfūẓ al-Sanhūrī
Edited and translated by Humphrey Davies (2016)

A Hundred and One Nights
Edited and translated by Bruce Fudge (2016)

The Excellence of the Arabs, by Ibn Qutaybah
Edited by James E. Montgomery and Peter Webb
Translated by Sarah Bowen Savant and Peter Webb (2017)

Scents and Flavors: A Syrian Cookbook
Edited and translated by Charles Perry (2017)

Arabian Satire: Poetry from 18th-Century Najd, by Ḥmēdān al-Shwēʿir
Edited and translated by Marcel Kurpershoek (2017)

In Darfur: An Account of the Sultanate and Its People, by Muḥammad ibn ʿUmar al-Tūnisī
Edited and translated by Humphrey Davies (2 volumes; 2018)

War Songs, by ʿAntarah ibn Shaddād
Edited by James E. Montgomery
Translated by James E. Montgomery with Richard Sieburth (2018)

Arabian Romantic: Poems on Bedouin Life and Love, by ʿAbdallāh ibn Sbayyil
Edited and translated by Marcel Kurpershoek (2018)

Dīwān ʿAntarah ibn Shaddād: A Literary-Historical Study
By James E. Montgomery (2018)

Stories of Piety and Prayer: Deliverance Follows Adversity, by al-Muḥassin ibn ʿAlī al-Tanūkhī
Edited and translated by Julia Bray (2019)

The Philosopher Responds: An Intellectual Correspondence from the Tenth Century, by Abū Ḥayyān al-Tawḥīdī and Abū ʿAlī Miskawayh
Edited by Bilal Orfali and Maurice A. Pomerantz
Translated by Sophia Vasalou and James E. Montgomery (2 volumes; 2019)

Tajrīd sayf al-himmah li-stikhrāj mā fī dhimmat al-dhimmah: A Scholarly Edition of ʿUthmān ibn Ibrāhīm al-Nābulusī's Text
By Luke Yarbrough (2020)

The Discourses: Reflections on History, Sufism, Theology, and Literature—Volume One, by al-Ḥasan al-Yūsī
Edited and translated by Justin Stearns (2020)

Impostures, by al-Ḥarīrī
Translated by Michael Cooperson (2020)

Maqāmāt Abī Zayd al-Sarūjī, by al-Ḥarīrī
Edited by Michael Cooperson (2020)

The Yoga Sutras of Patañjali, by Abū Rayḥān al-Bīrūnī
Edited and translated by Mario Kozah (2020)

The Book of Charlatans, by Jamāl al-Dīn ʿAbd al-Raḥīm al-Jawbarī
Edited by Manuela Dengler
Translated by Humphrey Davies (2020)

A Physician on the Nile: A Description of Egypt and Journal of the Famine Years, by ʿAbd al-Laṭīf al-Baghdādī
Edited and translated by Tim Mackintosh-Smith **(2021)**

The Book of Travels, by Ḥannā Diyāb
Edited by Johannes Stephan
Translated by Elias Muhanna **(2 volumes; 2021)**

Kalīlah and Dimnah: Fables of Virtue and Vice, by Ibn al-Muqaffaʿ
Edited by Michael Fishbein
Translated by Michael Fishbein and James E. Montgomery **(2021)**

Love, Death, Fame: Poetry and Lore from the Emirati Oral Tradition, by al-Māyidī ibn Ẓāhir
Edited and translated by Marcel Kurpershoek **(2022)**

The Essence of Reality: A Defense of Philosophical Sufism, by ʿAyn al-Quḍāt
Edited and translated by Mohammed Rustom **(2022)**

The Requirements of the Sufi Path: A Defense of the Mystical Tradition, by Ibn Khaldūn
Edited and translated by Carolyn Baugh **(2022)**

The Doctors' Dinner Party, by Ibn Buṭlān
Edited and translated by Philip F. Kennedy and Jeremy Farrell **(2023)**

Fate the Hunter: Early Arabic Hunting Poems
Edited and translated by James E. Montgomery **(2023)**

The Book of Monasteries, by al-Shābushtī
Edited and translated by Hilary Kilpatrick **(2023)**

In Deadly Embrace: Arabic Hunting Poems, by Ibn al-Muʿtazz
Edited and translated by James E. Montgomery **(2023)**

The Divine Names: A Mystical Theology of the Names of God in the Qur'an, by ʿAfīf al-Dīn al-Tilimsānī
Edited and translated by Yousef Casewit **(2023)**

Bedouin Poets of the Nafūd Desert, by Khalaf Abū Zwayyid, ʿAdwān al-Hirbīd, and ʿAjlān ibn Rmāl
Edited and translated by Marcel Kurpershoek **(2024)**

The Rules of Logic, by Najm al-Dīn al-Kātibī
Edited and translated by Tony Street **(2024)**

Najm al-Dīn al-Kātibī's Al-Risālah al-Shamsiyyah: An Edition and Translation with Commentary
By Tony Street **(2024)**

Arabian Hero: Oral Poetry and Narrative Lore from Northern Arabia, by Shāyiʿ al-Amsaḥ
Edited and translated by Marcel Kurpershoek **(2024)**

A Demon Spirit: Arabic Hunting Poems, by Abū Nuwās
Edited and translated by James E. Montgomery **(2024)**

English-only Paperbacks

Leg over Leg, by Aḥmad Fāris al-Shidyāq **(2 volumes; 2015)**
The Expeditions: An Early Biography of Muḥammad, by Maʿmar ibn Rāshid **(2015)**
The Epistle on Legal Theory: A Translation of al-Shāfiʿī's *Risālah*, by al-Shāfiʿī **(2015)**
The Epistle of Forgiveness, by Abū l-ʿAlāʾ al-Maʿarrī **(2016)**
The Principles of Sufism, by ʿĀʾishah al-Bāʿūniyyah **(2016)**
A Treasury of Virtues: Sayings, Sermons, and Teachings of ʿAlī, by al-Qāḍī al-Quḍāʿī, with the **One Hundred Proverbs** attributed to al-Jāḥiẓ **(2016)**
The Life of Ibn Ḥanbal, by Ibn al-Jawzī **(2016)**
Mission to the Volga, by Ibn Faḍlān **(2017)**
Accounts of China and India, by Abū Zayd al-Sīrāfī **(2017)**
A Hundred and One Nights (2017)
Consorts of the Caliphs: Women and the Court of Baghdad, by Ibn al-Sāʿī **(2017)**
Disagreements of the Jurists: A Manual of Islamic Legal Theory, by al-Qāḍī al-Nuʿmān **(2017)**
What ʿĪsā ibn Hishām Told Us, by Muḥammad al-Muwayliḥī **(2018)**
War Songs, by ʿAntarah ibn Shaddād **(2018)**
The Life and Times of Abū Tammām, by Abū Bakr Muḥammad ibn Yaḥyā al-Ṣūlī **(2018)**
The Sword of Ambition, by ʿUthmān ibn Ibrāhīm al-Nābulusī **(2019)**

Brains Confounded by the Ode of Abū Shādūf Expounded: Volume One, by Yūsuf al-Shirbīnī (2019)

Brains Confounded by the Ode of Abū Shādūf Expounded: Volume Two, by Yūsuf al-Shirbīnī and **Risible Rhymes**, by Muḥammad ibn Maḥfūẓ al-Sanhūrī (2019)

The Excellence of the Arabs, by Ibn Qutaybah (2019)

Light in the Heavens: Sayings of the Prophet Muḥammad, by al-Qāḍī al-Quḍāʿī (2019)

Scents and Flavors: A Syrian Cookbook (2020)

Arabian Satire: Poetry from 18th-Century Najd, by Ḥmēdān al-Shwēʿir (2020)

In Darfur: An Account of the Sultanate and Its People, by Muḥammad al-Tūnisī (2020)

Arabian Romantic: Poems on Bedouin Life and Love, by ʿAbdallāh ibn Sbayyil (2020)

The Philosopher Responds, by Abū Ḥayyān al-Tawḥīdī and Abū ʿAlī Miskawayh (2021)

Impostures, by al-Ḥarīrī (2021)

The Discourses: Reflections on History, Sufism, Theology, and Literature—Volume One, by al-Ḥasan al-Yūsī (2021)

The Book of Charlatans, by Jamāl al-Dīn ʿAbd al-Raḥīm al-Jawbarī (2022)

The Yoga Sutras of Patañjali, by Abū Rayḥān al-Bīrūnī (2022)

The Book of Travels, by Ḥannā Diyāb (2022)

A Physician on the Nile: A Description of Egypt and Journal of the Famine Years, by ʿAbd al-Laṭīf al-Baghdādī (2022)

Kalīlah and Dimnah: Fables of Virtue and Vice, by Ibn al-Muqaffaʿ (2023)

Love, Death, Fame: Poetry and Lore from the Emirati Oral Tradition, by al-Māyidī ibn Ẓāhir (2023)

The Essence of Reality: A Defense of Philosophical Sufism, by ʿAyn al-Quḍāt (2023)

The Doctors' Dinner Party, by Ibn Buṭlān (2024)

The Requirements of the Sufi Path: A Defense of the Mystical Tradition, by Ibn Khaldūn (2024)

Fate the Hunter: Early Arabic Hunting Poems (2024)

About the Editor–Translator

Marcel Kurpershoek is a specialist in the oral traditions and poetry of Arabia and a former senior research fellow at New York University Abu Dhabi. He obtained his PhD in modern Arabic literature at the University of Leiden. He has written a number of books on historical, cultural, and contemporary topics in the Middle East, including the five-volume *Oral Poetry and Narratives from Central Arabia* (1994–2005), which draws on his recordings of Bedouin tribes. For the Library of Arabic Literature, he has edited and translated *Arabian Satire* by Ḥmēdān al-Shwēʿir (2017), *Arabian Romantic* by ʿAbdallāh ibn Sbayyil (2018), *Love, Death, Fame* by al-Māyidī ibn Ẓāhir (2022), and *Bedouin Poets of the Nafūd Desert* (2024). In 2016, Al Arabiya television broadcast an eight-part documentary series based on the travelogue of fieldwork he had undertaken in the Nafūd desert of northern Arabia for his book *Arabia of the Bedouins* (in Arabic translation *The Last Bedouin*). In 2018, Al Arabiya broadcast his five-part documentary on Najdī poetry. He spent his career as a diplomat for the Netherlands, having served as ambassador to Pakistan, Afghanistan, Turkey, Poland, and special envoy for Syria until 2015. From 1996 to 2002, he held a chair as professor of literature and politics in the Arab world at the University of Leiden.

www.ingramcontent.com/pod-product-compliance
Lightning Source LLC
Chambersburg PA
CBHW021846090426
42811CB00033B/2154/J
* 9 7 8 1 4 7 9 8 3 4 1 6 7 *